Workbook
HIGH BEGINNING

OXFORD

PICTURE

DICTIONARY

THIRD EDITION

Marjorie Fuchs

OXFORD
UNIVERSITY PRESS

198 Madison Avenue
New York, NY 10016 USA

Great Clarendon Street, Oxford, OX2 6DP, United Kingdom

Oxford University Press is a department of the University of Oxford.
It furthers the University's objective of excellence in research, scholarship,
and education by publishing worldwide. Oxford is a registered trade
mark of Oxford University Press in the UK and in certain other countries

ISBN: 978 0 19 451122 3

Printed in China

This book is printed on paper from certified and well-managed sources

ACKNOWLEDGEMENTS

Illustrations by: Gary Antonetti/Ortelius Design: 13, 216; Argosy: 18, 46, 80, 91, 94,
102, 104, 105, 108, 115, 120, 155, 161, 206; Sally Bansusen: 217; Barb Bastian: 14;
40 (chart), 50, 54, 57, 67, 74, 92, 95, 98, 116, 148, 192, 223 (chart); Ken Batelman:
23, 38, 53, 66 (bottom), 70 (meat and poultry), 100 (sewing box), 110, 138, 221,
230, 233, 246; Kevin Brown: 248, 249, 259; Andrea Champlin: 6 (desk with school
supplies), 55, 123, 188; Annie Bissett: 65, 77 (h. turn on oven), 90 (catalog and
text), 131, 136, 154, 162, 171; Mary Chandler: 71, 219, 252; Jim Delapine: 77, 109,
220, 241; Vilma Ortiz-Dillon: 2 (top); Mark Duffin (phone): 94; Jody Emery: 17
(books), 24, 47, 48, 78, 83, 84, 129, 145 (TV Guide), 156, 186, 242; Mike Gardner:
7, 10, 35, 139, 145, 212 (icons); Garth Glazier: 107; Dennis Godfrey/Mike Wepplo:
214 (island); Glenn Gustafson: 27 (top), 75, 76, 79, 101, 119, 130, 159; Barbara
Harmon: 216; Shelley Himmelstein: 214; Kev Hopgood: 42; Janos Jantner/Beehive
Illustration: 11, 112; Pamela Johnson: 250, 258; Ken Joudrey/Munro Campagna:
68, 69, 187, 224, 245; Bob Kaganich/Deborah Wolfe: 41; Uldis Klavins/Hankins
& Tegenborg, Ltd.: 253; Deb LoFaso: 24, 52, 167, 168, 175, 181, 211, 212, 213,
240, 241; Scott MacNeill: 51, 61, 114, 231, 244; Alan Male: 216, 218; Mohammad
Masoor: 194, 196; Paul Mirocha: 222, 223; Karen Minot: 21, 32, 82 (Guest Check),
97, 135; Chris Pavely: 251; Tony Randazzo: 160, 238; Mike Renwick/Creative
Eye: 28, 56, 62, 66 (top); 73, 85, 89, 126, 138, 141, 146; Zina Saunders: 22, 33,
40, 59, 60, 81, 82, 86, 99, 100 (skirts), 107 (top), 127, 196 (adhesive); Jeff Sanson:
246 (top); Ben Shannon: 12, 26, 64, 96, 105, 152, 165, 179, 197, 256, 257; Stacey
Schuett: 72; Rob Schuster: 170, 172, 189, 207, 220, 232, 234, 240; Anna Veltfort:
254, 255; Samuel Velasco (5W Infographics): 38 (phone), 130, 155 (boarding
pass), 174, 210, 232, 260 (phone); Ralph Voltz/Deborah Wolfe: 90, 158, 166; Nina
Wallace: 63; Simon Williams/Illustration Ltd.: 38 (top right); 39, 44, 45.

Chapter icons: Anna Sereda

Pronk&Associates: 4, 5, 6 (Back to School and Spelling Test), 8, 9, 15, 16, 17 (pie
chart), 19, 20, 25, 27 (Be a Smart Shopper), 29, 30, 33, 35 (note at bottom), 36, 37
(crossword), 38 (To Do List), 43, 47 (Home Preference Checklist), 49, 52, 60 (To Do
List), 61 (To Buy), 63, 66 (shopping list), 68 (web browser), 68 (chart), 69 (chart), 70
(chart), 73 (Grocery List), 81 (Food Order Form), 86 (Clothing Rules), 88, 89 (Hotel
Stationary), 91 (receipt), 97 (receipt), 100 (form), 102 (price stickers), 103, 105
(Patient Form), 108 (list), 109 (To Buy list), 110 (Patient Form), 111, 112 (forms), 119
(check list), 123 (Supply List), 125, 132 (Mall Directory), 133, 134, 140 (chart), 141, 145
(forms), 149 (newspaper headlines), 150 (Emergency Plan and Disaster Checklist),
152 (Oak Street Association), 153, 156, 160 (chart), 161 (list), 176, 179 (forms), 185,
183, 186 (checklist), 187 (chart), 197 (checklist), 195 (chart), 189 (clipboard), 199,
201, 202, 204, 208, 216 (chart), 220 (chart), 224 (newspaper headlines), 229, 235, 236,
237 (chart), 243, 247, 249 (crossword), 250 (word search), 258 (crossword puzzle),
260 (forms).

*The publishers would like to thank the following for their kind permission to reproduce
photographs:* p.2 OUP/PhotoAlto/Michele Constantini; p.3 Andresr/Shutterstock; p.26
(dime) mattesimages/Shutterstock, (dollar) nimon/Shutterstock, (five, ten, hundred)
Ivan Vdovin/Alamy Stock Photo, (half-dollar) Daniel D Malone/Shutterstock, (nickel,
quarter) Fat Jackey/Shutterstock, (penny) Sascha Burkard/Shutterstock, (twenty)
OUP/Dennis Kitchen Studio, Inc.; p.31 (top row) KidStock/Getty Images, MBI/
Alamy Stock Photo, Daniel Allan/Getty Images, (bottom row) pathdoc/Shutterstock,
Rebecca Emery/Getty Images, Gabriela Insuratelu/Alamy Stock Photo; p.32 (left to
right) CHAjAMP/Shutterstock, Andresr/Shutterstock, Blend Images/Shutterstock,
Wavebreak Media ltd/Alamy Stock Photo, OUP/Shutterstock/racorn; p.37 (clockwise
from top left) OUP/Dennis Kitchen Studio, Inc (5), Kitch Bain/AGE Fotostock, Monika
Ribbe/Getty Images; p.52 (clockwise from top left) OUP/Shutterstock/Songquan
Deng, Corbis/Superstock, Pat & Chuck Blackley/Alamy Stock Photo, Imagenet/
Shutterstock; p.58 OUP/Lisa S./Shutterstock; p.66 Blue Jean Images/Alamy Stock
Photo; p.71 Visconti, Paul/StockFood/AGE Fotostock; p.106 PhotosIndia.com LLC/
Alamy Stock Photo; p.115 Don Farrall/Getty Images; p.122 Juice Images/Superstock;
p.132 (from top left) dekzerphoto/Shutterstock, OUP/Dennis Kitchen Studio, Inc
(2), Hurst Photo/Shutterstock, JDPR/Shutterstock, Ange/Alamy Stock Photo, OUP/
Shutterstock/Kletr, Stanca Sanda/Alamy Stock Photo; p.137 Jose Luis Pelaez Inc/Getty
Images; p.138 Fotos593/Shutterstock; p.142 (from top left) Shawn Thew/AFP/Getty
Images, OUP/Comstock, Andreas Solaro/AFP/Getty Images, nik wheeler/Alamy Stock
Photo, Richard Levine/AGE fotostock; p.144 Corbis/Superstock; p.149 (from top left)
Igor Zh/Shutterstock, negaprion/Getty Images, Nancy Borowick-Pool/Getty Images,
AP Photo/Jack Smith, Andrew Yates/AFP/Getty Images, Terry Vine/Getty Images;
p.151 Jim Edds/Science Photo Library; p.155 Ivan Vdovin/Alamy Stock Photo; p.209
(from top left) Bettmann/Getty Images, Sovfoto/UIG via Getty Images, Sacagawea
with Lewis and Clark during their expedition of 1804-06 (colour litho), Wyeth,
Newell Convers (1882-1945)/Private Collection/Peter Newark American Pictures/
Bridgeman Images, Robert W. Kelley/The LIFE Picture Collection/Getty Images,
Universal History Archive/UIG via Getty Images, Alexander Nikitin/Shutterstock,
OUP/Goodshot, De Visu/Shutterstock, V&A Images/Alamy Stock Photo; p.211 OUP/
Tatuasha; p.241 OUP/Purestock.

*The publisher would like to thank the following for their permission to reproduce copyrighted
material:* 136–137: USPS Corporate Signature, Priority Mail, Express Mail, Media
Mail, Certified Mail, Ready Post, Airmail, Parcel Post, Letter Carrier Uniform, Postal
Clerk Uniform, Flag and Statue of Liberty, Postmark, Post Office Box, Automated
Postal Center, Parcel Drop Box, Round Top Collection Mailbox are trademarks of the
United States Postal Service and are used with permission. Flag and Statue of Liberty
© 2006 United States Postal Service. All Rights Reserved. Used with Permission.
155: MetroCard and the logo "MTA" are registered trademarks of the Metropolitan
Transportation Authority. Used with permission.

Welcome to the Oxford Picture Dictionary Third Edition Workbooks

The *Low Beginning, High Beginning,* and *Low Intermediate Workbooks* that accompany *The Oxford Picture Dictionary* have been designed to provide meaningful and enjoyable practice of the vocabulary that students are learning. These workbooks supply high-interest contexts and real information for enrichment and self-expression.

The Oxford Picture Dictionary Third Edition provides unparalleled support for vocabulary teaching and language development.

- New and expanded topics including job search, career planning, and digital literacy prepare students to meet the requirements of their daily lives.
- Updated activities prepare students for work, academic study, and citizenship.
- Oxford 3000 vocabulary ensures students learn the most useful and important words.

Page-for-page correlation with the Dictionary

The *Workbook* pages conveniently correspond to the pages of the *Picture Dictionary*. For example, if you are working on page 50 in the *Dictionary*, the activities for this topic, Apartments, will be found on page 50 in all three *Picture Dictionary Workbooks*.

Consistent easy-to-use format

All topics in the *High Beginning Workbook* follow the same format. Exercise 1 is always a "look in your dictionary" activity, where students are asked to complete a task while looking in their *Picture Dictionary*. The tasks include answering questions about the pictures, judging statements true or false, counting the number of illustrated occurrences of a vocabulary item, completing a time line, or speculating about who said what.

Following this activity are one or more content-rich contextualized exercises, including true or false, matching, categorizing, odd-one-out, and completion of forms. These exercises often feature graphs and charts with real data for students to work with as they practice the new vocabulary. Many topics include a personalization exercise that asks "What about you?" where students can use the new vocabulary to give information about their own lives or to express their opinions.

The final exercise for each topic is a Challenge, which can be assigned to students for additional work in class or as homework. Challenge activities provide higher-level speaking and writing practice, and for some topics will require students to interview classmates, conduct surveys, or find information outside of class by looking in the newspaper, for example, or online.

Each of the 12 units ends with Another Look, a review which allows students to practice vocabulary from all the topics of a unit in a game or puzzle-like activity, such as picture crosswords, word searches, and C-searches, where students search in a picture for items which begin with the letter *c*. These activities are at the back of the High Beginning Workbook on pages 248–259.

Throughout the *Workbook*, vocabulary is carefully controlled and recycled. Students should, however, be encouraged to use their *Picture Dictionaries* to look up words they do not recall, or, if they are doing topics out of sequence, may not yet have learned. *The Oxford Picture Dictionary Workbooks* can be used in the classroom or at home for self-study.

Acknowledgments

The publisher and author would like to acknowledge the following individuals for their invaluable feedback during the development of this workbook:

Patricia S. Bell, Lake Technical County ESOL, FL; Patricia Castro, Harvest English Institute, NJ; Druci Diaz, CARIBE Program and TBT, FL; Jill Gluck, Hollywood Community Adult School, CA; Frances Hardenbergh, Southside Programs for Adult and Continuing Ed, VA; Mercedes Hern, Tampa, FL; (Katie) Mary C. Hurter, North Harris College, TX; Karen Kipke, Antioch Freshman Academy, TN; Ivanna Mann-Thrower, Charlotte Mecklenburg Schools, NC; Holley Mayville, Charlotte Mecklenburg Schools, NC; Jonetta Myles, Salem High School, GA; Kathleen Reynolds, Albany Park Community Center, IL; Jan Salerno, Kennedy-San Fernando CAS, CA; Jenni Santamaria, ABC Adult School, CA; Geraldyne Scott, Truman College/ Lakeview Learning Center, IL; Sharada Sekar, Antioch Freshman Academy, TN; Terry Shearer, Region IV ESC, TX; Melissa Singler, Cape Fear Community College, NC; Cynthia Wiseman, Wiseman Language Consultants, NY

Table of Contents

Contents

11. Academic Study

12. Recreation

1. Look in your dictionary. Label the pictures.

a. *Shake hands.*

b. _____

c. _____

d. _____

e. _____

f. _____

2. Circle the answer.

a. **Say, "Hello."**

   Good evening.   (Hi.)   Fine, thanks.

b. **Introduce a friend.**

   Ana, this is Meng.   Hi, I'm Ana.   Nice to meet you, Ana.

c. **Greet people.**

   Luis, this is Mia.   Hello, everyone.   Fine, thanks.

d. **Say, "Goodbye."**

   Good evening.   Hello.   Good night.

3. What about you? Imagine Jessica is your friend. You see her in school. Check (✓) the things you do.

☐ Say, "Hello."   ☐ Ask, "How are you?"

☐ Introduce yourself.   ☐ Smile.

☐ Wave.   ☐ Hug.

☐ Kiss.   ☐ Bow.

☐ Shake hands.   ☐ Say, "Goodbye."

Jessica

4. **Look in your dictionary. *True* or *False*?**

   a. **Picture A:** He introduces himself. _____*false*_____

   b. **Picture D:** She introduces a friend. _____

   c. **Picture E:** He waves. _____

   d. **Picture F:** They hug. _____

   e. **Picture G:** She smiles. _____

   f. **Picture I:** They bow. _____

   g. **Picture J:** She introduces a friend. _____

   h. **Picture K:** They shake hands. _____

5. **What about you? Complete the conversations. Use the instructions in parentheses ( ).**

   a. **You:** _____*Hello, I'm*_____
        (Introduce yourself to Miguel.)

      Miguel: Hi. I'm Miguel.

   Miguel

   b. **You:** _____
        (Say, "Hello," to a friend.)

      Friend: Hi.

   c. **You:** _____
        (Ask your friend, "How are you?")

      Friend: Fine, thanks.

   d. **You:** _____
        (Introduce your friend to Miguel.)

      Miguel: Nice to meet you.

      Friend: Nice to meet you, Miguel.

   e. **You:** _____
        (Say, "Goodbye.")

      Miguel and Friend: Goodbye!

[CHALLENGE] Introduce yourself to two classmates. Then introduce the two classmates to each other.

1. Look in your dictionary. What is Carlos Soto's . . . ?

a. ZIP code ___33607-3614___   c. apartment number _____

b. area code _____   d. Social Security number _____

2. Match.

__9__ a. middle initial   1. female

____ b. signature   2. California

____ c. city   3. (310)

____ d. gender   4. 548-00-0000

____ e. area code   5. Los Angeles

____ f. Social Security number 6. Miriam S. Shakter

____ g. name   7. 90049-1000

____ h. ZIP code   8. *Miriam S. Shakter*

____ i. state   9. S.

3. What about you? Fill out the form. Use your own information.

L.A. Adult Center

REGISTRATION FORM
(Please print.)

Last name _____   First name _____   Middle initial _____

Gender: ☐ Male ☐ Female

Place of birth _____   Date of birth _____

Address _____   Apartment number _____

_____   _____
(City)   (State)   (ZIP code)

Home phone _____   Cell phone _____

_____
Signature

CHALLENGE Interview a classmate. Find out his or her last name, first name, middle initial, address, and place of birth.

1. Look in your dictionary. Put the words in the correct columns.

People	Places	
principal	_quad_	

2. Look at the floor plan. Match the rooms on the directory with the letters.

Directory

	Room(s)
Auditorium	C
Cafeteria	
Classrooms	
Gym	
Library	
Lockers	
Restrooms	
Men's	
Women's	

3. What about you? Check (✓) the places your school has.

☐ auditorium   ☐ library   ☐ track   ☐ computer lab   ☐ cafeteria

[CHALLENGE] Draw a floor plan or write a directory for your school.

1. **Look at the top picture in your dictionary. How many . . . are in the classroom?**

a. teachers ___1___

c. students ____

e. bookcases ____

b. computers ____

d. desks ____

f. chairs ____

2. **Look at the list of school supplies. Check (✓) the items you see in the picture.**

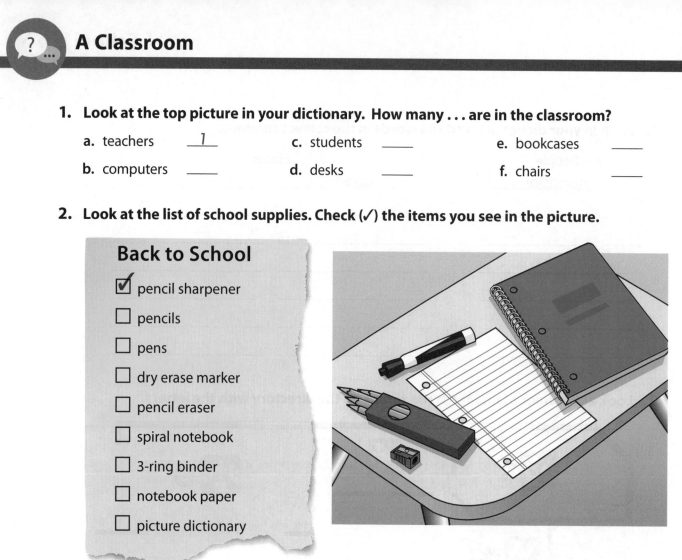

Back to School

- ✓ pencil sharpener
- ☐ pencils
- ☐ pens
- ☐ dry erase marker
- ☐ pencil eraser
- ☐ spiral notebook
- ☐ 3-ring binder
- ☐ notebook paper
- ☐ picture dictionary

3. **Complete the spelling test.**

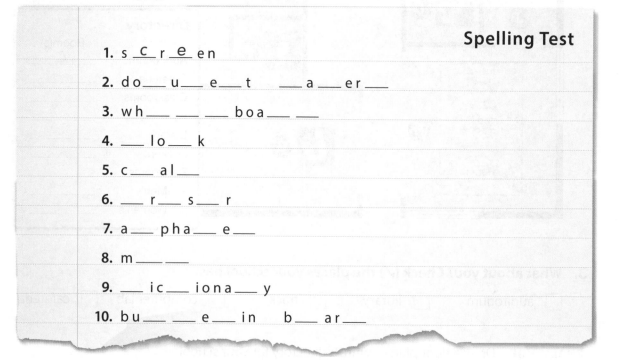

Spelling Test

1. s _c_ r _e_ en

2. d o __ u __ e __ t __ a __ e r __

3. w h __ __ __ b o a __ __

4. __ l o __ k

5. c __ a l __

6. __ r __ s __ r

7. a __ p h a __ e __

8. m __ __

9. __ i c __ i o n a __ y

10. b u __ __ e __ i n b __ a r __

4. Label the pictures. Use the words in the box.

Listen to a recording.	~~Open your workbook.~~	Stand up.
Pick up your pencil.	Close your workbook.	Put down your pencil.
Take a seat.	Raise your hand.	Talk to the teacher.

a. *Open your workbook.*

b. _____

c. _____

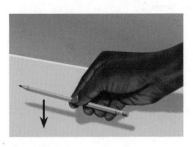

d. _____

e. _____

f. _____

g. _____

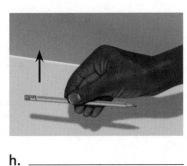

h. _____

i. _____

5. What about you? Check (✓) the items you use in your classroom.

- ☐ pencils
- ☐ spiral notebook
- ☐ pencil sharpener
- ☐ dictionary
- ☐ textbook
- ☐ Other: _____

- ☐ headphones
- ☐ permanent markers
- ☐ notebook paper
- ☐ picture dictionary
- ☐ computer

- ☐ pens
- ☐ 3-ring binder
- ☐ document camera
- ☐ workbook
- ☐ chalkboard

CHALLENGE Write about the items in Exercise 5. **Example:** *I have one dictionary. I have two pens. I don't have any pencils.*

1. **Look in your dictionary.** *True* or *False*?

   a. **Picture A:** The student is copying a word. _____*false*_____

   b. **Picture C:** The student is translating the word. _____

   c. **Picture J:** The students are sharing a book. _____

   d. **Picture K:** The woman is asking a question. _____

   e. **Picture M:** The students are putting away their books. _____

   f. **Picture N:** The man is dictating a sentence. _____

2. **Match.**

   _3_ a. Ask a question.

   ___ b. Answer the question.

   ___ c. Look up the word.

   ___ d. Translate the word.

   ___ e. Check the pronunciation.

   ___ f. Copy the word.

   ___ g. Draw a picture of the word.

   ___ h. Circle the answer.

   1. **pencil**/'pensl/

   2. pencil

      pencil

   3. What's a pencil?

   4.

   5. **pence** /pens/ *n.* (*pl.*) pennies.
      pencil/'pensl/ *n.* instrument for writing and drawing, made of a thin piece of wood with lead inside it.
      penetrate /'penɪtreɪt/ *v.* go into or through something: *A nail penetrated the car tire.*

   6. A pencil is something you write with.

   7. This is a pen /pencil.

   8. pencil = えんぴつ

3. Complete this test.

Name: _____   Class: _____

1. Fill in the blanks. Use the words in the box.

| away | ~~in~~ | out |

a. I'm filling _____*in*_____ the blanks.

b. The students are taking _____ their picture dictionaries.

c. The teacher is putting _____ the books.

2. Cross out the word that doesn't belong.

a. help   share   ~~match~~   brainstorm

b. ask   underline   circle   fill in

c. brainstorm copy   dictate   discuss

3. Underline the words that begin with _c_. Circle the words that begin with _d_.

read   <u>copy</u>   (draw)   share   help

dictate   circle   check   discuss   choose

4. Match.

__3__ a. Look up   1. a picture.

____ b. Draw   2. a question.

____ c. Ask   3. a word.

5. Unscramble the words.

a. tedicta ___*dictate*___   c. scudiss _____

b. wrad _____   d. lastetran _____

---

4. What about you? Look in your dictionary. Which classroom activities do you like to do? Which activities don't you like to do? Make two lists.

CHALLENGE Look up the word _thimble_ in your dictionary.
  a. Translate the word.
  b. Draw a picture of a thimble.
  c. Label the picture.

1. Look in your dictionary. *True* or *False*?

   a. Picture A: Sergio is taking notes.   *false*

   b. Picture B: He is participating in class.   _____

   c. Picture D: He is studying at home.   _____

   d. Picture G: He is not making progress.   _____

   e. Picture H: He is getting good grades.   _____

   f. Picture J: He is asking for help.   _____

   g. Picture K: He is taking a test.   _____

   h. Picture L: He is not checking his work.   _____

   i. Picture N: He is correcting the mistake.   _____

2. Sergio is taking a test. Number the activities in the correct order. (1 = the first thing Sergio does)

   ____ **a.** He checks his work.

   ____ **b.** He bubbles in the answer on the answer sheet.

   ____ **c.** He hands in his test.

   _1_ **d.** He clears off his desk.

   ____ **e.** He corrects the mistake.

   ____ **f.** He passes the test.

   ____ **g.** He erases the mistake.

3. What about you? Check (✓) the things you do.

   ☐ set goals   ☐ bubble in answers

   ☐ participate in class   ☐ check my work

   ☐ take notes   ☐ ask my teacher for help

   ☐ study at home   ☐ ask my classmates for help

CHALLENGE Write three study goals. **Example:** *Learn five words a day.*

   a. _____

   b. _____

   c. _____

1. Look in your dictionary. Circle the words to complete the sentences.

a. Five students (enter the room) / leave the room.

b. The teacher runs to class / turns on the light.

c. One student is carrying books / trash.

d. He's delivering them to room 102 / 202.

e. Two teachers have a conversation / buy a snack during the break.

f. After the break, they leave / go back to class.

2. Look at the pictures. Match.

1.
2.
3.
4.
5.
6.

____ **a.** The students leave the room.

____ **b.** The students enter the room.

____ **c.** The class takes a break.

____ **d.** The teacher turns off the lights.

_1_ **e.** The students walk to school.

____ **f.** The students go back to class.

3. What about you? Check (✓) the things you do at school.

☐ walk to class   ☐ run to class

☐ carry books   ☐ turn off the light

☐ take a break   ☐ buy a snack

☐ eat   ☐ drink

☐ throw away trash   ☐ lift books

CHALLENGE Look in your dictionary. Write sentences about picture H–L. What are people eating? What are they drinking? What are the teachers having a conversation about?

? Everyday Conversation

1. **Look in your dictionary. Circle the correct words.**

a. [Hi. I'm Danny.]   make small talk / (start a conversation)

b. [Is that *Donny*?]   check your understanding / explain something

c. [Nice day, isn't it?]   compliment someone / make small talk

d. [That's a nice jacket.]   agree / compliment someone

e. [I'm having a party tonight. Please come.]   accept an invitation / invite someone

2. **Complete the conversations from Amy's party. Use the sentences in the box.**

This food is great!	~~Coats go in there.~~	Oh! Sorry!	There?
No. It's very bad!	Here's a napkin.	Thanks!	That's OK.

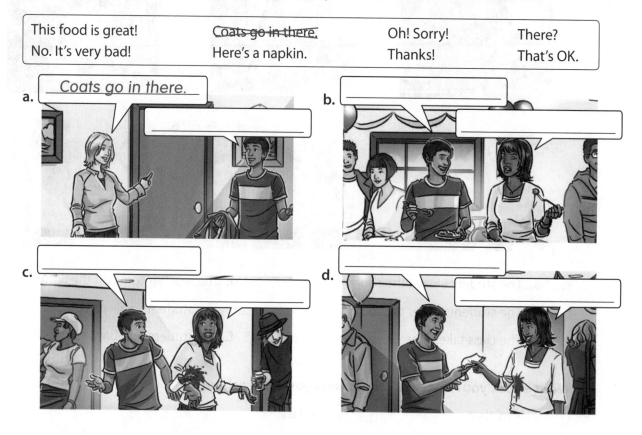

a. *Coats go in there.*

b.

c.

d.

3. **Look at Exercise 2. In which picture is someone . . . ?**

1. accepting an apology   _c_
2. apologizing   ___
3. checking understanding   ___
4. disagreeing   ___
5. offering something   ___
6. thanking someone   ___

[CHALLENGE] What are good topics for small talk? What are bad topics? Make a list.

1. Look in your dictionary. Describe the temperatures.

a. Fahrenheit: 95° ___*hot*___   35° _____   60° _____

b. Celsius: 25° _____   −10° _____   40° _____

2. Look at the weather map. Circle the words to complete the sentences.

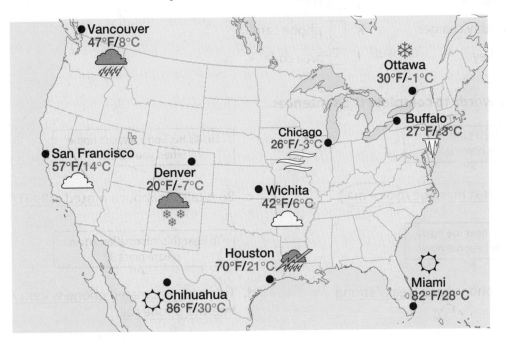

a. It's <u>foggy</u> / (windy) in Chicago.

b. There's a <u>heat wave / snowstorm</u> in Denver.

c. Houston is having a <u>dust storm / thunderstorm</u>.

d. It's <u>clear / cloudy</u> in Chihuahua.

e. The temperature is <u>cold / freezing</u> in Ottawa.

f. There's <u>rain / snow</u> in Vancouver.

g. It's <u>icy / smoggy</u> in Buffalo.

h. It's <u>cloudy / sunny</u> in San Francisco.

i. It's <u>hot / warm</u> and sunny in Miami.

j. It's cloudy and <u>cool / cold</u> in Wichita.

3. What about you? What kinds of weather do you like? Check (✓) the columns.

	I like it.	It's OK.	I don't like it.
humid			
cool and foggy			
rain and lightning			
warm and sunny			
hail			

CHALLENGE Write a weather report for your city. **Example:** *Monday, January 25. Today it's sunny and warm in San Antonio. The temperature is . . . .*

1. **Look at pages 14–15 in your dictionary. Check (✓) the things with numbers.**

   a. ✓ phone bill

   b. ☐ phone jack

   c. ☐ charger plug

   d. ☐ contact list

   e. ☐ monthly charges

   f. ☐ star key

   g. ☐ base

   h. ☐ handset

   i. ☐ keypad

   j. ☐ data

   k. ☐ phone card

   l. ☐ area code

2. **Circle the words to complete the sentences.**

   > Hi. It's me.
   > I'll be home late.

   a. This is a text message /(voice mail).

   > Can you hear me now?
   > Can you hear me now?

   b. The cell phone has a weak / strong signal.

   > Hi, it's Bo. Sorry I wasn't home when you called.

   c. Bo is talking about a missed call / TDD.

   > To hear this information again, please press 3.

   d. This is an automated phone system / Internet phone call.

3. **Look at pages 14–15 in your dictionary. Match.**

   _10_ a. 555-1357

   ___ b. 823

   ___ c. May 15, 2018–June 14, 2018

   ___ d. 911

   ___ e. 0

   ___ f. *

   ___ g. Horizon

   ___ h. #

   ___ i. $40.00

   ___ j. 1531-5471-2923-889

   ___ k. 411

   1. pound key

   2. emergency call

   3. billing period

   4. operator

   5. access number

   6. directory assistance

   7. star key

   8. monthly charges

   9. area code

   10. phone number

   11. carrier

4. Look in your dictionary. Cross out the word that doesn't belong.

a. **Keys on the keypad**   star   pound   operator   ~~carrier~~

b. **Types of calls**   long-distance   local   data   Internet

c. **Things with cords**   contact list   base   headset   cell phone

d. **Parts of a phone**   keypad   handset   TDD   base

e. **Things to read**   voice mail   contact list   phone bill   text message

5. Circle the words to complete the instructions.

Follow these instructions for an (emergency)/ international call:
   a.

First, dial 411 / 911. Give your contact list / name to the operator.
   b.   c.

Then state the emergency / press talk. Is there a fire? Do you need a doctor? Tell the operator.
   d.

Stay on the line. Hang up / Don't hang up! The operator will ask you more questions.
   e.

6. What about you? Complete the chart.

Important Phone Numbers		
	Emergency	911
	Non-emergency	
	Directory assistance (local calls)	
	Doctor	
	School	
	Other: _____	

CHALLENGE   Find out the area codes for five cities. Use the Internet or ask your classmates.
   Example: *San Antonio—713 and 830*

Numbers

1. Look in your dictionary. Write the types of numbers. What comes next?

a. ___Ordinal numbers___ : tenth, twentieth, thirtieth, ___fortieth___

b. _____ : VI, VII, VIII, _____

c. _____ : 70, 80, 90, _____

2. Complete the chart.

Word	Number	Roman Numeral
ten	10	X
		III
	15	
		L
	20	
one hundred		
		D
one thousand		

3. Look at the bar graph. Ana is first (= best) in her class. What about the other students? Complete the sentences.

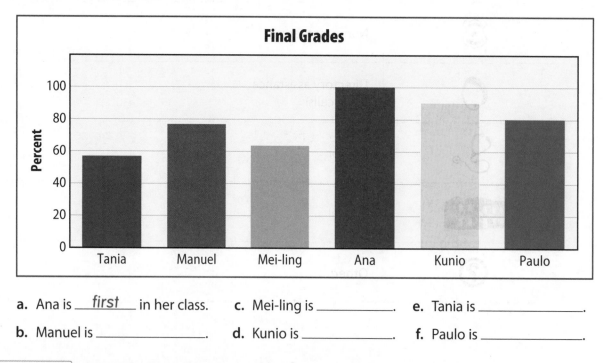

Final Grades

a. Ana is ___first___ in her class.   c. Mei-ling is _____.   e. Tania is _____.

b. Manuel is _____.   d. Kunio is _____.   f. Paulo is _____.

CHALLENGE   Work with a partner. Where can you see cardinal numbers? Ordinal numbers? Roman numerals? Write sentences. Compare your answers.
Example: *Telephone numbers have cardinal numbers.*

1. **Look in your dictionary. What kind of numbers are these?**

   a. 1/5 ___*fraction*___   b. 20% _____   c. .20 _____

2. **Look at the chart. Complete the sentences.**

   a. ___*Sixty-two percent*___ speak Spanish.

   b. _____ speak French.

   c. _____ speak Tagalog.

   d. _____ speak Chinese.

   e. _____ speak Vietnamese.

   f. _____ speak other languages.

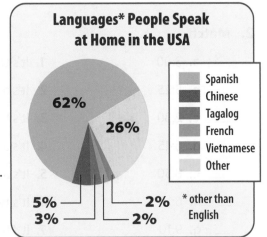

Languages* People Speak at Home in the USA

62%   26%

Spanish
Chinese
Tagalog
French
Vietnamese
Other

5%   2%
3%   2%

* other than English

Based on information from: *US Census Bureau, American Community Survey Reports, 2011.*

3. **Look at the books. Complete the sentences.**

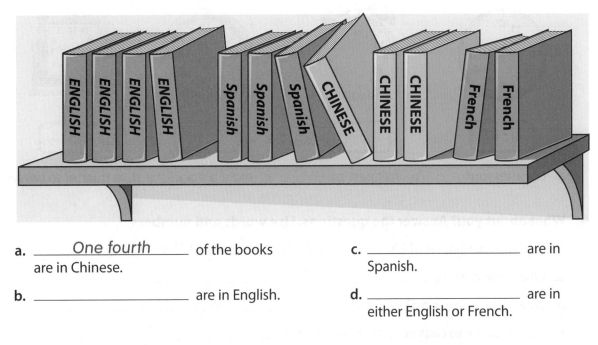

   a. ___*One fourth*___ of the books are in Chinese.

   b. _____ are in English.

   c. _____ are in Spanish.

   d. _____ are in either English or French.

4. **What about you? Measure a bookcase in school or at home. Write the measurements.**

   width _____   height _____   depth _____

   CHALLENGE How many students in your class speak your language? How many students speak other languages? Calculate the percents. **Example:** *There are twenty students in my class. Ten students speak Spanish. That's fifty percent.*

Time

1. Look in your dictionary. What's another way to say . . . ?

    a. ten-thirty   _half past ten_   **c.** a quarter after three   _____

    b. two-forty-five   _____   **d.** twenty after six   _____

2. Match.

   _3_ **a.** 3:00   **1.** It's ten to nine.

   ___ **b.** 5:25   **2.** It's a quarter to seven.

   ___ **c.** 2:30   **3.** It's three o'clock.

   ___ **d.** 6:45   **4.** It's a quarter after six.

   ___ **e.** 8:50   **5.** It's a quarter to six.

   ___ **f.** 6:15   **6.** It's two-thirty.

   ___ **g.** 9:10   **7.** It's five-twenty-five.

   ___ **h.** 5:45   **8.** It's ten after nine.

3. Complete the clocks.

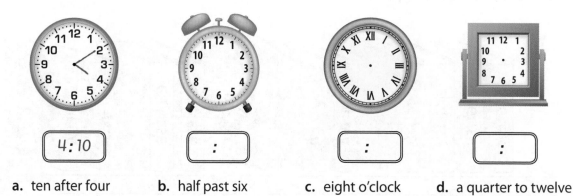

    a. ten after four   **b.** half past six   **c.** eight o'clock   **d.** a quarter to twelve

4. What about you? Answer the questions. Use words and numbers.

    Example: What time is it? It's _____ _four-fifteen p.m. (4:15 p.m.)_ _____.

    a. What time is it? It's _____.

    b. What time is your class? It's from _____ to _____.

    c. Do you come to class early, on time, or late? _____.

        If you come early or late, at what time? At _____.

    d. What time do you leave class? At _____.

    e. What time do you get home? At _____.

5. Look at the map in your dictionary. In which time zone is . . . ?

a. Caracas _____Atlantic_____   c. Denver _____

b. Chicago _____   d. Vancouver _____

6. Look at the chart. It's 12:00 noon in New York City. What time is it in . . . ?
Use numbers and the words in the box.

At 12:00 noon, Eastern Standard Time, the time in . . . is . . .			
Athens	7 P.M.	Mexico City	11 A.M.
Baghdad	8 P.M.	Montreal	12 noon
Bangkok	12 midnight*	New York City	12 noon
Barcelona	6 P.M.	Panama	12 noon
Buenos Aires	3 P.M.	Paris	6 P.M.
Frankfurt	6 P.M.	Rio de Janeiro	3 P.M.
Halifax	1 P.M.	Riyadh	8 P.M.
Hanoi	12 midnight*	Rome	6 P.M.
Havana	12 noon	St. Petersburg	8. P.M.
Hong Kong	1 A.M.*	San Juan	1 P.M.
Houston	11 A.M.	Seoul	2 A.M.*
Kolkata	10:30 P.M.	Sydney	4 A.M.*
London	5 P.M.	Tel Aviv	7 P.M.
Los Angeles	9 A.M.	Tokyo	2 A.M.*
Mecca	8 P.M.	Zurich	6 P.M.
* = the next day			

| in the morning   in the afternoon   in the evening   at night   noon   midnight |

a. Athens ____7:00 in the evening____   g. St. Petersburg _____

b. London _____   h. Bangkok _____

c. Kolkata _____   i. Mexico City _____

d. Panama _____   j. Frankfurt _____

e. Halifax _____   k. Los Angeles _____

f. Tokyo _____   l. Hanoi _____

7. What about you? Does your native country have . . . ? Write *Yes* or *No*.

a. different time zones? _____   b. daylight saving time? _____

CHALLENGE   Find out the time for sunrise and sunset in your area. Look in a newspaper or online.

The Calendar

1. **Look in your dictionary. In May, how many . . . are there?**

   a. days   <u>31</u>

   b. Mondays   ___

   c. Thursdays   ___

   d. weekdays   ___

   e. two-day weekends   ___

   f. seven-day weeks   ___

2. **Unscramble the months. Then number them in order. (1 = the first month)**

   a. r a J n y u a   <u>January</u>   <u>1</u>

   b. y a M   _____   ___

   c. m e D b r e c e   _____   ___

   d. n u J e   _____   ___

   e. c h a r M   _____   ___

   f. b r e t o c O   _____   ___

   g. l i p r A   _____   ___

   h. l y J u   _____   ___

   i. p r e S e t m e b   _____   ___

   j. b r u F y e a r   _____   ___

   k. s A t u g u   _____   ___

   l. v e N o m b e r   _____   ___

3. **Write the seasons.**

Seasons in the United States			
December 21 – March 20	March 21 – June 20	June 21 – September 20	September 21 – December 20

   a. <u>winter</u>   b. _____   c. _____   d. _____

4. **Look at the dates. Write the seasons. Use the information from Exercise 3.**

   a. January 5   <u>winter</u>

   b. November 28   _____

   c. March 22   _____

   d. May 6   _____

   e. December 19   _____

   f. June 25   _____

5. Look at Antonio's calendar. *True* or *False*?

			March			
SUN.	MON.	TUES.	WED.	THURS.	FRI.	SAT.
	1 Science Lab English	2 Computer Lab Math	3 English	4 Gym Math	5 Language Lab English	6 To Los Angeles!
7 Daylight Saving Time	8	9	10 NO CLASSES	11	12 To N.Y.	13 Ana 7:00 p.m.
14	15 Science Lab English	16 Auditorium 2:00 Math	17 English	18 Gym Math	19 Language Lab English	20 Track & Field
21 Mary 6:00 p.m.	22 Science Lab English	23 Counselor's Office 3:15 Math	24 English	25 Gym Math	26 Language Lab English	27 Library with Frank
28	29 Science Lab English	30	31			

TODAY'S DATE (19)

a. Antonio has class every day this month.   *false*

b. He has Math twice a week.   _____

c. He has Math on Wednesday and Friday.   _____

d. He has English three times a week.   _____

e. He has Gym once a week.   _____

f. He was in Los Angeles last weekend.   _____

g. Tomorrow he has Track & Field.   _____

h. Yesterday was Tuesday.   _____

i. He sees Mary Saturday night.   _____

j. He sees Mary every weekend.   _____

k. There were no classes last week.   _____

l. Daylight saving time begins this week.   _____

m. Next week Antonio sees the school counselor.   _____

CHALLENGE Make a calendar of your monthly activities. Write ten sentences about your calendar.

Calendar Events

1. **Look in your dictionary. Number the legal holidays in order.**
   (1 = the first holiday in the year)

   ____ **a.** Labor Day   ____ **e.** Memorial Day

   ____ **b.** Christmas   ____ **f.** Presidents' Day

   ____ **c.** Fourth of July   ____ **g.** Thanksgiving

   _1_ **d.** New Year's Day   ____ **h.** Martin Luther King Jr. Day

2. **Look at the pictures. Match.**

   _2_ **a.** Luisa's first doctor's appointment   ____ **d.** Our tenth anniversary

   ____ **b.** Our wedding   ____ **e.** Thanksgiving

   ____ **c.** Vacation, summer 2012   ____ **f.** Luisa's eighth birthday

CHALLENGE Bring some photos to class. Write captions on your own paper.

1. Look in your dictionary. Write the opposites.

a. big _____little_____

b. same _____

c. heavy _____

d. cheap _____

e. ugly _____

f. slow _____

2. Look at the classroom. *True* or *False*? Change the <u>underlined</u> word in the false sentences. Make the sentences true.

a. The chairs are <u>soft</u>.   _*False. The chairs are hard.*_

b. There's a <u>big</u> clock in the room.   _____

c. Bob is a <u>good</u> student.   _____

d. His book is <u>thin</u>.   _____

e. The teacher's glass is <u>empty</u>.   _____

f. The words on the board are <u>easy</u>.   _____

g. The classroom is <u>noisy</u>.   _____

3. What about you? Check (✓) the words that describe your classroom.

☐ beautiful   ☐ big   ☐ quiet

☐ noisy   ☐ ugly   ☐ Other: _____

CHALLENGE   Describe your classroom. Write six sentences.

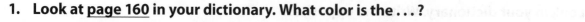

1. Look at <u>page 160</u> in your dictionary. What color is the . . . ?

    a. convertible   <u>   red   </u>   **c.** hatchback   <u>   </u>

    b. school bus   <u>   </u>   **d.** pickup truck   <u>   </u>

2. Look at the pie charts. Put the colors in order. (1 = favorite)

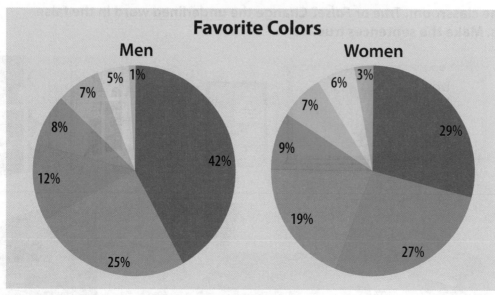

Based on information from: *LiveScience.com* (2012).

Men's Favorite Colors	Women's Favorite Colors
1. <u> blue </u>	1. <u> </u>
2. <u> </u>	2. <u> </u>
3. <u> </u>	3. <u> </u>
4. <u> </u>	4. <u> </u>
5. <u> </u>	5. <u> </u>
6. <u> </u>	6. <u> </u>
7. <u> </u>	7. <u> </u>

3. What about you? Put the colors in order. (1 = your favorite)

   <u>   </u> red   <u>   </u> turquoise   <u>   </u> yellow   <u>   </u> pink   <u>   </u> violet

   <u>   </u> brown   <u>   </u> light blue   <u>   </u> dark blue   <u>   </u> orange   <u>   </u> beige

CHALLENGE   Make a list of the colors in Exercise 2. Ask five men and five women their favorite colors. Do their answers agree with the information in Exercise 2?

1. **Look at <u>page 24</u> in your dictionary. *True* or *False*?**

   a. The red sweaters are above the yellow sweaters.   _____*true*_____

   b. The purple sweaters are next to the orange sweaters.   _____

   c. The white sweaters are between the black and gray sweaters.   _____

   d. The brown sweaters are on the left.   _____

   e. The dark blue sweaters are below the turquoise sweaters.   _____

2. **Follow the instructions below.**

   a. Put the letter **W** in the pink box.

   b. Put a **Y** below it.

   c. Put an **E** in the yellow box.

   d. Put an **I** above the **E**.

   e. Put a **P** next to the **E**, on the left.

   f. Put a **U** in the green box.

   g. Put an **O** between the **Y** and the **U**.

   h. Put an **E** above the **U**.

   i. Put an **R** next to the **U**, on the right.

   j. Put an **H** between the **W** and the **E**.

   k. Put the letters **E**, **N**, **R**, and **S** in the correct boxes to complete the question.

3. **What about you? Look at Exercise 2. Answer the question.**

   _____

   CHALLENGE Draw a picture of your classroom. Write about the locations of the classroom
   items in your picture. **Example**: *The map is next to the board, on the right.*

1. **Look in your dictionary. How much money is there in . . . ?**

a. coins ___$1.91___   **b.** bills _____   **c.** coins and bills _____

2. **Look at the money. How much is it? Use numbers.**

a. _____$5.10_____   **b.** _____ or _____   **c.** _____ or _____

d. _____   **e.** _____   **f.** _____

3. **Read the cartoon. Who . . . ? Check (✓) the correct column.**

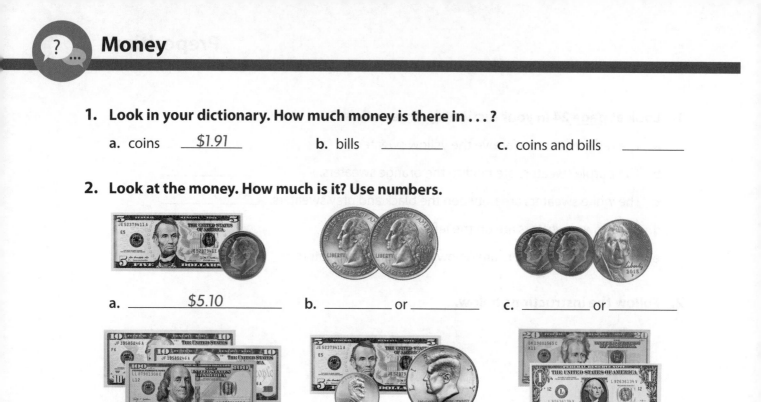

I need a quarter. Do you have change for $1.00?

No, sorry. But here's a quarter.

Here's your quarter.

Oh, thanks!

	The Man	The Woman
a. wants to gets change	✓	☐
b. lends money	☐	☐
c. borrows money	☐	☐
d. pays back money	☐	☐

CHALLENGE How many different ways can you get change for a dollar? **Example:** *four quarters*

1. Look in your dictionary. Match.

1.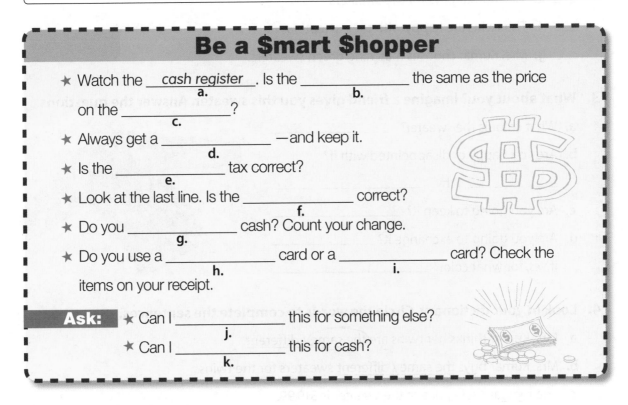

2.

3.

4.

5.

6.

___3___ **a.** SKU number   ____ **c.** use a debit card   ____ **e.** sales tax

____ **b.** bar code   ____ **d.** use a gift card   ____ **f.** regular price

2. Complete the shopping tips. Use the words in the box.

~~cash register~~	credit	debit	exchange	pay	total
price	price tag	receipt	return	sales	

Be a $mart $hopper

★ Watch the ___cash register___. Is the _____ the same as the price
             a.   **b.**
   on the _____?
           c.

★ Always get a _____ —and keep it.
               d.

★ Is the _____ tax correct?
          e.

★ Look at the last line. Is the _____ correct?
                         f.

★ Do you _____ cash? Count your change.
             g.

★ Do you use a _____ card or a _____ card? Check the
                 h.   **i.**
   items on your receipt.

Ask: ★ Can I _____ this for something else?
                j.
      ★ Can I _____ this for cash?
                  k.

3. What about you? What has sales tax in your state? How much is it?

CHALLENGE Look at page 260 in this book. Complete the sales slip.

Go to page 248 for Another Look (Unit 1).

1. Look in your dictionary. *True* or *False*?

    a. Anya and Manda are twins.   ____*true*____

    b. Mrs. Kumar is shopping for matching sweaters.   _____

    c. She buys two navy blue sweaters.   _____

    d. Manda is happy with her sweater.   _____

    e. Anya is happy with her sweater.   _____

    f. Mrs. Kumar looks disappointed.   _____

    g. Anya keeps her sweater.   _____

2. Put the sentences in order. (1 = the first event) Use your dictionary for help.

    ____ **a.** The twins look at the sweaters.

    _1_ **b.** Mrs. Kumar shops for Manda and Anya.

    ____ **c.** Anya exchanges her sweater.

    ____ **d.** Manda is happy with the sweater, but Anya is a little disappointed.

    ____ **e.** Mrs. Kumar pays for the sweaters.

    ____ **f.** The twins are happy with their sweaters.

    ____ **g.** Mrs. Kumar chooses matching green sweaters.

3. What about you? Imagine a friend gives you this sweater. Answer the questions.

    a. What color is the sweater? _____

    b. Are you happy or disappointed with it?

    _____ Why? _____

    c. Are you going to keep it? _____

    d. Are you going to exchange it? _____

    If *yes*, for what color? _____

4. Look in your dictionary. Circle the words to complete the sentences.

    a. Mrs. Kumar thinks her twins are (the same) / different.

    b. Mrs. Kumar buys the same / different sweaters for the twins.

    c. The regular / sale price of the sweater is $19.99.

    d. The total / sales tax is $43.38.

    e. Mrs. Kumar pays cash / uses a credit card.

    f. Manda exchanges / keeps the sweater.

5. Look in your dictionary. Complete the receipt. Write the total and the change.

```
         A&G
   DATE: ___10/20/16___
  ******************************
  ITEM
  1 GREEN SWEATER    $_____

  _____       $_____

  SUBTOTAL           $ 39.98

  SALES TAX          $  3.40

  TOTAL              $_____

  CASH               $ 45.00

  CHANGE             $_____

  ******************************
  THANK YOU FOR SHOPPING WITH US.
```

6. Complete Manda's journal entry. Use the words in the box.

| disappointed | happy | keep | matching |
| navy blue | ~~shop~~ | sweaters | twins |

October 22

Mom really likes to _____shop_____ for us! Yesterday, she gave us two beautiful
          a.

_____ green _____. I'm very _____ with my sweater.
  b.   **c.**   **d.**

I love the color, and it's thick and warm. Anya was a little _____.
                        e.

She wants to be different. I'm going to _____ my sweater, but Anya
              f.

exchanged her sweater for a _____ sweater. Anya said to Mom,
              g.

"Our sweaters are now different colors, but they are still the same sweaters."

And Mom said, "You're different people, but you're still _____!"
                                 h.

7. What about you? Look in your dictionary. Which color sweater do you like?

CHALLENGE Imagine you are Anya. Write a journal entry about the sweaters.

Adults and Children

1. **Look in your dictionary. How many . . . are there?**

   a. men   <u>3</u>

   b. women   __

   c. senior citizens   __

   d. infants   __

   e. teenagers   __

   f. girls   __

2. **Which words are for males? Which words are for females? Which words are for both? Put the words in the box in the correct spaces in the circles.**

~~baby~~	infant	teen
boy	man	toddler
girl	senior citizen	woman

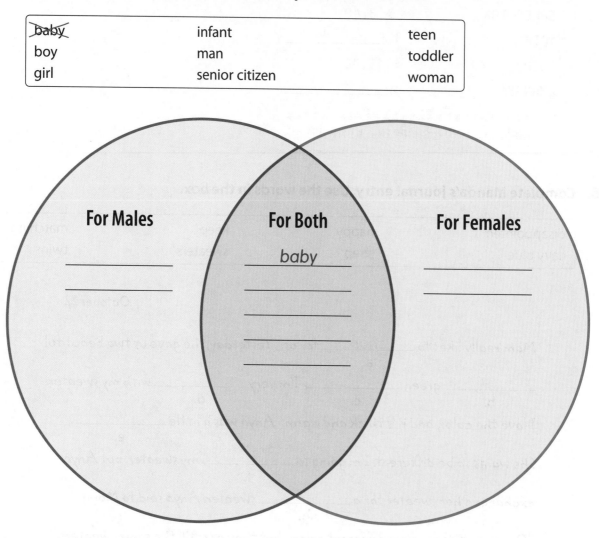

For Males

For Both

baby

For Females

3. **What about you? How many . . . are in your class?**

   men   __

   women   __

   senior citizens   __

   teenagers   __

4. Look in your dictionary. *True* or *False*? Write a question mark (?) if you don't know.

a. The senior citizen is a woman. _____true_____

b. The toddler is a girl. _____

c. The infant is a boy. _____

d. The teenager is sitting next to a 10-year-old boy. _____

e. The baby is sitting next to a woman. _____

f. A man is holding the infant. _____

5. Match.

_2_ a. man   **1.** 78 years old

___ b. toddler   **2.** 40 years old

___ c. teen   **3.** 10 years old

___ d. girl   **4.** 2 months old

___ e. infant   **5.** 2 years old

___ f. senior citizen   **6.** 17 years old

6. Label the pictures. Use the words from Exercise 5.

a. _____teen_____   b. _____   c. _____

d. _____   e. _____   f. _____

CHALLENGE Look in your dictionary. How old are the people? Discuss your answers with a classmate. **Example:** *A: I think this man is 40. What about you? B: I think he's only 30.*

Describing People

1. Look in your dictionary. Write the opposites.

a. young   *elderly*

b. tall   _____

c. thin   _____ or _____

2. Look at the ads. Circle the words that describe age and appearance. Match the ads with the photos.

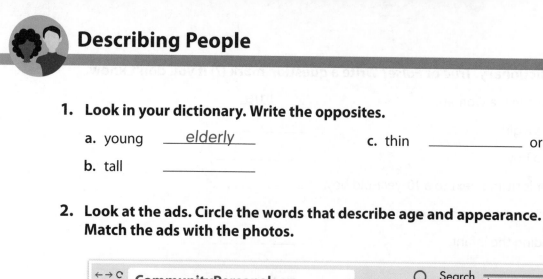

← → C   **CommunityPersonals.us**   🔍 Search our Site | ☰

① ② ③ ④ ⑤

___3___ a. **Hi!:** I'm a (short) attractive middle-aged woman. You're smart, nice and funny. Appearance not important.   cutiepie@mid.us

_____ b. **Attractive:** Slender, elderly woman looking for relationship with honest man.   happyface@lcd.us

_____ c. **Young and Attractive:** Physically challenged man looking for someone to share the great things in life.   travelfun@eol.us

_____ d. **Short and Sweet:** Cute young woman of average weight seeks nice fun-loving man. No tattoos please!   sallyo@rcd.us

_____ e. **Friendly and Fun:** Great guy of average height and average weight. Looking for a happy woman who loves life.   ff@eol.us

3. Look at the photos in Exercise 2. Do people have . . . ? Check (✓) the boxes. For the boxes with checks, write the number of the picture.

✓ pierced ears _3_   ☐ a mole ____   ☐ a tattoo ____

CHALLENGE   Name a famous person who was or is . . . .
a. physically challenged   b. sight impaired   c. hearing impaired

1. **Look at the top picture in your dictionary. How many . . . do you see?**

   a. combs   _5_   **c.** blow dryers   ___   **e.** sanitizing jars   ___

   b. rollers   ___   **d.** brushes   ___   **f.** shears   ___

2. **Look at the pictures of Cindi. Check (✓) the things The Hair Salon did to Cindi's hair.**

3. **Circle the words to complete the paragraph about Cindi.**

   Cindi is very happy with her new hairstyle. Before, she had short /(long,) curly / straight,
                                                                a.   **b.**

   blond / brown hair with corn rows / bangs and a part / no part. Now she has very
         c.   **d.**   **e.**

   long / short, curly / straight, red / black hair. Cindi looks great!
       f.   **g.**   **h.**

4. **What about you? Draw a picture of a friend's hair. Check (✓) the correct boxes.**
   My friend has . . . .

  ☐ short hair   ☐ shoulder-length hair   ☐ long hair

  ☐ no hair (bald)   ☐ straight hair   ☐ wavy hair

  ☐ curly hair   ☐ a part   ☐ bangs

  ☐ corn rows   ☐ a mustache   ☐ a beard

  ☐ sideburns   ☐ _____ hair
                                 (list hair color)

CHALLENGE   Find three pictures of hairstyles in your dictionary, a newspaper or magazine, or online. Write descriptions.

Families

1. **Look in your dictionary. Put the words in the box in the correct category.**

| aunt~~ ~~ | brother-in-law | cousin | daughter | grandmother |
| husband | niece | parent | son | uncle |

Male	Female	Male or Female
_____	*aunt*	_____
_____	_____	_____
_____	_____	
_____	_____	

2. **Look in your dictionary. *True* or *False*?**

Tim Lee's family:

a. Tim has two sisters.   *false*

b. Min is Lu's wife.   _____

c. Dan is Min and Lu's nephew.   _____

d. Tim and Emily have the same grandparents.   _____

e. Rose is Emily's aunt.   _____

Ana Garcia's family:

f. Ana is Carlos's sister-in-law.   _____

g. Sara is Eva and Sam's granddaughter.   _____

h. Felix is Alice's brother.   _____

i. Marta is Eddie's mother-in-law.   _____

j. Marta is Eva and Sam's daughter-in-law.   _____

3. **What about you? What is your . . . ? Answer the questions.**

a. name: _____

b. mother's name: _____

c. father's name: _____

d. marital status: ☐ single ☐ married ☐ divorced

     If you are married, what is your husband's or wife's name? _____

e. **Do you have children?** ☐ yes ☐ no

     If *yes*, what are their names? _____

4. Look in your dictionary. Circle the answers.

a. Carol was Bruce's (wife)/ sister.

b. Sue is Kim's stepmother / mother.

c. Rick is a single father / father.

d. David is Mary's brother / half brother.

e. Lisa is Bill's half sister / stepsister.

f. Bruce is Bill and Kim's father / stepfather.

5. Look at Megan's pictures. Put the sentences in order.

1.

Megan and Chet—2010

2.

Megan, Chet, and Nicole—2011

3.

Megan   Chet

4.

Megan and Nicole—2013

5.

Megan, Brian, Nicole, and Jason—2015

6.

Megan, Nicole, and Jason—2015

____ a. Megan is remarried.

____ b. Megan is a stepmother.

_1_ c. Megan is married.

____ d. Megan has a baby.

____ e. Megan is a single mother.

____ f. Megan is divorced.

6. Complete Nicole's story. Use the information in Exercise 5.

Name: Nicole Parker   October 10, 2018

My name is Nicole. My _____*mother*_____'s name is Megan.
                                          a.
My _____'s name is Chet. I have a _____.
              b.   c.
His name is Brian. Brian has a _____.
                                          d.
His name is Jason. Jason is my _____.
                                          e.

CHALLENGE Draw your family tree. Use the family trees in your dictionary as a model.

Childcare and Parenting

1. Look in your dictionary. Who is . . . the child? Check (✓) the answers.

	Mother	Father	Grandmother
a. bathing	✓	☐	☐
b. reading to	☐	☐	☐
c. disciplining	☐	☐	☐
d. holding	☐	☐	☐
e. kissing	☐	☐	☐
f. undressing	☐	☐	☐
g. rocking	☐	☐	☐
h. buckling up	☐	☐	☐
i. feeding	☐	☐	☐
j. dressing	☐	☐	☐
k. praising	☐	☐	☐

2. Look at Sofia's *To Do* list. What is Sofia doing? Write sentences.

a. It's 10:00. *She's bathing the baby.*

b. It's 12:00. _____

c. It's 11:30. _____

d. It's 10:30. _____

e. It's 1:15. _____

TO DO

10:00 a.m. bathe Luisa

10:30 a.m. dress her

11:00–11:45 a.m. play with her

12:00 p.m. feed her

1:00–1:30 p.m. read to her

3. What about you? Check (✓) the things you can do.

	Yes	No
a. comfort a baby	☐	☐
b. read nursery rhymes to a child	☐	☐
c. feed baby food to a child	☐	☐
d. dress a child in training pants	☐	☐
e. change a cloth diaper	☐	☐
f. rock a baby to sleep	☐	☐

4. Cross out the word that doesn't belong.

a. Places to sit   high chair   ~~diaper pail~~   potty seat

b. Things a baby wears   pacifier   bib   disposable diaper

c. Things a baby eats   formula   baby food   baby lotion

d. Things with wheels   rocking chair   carriage   stroller

e. Things to put in a baby's mouth   teething ring   diaper bag   nipple

f. Things for changing diapers   baby powder   training pants   wipes

g. Things a baby plays with   night light   rattle   teddy bear

h. Things that hold a baby   safety pins   baby carrier   car safety seat

5. There are eight childcare and parenting words. They go across (→) and down (↓). Find and circle six more. Use the pictures as clues.

```
P  A  C  I  F  I  E  R  D
Y  W  R  E  N  S  S  A  I
N  I  X  S  L  E  N  T  A
E  P  R  N  H  Y  A  T  P
X  E  M  B  O  T  T  L  E
E  S  T  R  O  L  L  E  R
R  H  C  E  B  R  B  M  L
C  A  R  R  I  A  G  E  O
H  A  L  R  B  R  U  L  N
```

[CHALLENGE] Make a list of things to put in a diaper bag. What can you use them for?
Example: *bottle—to feed the baby*

1. Look in your dictionary. Complete Dan Lim's schedule.

Schedule	12:34 PM
6:00 A.M.	wake up
6:30 A.M.	get dressed
7:00 A.M.	_____
7:30 A.M.	_____
_____	drive to work
5:00 P.M.	_____
_____	exercise at the gym
	have dinner
8:00 P.M.	_____
8:30 P.M.	_____
_____	go to sleep

2. Look at the picture of the Lims' things. Match each item with the correct activity.

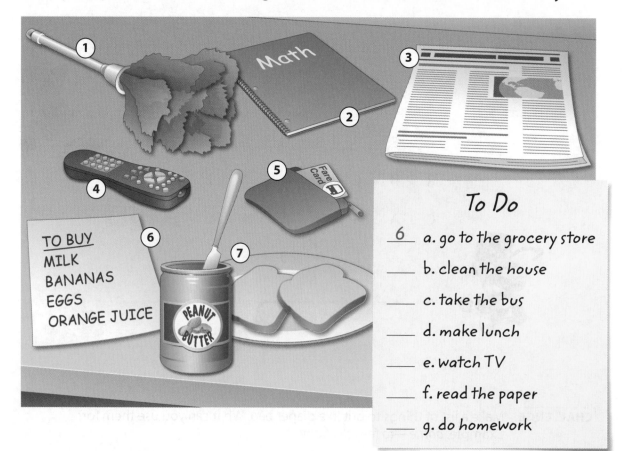

To Do

6   a. go to the grocery store

_____ b. clean the house

_____ c. take the bus

_____ d. make lunch

_____ e. watch TV

_____ f. read the paper

_____ g. do homework

3. **Read about Nora Lim. Complete the story. Use the words in the boxes.**

checks	eats	gets up	~~relaxes~~	takes

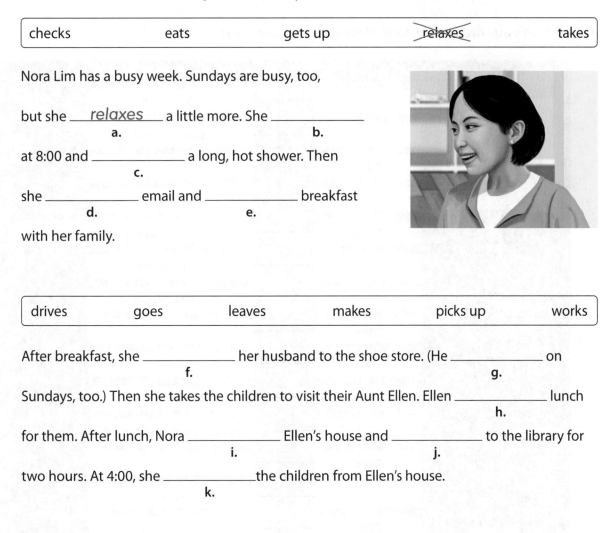

Nora Lim has a busy week. Sundays are busy, too,

but she ___*relaxes*___ a little more. She _____
        a.   **b.**

at 8:00 and _____ a long, hot shower. Then
                c.

she _____ email and _____ breakfast
      d.   **e.**

with her family.

drives	goes	leaves	makes	picks up	works

After breakfast, she _____ her husband to the shoe store. (He _____ on
                f.   **g.**

Sundays, too.) Then she takes the children to visit their Aunt Ellen. Ellen _____ lunch
                                                                       h.

for them. After lunch, Nora _____ Ellen's house and _____ to the library for
                                i.   **j.**

two hours. At 4:00, she _____ the children from Ellen's house.
                            k.

cooks	gets	goes	has	takes	watches

Nora _____ home at 5:00 and _____ dinner for her family. Her daughter,
           l.   **m.**

Sara, helps her. Dan _____ the bus home. The family _____ dinner at 6:00.
                    n.   **o.**

They talk about their day. After dinner, Nora _____ TV with her family. At 10:00,
                                          p.

Nora _____ to bed.
        q.

4. **What about you? Complete your weekday or weekend schedule. Use the schedule in Exercise 1 as an example.**

CHALLENGE   Interview someone you know (a friend, family member, or classmate). Write a schedule of his or her daily routine.

Life Events and Documents

1. Look in your dictionary. Complete the timeline for Martin Perez.

YEARS	LIFE EVENTS
1935	*be born*
1940	**start school**
1950	
	graduate
1954	**and become a citizen**
	go to college
	get engaged
1959	
1961	
	buy a home
	become a grandparent
2000	
	travel
2008	

2. Complete the story about Rosa Lopez. Use the words in the box.

~~was~~	died	fell	got	graduated	had	got	learned

Rosa Lopez _____*was*_____ born in the United States in 1938. She _____ from
　　　　　　　　a.　　　　　　　　　　　　　　　　　　　**b.**

high school in 1955. In 1956, she _____ to drive and _____
　　　　　　　　　　　　　　　　　　　c.　　　　　　　**d.**

a job in Los Angeles. Then she met Martin.

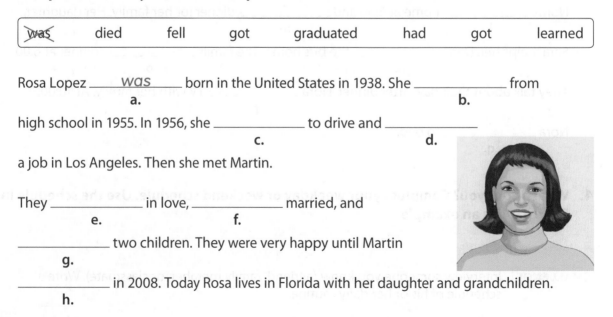

They _____ in love, _____ married, and
　　　e.　　　　　　　**f.**

_____ two children. They were very happy until Martin
g.

_____ in 2008. Today Rosa lives in Florida with her daughter and grandchildren.
h.

40

3. Look at the documents. Answer the questions.

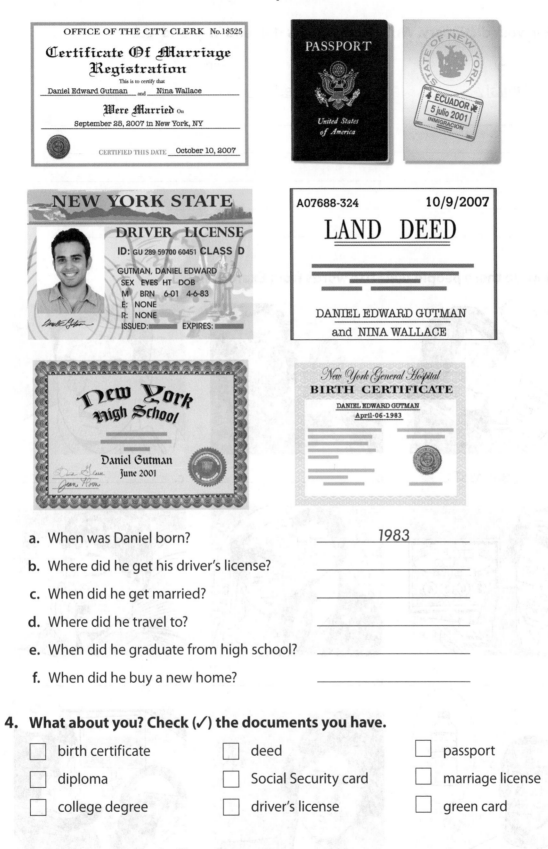

a. When was Daniel born? <u>   1983   </u>

b. Where did he get his driver's license? _____

c. When did he get married? _____

d. Where did he travel to? _____

e. When did he graduate from high school? _____

f. When did he buy a new home? _____

4. What about you? Check (✓) the documents you have.

☐ birth certificate   ☐ deed   ☐ passport

☐ diploma   ☐ Social Security card   ☐ marriage license

☐ college degree   ☐ driver's license   ☐ green card

CHALLENGE Draw a timeline for important events in your life. Use the timeline in Exercise 1 for ideas.

1. **Look in your dictionary. Write all the words that end in -y and -ed.**

-y	-ed	
thirsty	satisfied	

2. **How do these people feel? Use words from Exercise 1.**

Phew!

a. _relieved_

b. _____

c. _____

d. _____

e. _____

f. _____

g. _____

h. _____

i. _____

3. Put the words in the correct columns.

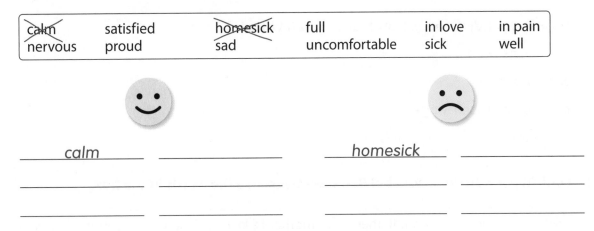

| calm | satisfied | homesick | full | in love | in pain |
| nervous | proud | sad | uncomfortable | sick | well |

(calm and homesick crossed out; homesick and sad crossed out)

😊   ☹️

_____calm_____   _____   ____homesick____   _____

_____   _____   _____   _____

_____   _____   _____   _____

4. Complete the conversations. Use words from Exercise 3.

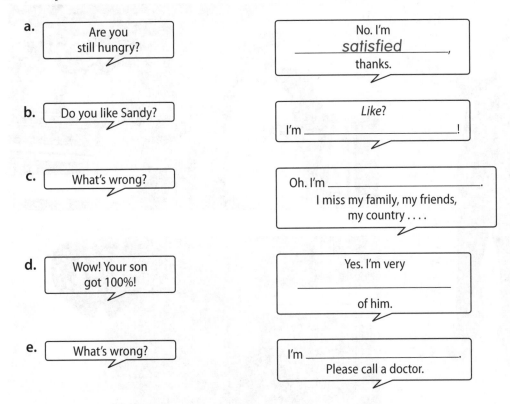

a. Are you still hungry?

No. I'm _____satisfied_____, thanks.

b. Do you like Sandy?

Like? I'm _____!

c. What's wrong?

Oh. I'm _____. I miss my family, my friends, my country . . . .

d. Wow! Your son got 100%!

Yes. I'm very _____ of him.

e. What's wrong?

I'm _____. Please call a doctor.

5. What about you? How do you feel when you . . . ? Circle as many words as possible. Add new words, too.

a. wake up	sleepy	happy	calm	_____
b. start a new class	nervous	confused	excited	_____
c. have problems in school	worried	upset	homesick	_____
d. exercise	happy	proud	uncomfortable	_____

CHALLENGE What do you do when you feel nervous? Bored? Homesick? Confused? Angry? Discuss your answers with a classmate.

Go to page 249 for Another Look (Unit 2).

1. **Look in your dictionary. How many . . . can you see?**

   a. banners   _1_

   b. balloons   ___

   c. children misbehaving   ___

   d. relatives   ___

2. **Look in your dictionary. Label Ben's relatives. Use the words in the box.**

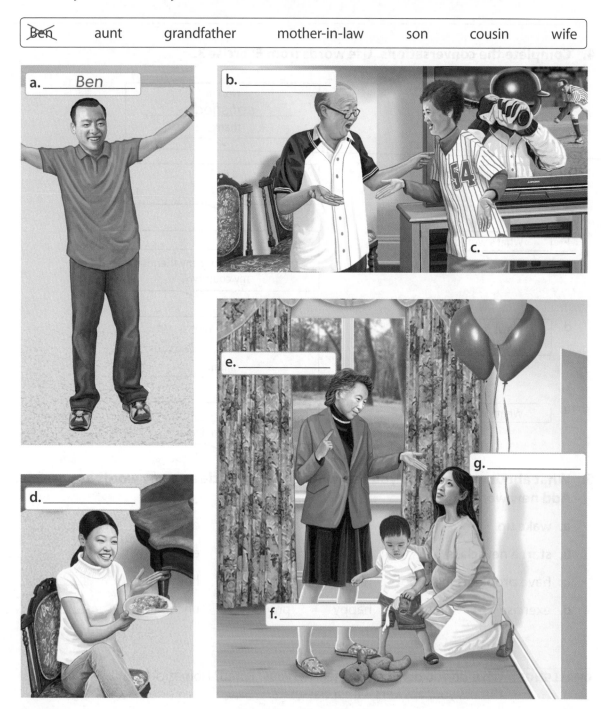

| ~~Ben~~ | aunt | grandfather | mother-in-law | son | cousin | wife |

a. _Ben_

b. _____

c. _____

d. _____

e. _____

f. _____

g. _____

3. **Look in your dictionary. Who are Ben's other relatives? Guess. Complete the sentences. Then discuss your answers with a classmate. Do you and your classmate agree?**

   a. The woman to the right of Ben is his ___cousin (or aunt or sister)___.

   b. The physically-challenged man is his _____.

   c. The little girl near the food table is his _____.

   d. The boy watching TV is his _____.

4. **Look in your dictionary. What did people do at the reunion? Check (✓) the answers.**

✓ eat	☐ misbehave
☐ clean	☐ laugh
☐ go to sleep	☐ exercise
☐ cook	☐ check email
☐ talk	☐ read
☐ watch TV	☐ play baseball
☐ sing	

5. **Look in your dictionary. Circle the words to complete the sentences.**

   a. Ben Lu is single / (married).

   b. He has a family reunion every year / month.

   c. The reunion is at Ben's / his aunt's house.

   d. Ben is talking to relatives / watching TV.

   e. His grandfather and aunt have the same / different opinions about the baseball game.

   f. His grandfather has a beard / gray hair.

   g. His mother / son is misbehaving.

   h. Ben is glad / sad his family is all there.

6. **What about you? Imagine you are at Ben's family reunion. Who do you want to talk to? Why?**

   Example: *I want to talk to Ben's aunt and grandfather. I like baseball, too.*

   CHALLENGE Look in your dictionary. Choose three of Ben's relatives. Describe them to a partner. Your partner will point to the correct picture. **Example:** *She is elderly and has gray hair. She is near the food.*

1. Look in your dictionary. *True* or *False*?

   a. This home has three bedrooms.   *true*

   b. There's a door between the bedroom and the bathroom.   _____

   c. The baby's room is next to the parents' bedroom.   _____

   d. There's an attic under the roof.   _____

   e. The kitchen is under the kids' bedroom.   _____

   f. There's a window in the bathroom.   _____

   g. There are books on the floor in the kids' bedroom.   _____

2. Look at the pictures. Which rooms do they go in? Match.

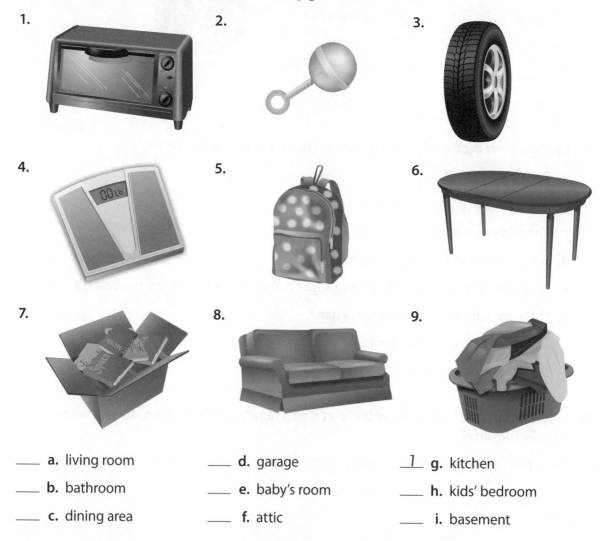

1.

2.

3.

4.

5.

6.

7.

8.

9.

  ___ **a.** living room   ___ **d.** garage   *1* **g.** kitchen

  ___ **b.** bathroom   ___ **e.** baby's room   ___ **h.** kids' bedroom

  ___ **c.** dining area   ___ **f.** attic   ___ **i.** basement

3. What about you? Do you like the house in your dictionary? Why or why not? Talk about it with a partner.

4. Look in your dictionary. Complete the sentences.

a. The mother is in the _____ *living room* _____.

b. The father is in the _____.

c. The teenage daughter is in the _____.

d. The 10-year-old girl is in the _____.

e. The baby is in the _____.

f. The car is in the _____.

5. Look in your dictionary. Correct the mistakes in the ad.

FOR SALE

~~4~~ 3 bedroom house with 2 bathrooms

Large kitchen and dining area. Attic and basement.

2-car garage. Large yard. Good for a family. Call 555-3434.

6. What about you? What's important to you in a home? Complete the chart.

Home Preference Checklist

J&R REALTORS

Number of bedrooms _____ Number of bathrooms _____

	very important	important	not important
Kitchen with a dining area?	☐	☐	☐
Window in the kitchen?	☐	☐	☐
Window in the bathroom?	☐	☐	☐
A basement?	☐	☐	☐
A yard?	☐	☐	☐
A garage?	☐	☐	☐

CHALLENGE Write an ad for a home. It can be for your home, a home that you know, or for the home on <u>page 53</u> of this workbook. Use the ad in Exercise 5 as an example.

1. **Look at pictures 1 and 2 in your dictionary.** *True* **or** *False*?

   Apartment Search Tool

   a. The search tool is for a house.   *false*

   b. It's at 54 Greenwood Ln.   _____

   c. The ZIP code is 66611.   _____

   Listing / Classified Ad

   d. The rent is $950 a month.   _____

   e. It does not have AC.   _____

   f. It has two bathrooms.   _____

2. **Check (✓) the things people do when they rent an apartment and / or buy a house.**

	Rent an Apartment	Buy a House
a. make an offer	☐	✓
b. sign a rental agreement	✓	☐
c. get a loan	☐	☐
d. ask about the features	☐	☐
e. take ownership	☐	☐
f. move in	☐	☐
g. pay the rent	☐	☐
h. make a mortgage payment	☐	☐
i. unpack	☐	☐
j. arrange the furniture	☐	☐
k. meet with a realtor	☐	☐
l. put the utilities in their name	☐	☐
m. meet the neighbors	☐	☐
n. submit an application	☐	☐

3. **What about you? Look at the apartment search tool and the classified ad in your dictionary. Which way is better to find an apartment? Why? Tell a partner.**

4. Look in your dictionary. Circle the words to complete the sentences.

a. The woman in picture A wants to buy / (rent) an apartment.

b. She talks to the manager / realtor.

c. The rent is $950 / $1,900 a month.

d. The man and woman in picture H are looking at a new apartment / house.

e. The realtor makes / man and woman make an offer.

f. The rent / mortgage is $1,137.90 a month.

5. Look at the listings. *True* or *False*?

708 Apartments for rent	708 Apartments for rent
Westside Apartments	**Eastside Apartments**
3 br 2 ba furn apt New kit $1000/mo Util incl Call mgr	2 br 1 ba unfurn apt Large yd $850/mo Util incl Call mgr
555-1002 eves	**555-1002 eves**

a. The Westside apartment is furnished. _____true_____

b. The Eastside apartment has a new kitchen. _____

c. The Eastside apartment has more bedrooms. _____

d. The Westside apartment has more bathrooms. _____

e. The Eastside apartment's rent is more. _____

f. Utilities are included for both apartments. _____

g. Both apartments have the same manager. _____

h. You can call the manager in the morning. _____

6. What about you? Check (✓) the things you and your family did the last time you moved.

☐ rented an apartment   ☐ looked at houses

☐ submitted an application   ☐ signed a rental agreement

☐ paid rent   ☐ met with a realtor

☐ made an offer   ☐ got a loan

☐ made a mortgage payment   ☐ called a manager

☐ painted   ☐ met the neighbors

CHALLENGE   How did you find your home? Write a paragraph.

1. **Look at page 50 in your dictionary. Circle the words to complete the sentences.**

   a. There's a fire escape on the first / (second) floor.

   b. The building on the right has a playground / roof garden.

   c. A tenant / The manager is hanging a vacancy sign.

   d. A tenant / The manager is entering the building.

   e. There's an intercom in the entrance / lobby.

   f. The mailboxes are in the entrance / lobby.

   g. A tenant is using the elevator / stairs.

   h. There's a big-screen TV in the laundry room / recreation room.

   i. There's a security camera in the garage / recreation room.

   j. There's a pool table / washer in the recreation room.

2. **Look at the sign. *True* or *False*?**

   a. The swimming pool is always open until 8:00 p.m. _____*false*_____

   b. You can use the washer and dryer all night. _____

   c. The garage is always open. _____

   d. The playground closes at different times each day. _____

   e. You can use the storage lockers at midnight. _____

   f. The recreation room is open twenty-four hours. _____

   g. You can watch a movie on the big-screen TV at 9:00 p.m. _____

3. **Look in your dictionary.** *True* or *False*? **Correct the underlined words in the false sentences.**

a. Each apartment has a ~~fire escape~~. *balcony* ___false___

b. The apartment complex has a <u>swimming pool and courtyard</u>. _____

c. The <u>trash chute</u> is in the alley. _____

d. The emergency exit is in the <u>hallway</u>. _____

e. The landlord is talking about a <u>lease</u>. _____

f. A tenant is using her <u>peephole</u>. _____

4. **Complete the signs. Use the words in the box.**

buzzer	elevator	~~emergency exit~~	intercom
mailbox	tenants	trash bin	trash chute

a.

IN CASE OF FIRE
use the
emergency exit
DO NOT
use the
_____

b.

NEW _____ :
Please put your
name on your
_____ .

c.

NOTICE Do not throw...
...down the _____ .
Put them in the _____
in the alley.

d.

ATTENTION
ALL TENANTS:
Do not allow strangers
into the building.
Always use the _____
BEFORE you use the _____ !

5. **What about you? Check (✓) the items in your home.**

☐ fire escape ☐ security camera ☐ laundry room

☐ garage ☐ balcony ☐ smoke detector

☐ lobby ☐ third floor ☐ security gate

☐ door chain ☐ dead-bolt lock ☐ peephole

[CHALLENGE] Look at Exercise 5. Which three items are most important to you? Why?
Tell a classmate.

Different Places to Live

1. Look in your dictionary. Where are they?

a. students   <u>college dormitory</u>

b. an elderly, physically-challenged woman   _____

c. a man with a newspaper   _____

2. Look at the photos. Circle the words to complete the sentences.

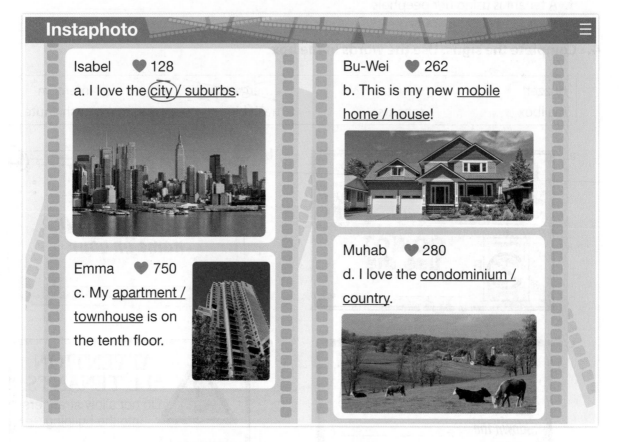

Instaphoto

Isabel ♥ 128
a. I love the (city) / suburbs.

Emma ♥ 750
c. My apartment / townhouse is on the tenth floor.

Bu-Wei ♥ 262
b. This is my new mobile home / house!

Muhab ♥ 280
d. I love the condominium / country.

3. What about you? Check (✓) the places you've lived.

☐ city   ☐ country   ☐ college dorm

☐ suburbs   ☐ farm   ☐ townhouse

☐ small town   ☐ ranch   ☐ mobile home

☐ senior housing   ☐ condo   ☐ Other: _____

CHALLENGE   Take a class survey. Where do your classmates live? Write the results.
Example: *Ten students live in the suburbs.*

1. **Look in your dictionary. Check (✓) the locations.**

	On the Lawn	On the Patio
a. patio furniture	☐	✓
b. hose	☐	☐
c. hammock	☐	☐
d. grill	☐	☐
e. compost pile	☐	☐
f. garbage can	☐	☐
g. sliding glass door	☐	☐

2. **Look at the house. *True* or *False*? Correct the <u>underlined</u> words in the false sentences.**

                steps

a. There are three ~~<u>mailboxes</u>~~ in front of the front door.   *false*

b. The <u>doorbell</u> is to the right of the doorknob.   _____

c. The <u>storm</u> door is open.   _____

d. The <u>porch light</u> is on.   _____

e. There's a <u>vegetable garden</u> in the front lawn.   _____

f. The <u>chimney</u> is blue.   _____

g. The satellite dish is near the <u>driveway</u>.   _____

h. The <u>front walk</u> stops at the steps.   _____

3. **What about you? Do you like this house? Check (✓) *Yes* or *No*.**

   ☐ Yes   ☐ No   Why? _____

CHALLENGE Draw a picture of your "dream house." Describe it to a partner.

A Kitchen

1. Look in your dictionary. Where can you find the . . . ? Use *on* or *under*.

a. paper towels _under the cabinet_

b. dish rack _____

c. coffee maker _____

d. pot _____

e. broiler _____

f. garbage disposal _____

2. Look at the bar graph. How long do things last? Put the words in the correct columns.

How Long Things Last

Based on information from: *This Old House Online* (2016).

5–9 Years	10–15 Years
coffee maker	_____
_____	_____
_____	_____

3. What about you? Check (✓) the items you have.

		Where is it?	How long have you had it?
☐	blender	_on the counter_	_two years_
☐	electric can opener	_____	_____
☐	coffee maker	_____	_____
☐	electric mixer	_____	_____
☐	food processor	_____	_____
☐	microwave	_____	_____
☐	teakettle	_____	_____
☐	toaster oven	_____	_____

CHALLENGE Look at the kitchen appliances in your dictionary. List the five you think are the most important. Compare your list with a partner's list.

1. **Look in your dictionary. *True* or *False*?**

    a. There's a teapot on the tray. _____true_____

    b. The fan has two light fixtures. _____

    c. The tablecloth is blue. _____

    d. There's a vase on the buffet. _____

    e. The salt shaker is on the table. _____

    f. There's a coffee mug on the dining room table. _____

    g. The sugar bowl and creamer are in the hutch. _____

2. **Look at the table setting. Complete the sentences.**

    a. The _____plate_____ is light blue.

    b. It's on a dark blue _____.

    c. A white _____ is on the plate.

    d. There are two _____ to the left of the plate.

    e. They're on the yellow _____.

    f. There are two _____. They're to the right of the plate.

    g. There's also a _____ to the right of the plate.

    h. There's a _____ above the spoons.

3. **What about you? What does *your* table setting look like? Draw a picture on your own paper. Then, complete the charts.**

Item	How Many?	Where?
knife		
fork		
spoon		
plate		
bowl		

Item	How Many?	Where?
teacup		
placemat		
napkin		
Other: _____		

CHALLENGE   Describe your table setting to a partner. Your partner will draw it. Does it look the same as your picture in Exercise 3?

1. **Look in your dictionary. How many . . . can you see?**

a. paintings ___2___   c. throw pillows ___   e. windows ___

b. walls ___   d. fireplaces ___   f. end tables ___

2. **Look at the Millers' new living room. Cross out the items they already have.**

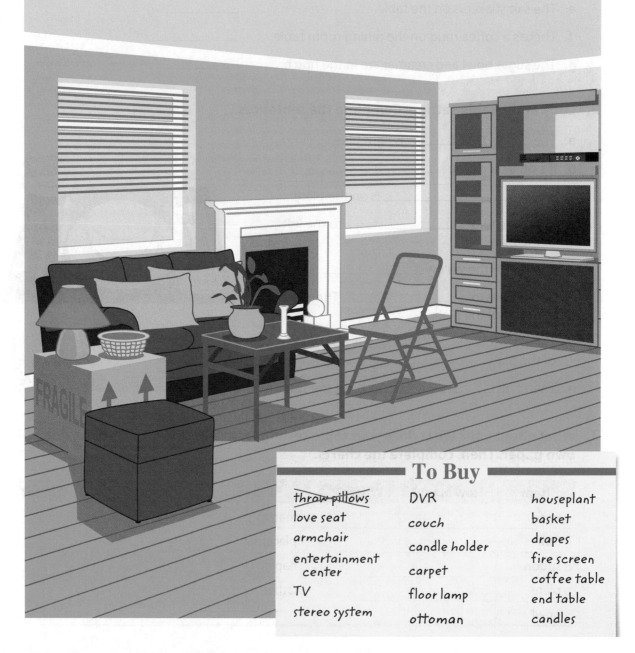

To Buy

~~throw pillows~~	DVR	houseplant
love seat	couch	basket
armchair	candle holder	drapes
entertainment center	carpet	fire screen
TV	floor lamp	coffee table
stereo system	ottoman	end table
		candles

3. **What about you? Look at the list in Exercise 2. List the items you have.**

CHALLENGE Write six sentences about the Millers' living room.
Example: *They have a couch, but they don't have a love seat.*

1. Look in your dictionary. Check (✓) the locations.

	Sink	Bathtub	Wall
a. hot and cold water	✓	✓	☐
b. towel racks	☐	☐	☐
c. shower curtain	☐	☐	☐
d. faucets	☐	☐	☐
e. tiles	☐	☐	☐
f. drains	☐	☐	☐
g. grab bar	☐	☐	☐
h. toilet paper	☐	☐	☐

2. Look at the ad. Circle the words to complete the sentences.

THE **BIG** SPLASH
The Place for Big Bath Buys

$18.99 $8.99 $9.99 $6.99
$44.99 $7.99 $5.99 $3.99 $4.99 $1.99
$.99 $4.99 $2.99 $37.99 $6.99

a. The (bath mat)/ rubber mat is $9.99.

b. The hamper / wastebasket is $6.99.

c. The bath towel / hand towel is $5.99.

d. The soap dish / soap is $2.99.

e. The toilet brush / toothbrush is $4.99.

f. The showerhead / washcloth is $3.99.

g. The mirror / scale is $37.99.

h. The toothbrush holder / soap dish is $4.99.

CHALLENGE What items do people put in a medicine cabinet? Make a list.

1. Look in your dictionary. What color is the . . . ?

    a. pillow _____white_____   **b.** mattress _____   **c.** dust ruffle _____

2. Cross out the word that doesn't belong.

a. They're electric.	~~mirror~~	outlet	light switch	lamp
b. They're soft.	pillowcase	quilt	headboard	blanket
c. They're part of a bed.	mattress	alarm clock	box spring	bed frame
d. They're on the wood floor.	dresser	lampshade	rug	night table
e. They make the room dark.	light switch	curtains	mini-blinds	flat sheet
f. You put things in them.	closet	drawer	photos	picture frame

3. Complete the conversations. Use words from Exercise 2.

    a. **Lee:**   What time is it?

        Mom: I don't know. There's an _alarm clock_
                   on the night table.

    b. **Tom:**   I'm cold.

        Ana: Here's an extra _____.

    c. **Ray:**   The bed's uncomfortable.

        Mia: The _____ is too soft.

    d. **Amir:**   There are no curtains.

        Marwa: No, but there are _____.

    e. **Bill:**   My sweater isn't in the drawer.

        Molly: Look in the _____.

4. What about you? Check (✓) the items that are on your bed.

    ☐ fitted sheet   Color: _____

    ☐ flat sheet   Color: _____

    ☐ quilt   Color: _____

    ☐ pillow(s)   How many? _____   Hard or soft? _____

    ☐ mattress   Hard or soft? _____

    ☐ blankets   How many? _____

CHALLENGE   Write a paragraph describing your bedroom.

1. **Look in your dictionary. Which three items are for safety?**

   a. _____bumper pad_____

   b. _____

   c. _____

2. **Look at Olivia and Emma's room. There are eleven dolls. Find and circle ten more.**

3. **Write the locations of the dolls. Use *on*, *under*, and *in*. Use your own paper.**

   Example: *on the chest of drawers*

4. **What about you? Check (✓) the things you had when you were a child.**

   ☐ dolls   ☐ mobile   ☐ crayons   ☐ Other: _____

   ☐ stuffed animals   ☐ balls   ☐ puzzles

   CHALLENGE   Look at the toys you checked in Exercise 4. Write a paragraph about your favorite one.

1. **Look in your dictionary. What are the people doing? Circle the words.**

   a. "Can we do this with magazines, too?"   recycling newspapers / taking out the garbage

   b. "Dad, does this truck go here?"   dusting the furniture / putting away the toys

   c. "I like this new blanket."   making the bed / sweeping the floor

   d. "Is this the last plate, Dad?"   cleaning the oven / drying the dishes

2. **Look at the room. Check (✓) the completed jobs.**

   To Do

   - ✓ wash the sheets
   - ☐ change the sheets
   - ☐ sweep the floor
   - ☐ empty the trash
   - ☐ polish the dresser
   - ☐ scrub the sink
   - ☐ mop the bathroom floor
   - ☐ take out the newspapers

3. **What about you? How often do you . . . ? Check (✓) the columns.**

	Every Day	Every Week	Every Month	Never
dust the furniture				
polish the furniture				
recycle the newspapers				
wash the dishes				
vacuum the carpet				
wipe the counter				
scrub the sink				
put away the toys				
Other: _____				

CHALLENGE   Write a *To Do* list of your housework for this week.

1. **Look in your dictionary. What can you use to clean the . . . ? There may be more correct answers than you can write here.**

Windows	Floor	Dishes
glass cleaner		

2. **Match each item with the correct coupon.**

TO BUY

_4_ a. feather duster
___ b. steel-wool soap pads
___ c. sponges
___ d. pail
___ e. multipurpose cleaner
___ f. trash bags
___ g. dishwashing liquid
___ h. rubber gloves
___ i. vacuum cleaner bags
___ j. disinfectant wipes

1. 50-33 gal. $2.99 Strongy 50 lg
2. 22 oz. SPARKLE $1.89
3. 9 qt. $1.99
4. $1.99
5. $2.99 Very Clean
6. 99¢/pair
7. $3.29
8. pk of 12 $1.99
9. $1.59 SCRUB EZ
10. 2-pack $3.19

3. **What about you? Look at the cleaning supplies in Exercise 2. Which ones do you have? What do you use them for?**

   Example: *feather duster—dust the desk*

CHALLENGE   Look in a store, online, or at newspaper ads. Write the prices of some cleaning supplies that you use.

Household Problems and Repairs

1. Look in your dictionary. Who said . . . ?

a. I'm up on the roof.   _roofer_

b. Good-bye, termites!   _____

c. I'm turning on the power again.   _____

d. I'll fix the toilet next.   _____

e. I'm fixing the lock on the front door.   _____

f. There's one more step to repair.   _____

g. I'm putting in new windows.   _____

2. Look at John's bathroom. There are seven problems. Find and circle six more.

3. Look at Exercise 2. *True* or *False*? Correct the underlined words in the false sentences.

bathtub

a. The ~~sink~~ faucet is dripping.   _false_

b. The window is broken.   _____

c. There are ants near the sink.   _____

d. The light isn't working.   _____

e. The sink is overflowing.   _____

f. The wall is cracked.   _____

4. Look at Exercise 2 and the ads below. Who should John call? Include the repair person, the problem(s), and the phone number on the list. (Hint: John will use some companies for more than one problem.)

CALL

1. _exterminator_ 555-4789
   a. _cockroaches_
2. _____
   a. _The faucet is dripping._
   b. _____
   c. _____
3. _____ 555-2656
   a. _____
4. _repairperson_
   a. _____
   b. _____

CHALLENGE Look at the problems in Exercise 2. Who fixes them in your home? Make a list.
Example: *toilet stopped up—my son*

Go to page 250 for Another Look (Unit 3). 63

The Tenant Meeting

1. Look in your dictionary. *True* or *False*?

a. Sally and Tina are roommates. _____true_____

b. They had a party in Apartment 3B. _____

c. A DJ played music. _____

d. Some people danced. _____

e. Sally and Tina were irritated by the noise. _____

f. The neighbors cleaned up the mess in the hallway. _____

g. Sally and Tina gave an invitation to the woman in Apartment 2C. _____

2. Look at the pictures. Check (✓) the answers.

Friday Night   Saturday Night

	Friday Night	Saturday Night
a. The party was in the rec room.	✓	☐
b. There was a DJ at the party.	☐	☐
c. The music was loud.	☐	☐
d. There was a mess on the floor.	☐	☐
e. People danced.	☐	☐
f. There was a lot of noise.	☐	☐
g. The roommates were at the party.	☐	☐
h. A neighbor was irritated.	☐	☐

3. **Look at the top picture on page 65 in your dictionary. Circle the words to complete the sentences.**

a. The man is Sally and Tina's (neighbor) / roommate.

b. He's <u>at the party</u> / <u>in his bedroom</u>.

c. He's <u>happy</u> / <u>irritated</u>.

d. It's <u>before</u> / <u>after</u> midnight.

e. Sally and Tina didn't give him <u>an invitation</u> / <u>the rules</u> to the party.

f. He can't sleep because of the <u>mess</u> / <u>noise</u>.

4. **Complete the sign. Use the words in the box.**

dance	DJs	mess	music	noise	parties	~~Rules~~

Building ___Rules___
a.

• No loud _____ after 10:00 p.m.
  b.

• Large _____ in rec room only.
  c.

• Please be quiet in the hallways. No _____!
  d.

• Please clean up your
  _____ in public areas.
  e.

• You can _____ in your apartment,
  f.
  but you must have carpet.

• No _____ at
  g.
  apartment parties.

Thank you,
The Manager

CHALLENGE Look at the rules in Exercise 4 and the parties in Exercise 2.
Did the people follow the rules? Talk about it with a partner.

Back from the Market

1. **Look in your dictionary. Where's the . . . ? Check (✓) the answers.**

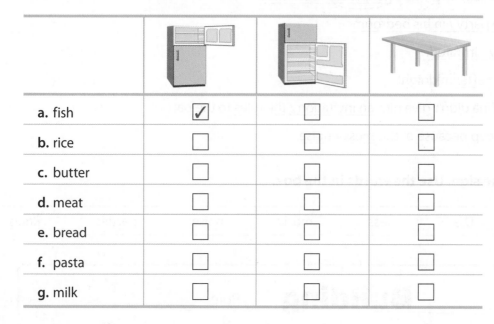

a. fish	✓	☐	☐
b. rice	☐	☐	☐
c. butter	☐	☐	☐
d. meat	☐	☐	☐
e. bread	☐	☐	☐
f. pasta	☐	☐	☐
g. milk	☐	☐	☐

2. **Complete Shao-fen's shopping list. Use your dictionary for help.**

- ✓ **a.** e _g_ _g_ s
- ☐ **b.** ___ r ___ i t
- ☐ **c.** v ___ g e ___ a ___ l ___ s
- ☐ **d.** r ___ ___ ___ e
- ☐ **e.** c ___ ___ ___ e ___ e
- ☐ **f.** ___ r e ___ d
- ☐ **g.** ___ a ___ ___ ___ a
- ☐ **h.** ___ h ___ c k ___ n

Shao-fen

3. **Look at the food that Shao-fen bought at the market. Check (✓) the items she bought on the shopping list in Exercise 2.**

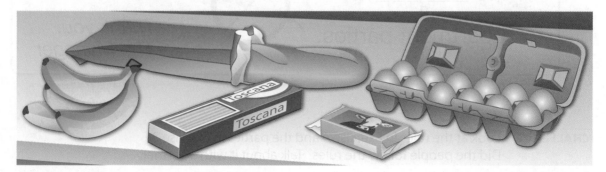

4. Look in your dictionary. *True* or *False*?

a. There are four grocery bags in the kitchen.   *false*

b. There's a shopping list on the table.   _____

c. The word *butter* is on the shopping list.   _____

d. There are coupons on the table.   _____

e. There are eggs on the table.   _____

f. There are vegetables in the refrigerator.   _____

g. There's fruit in the refrigerator.   _____

5. Complete the coupons. Write the names of the foods.

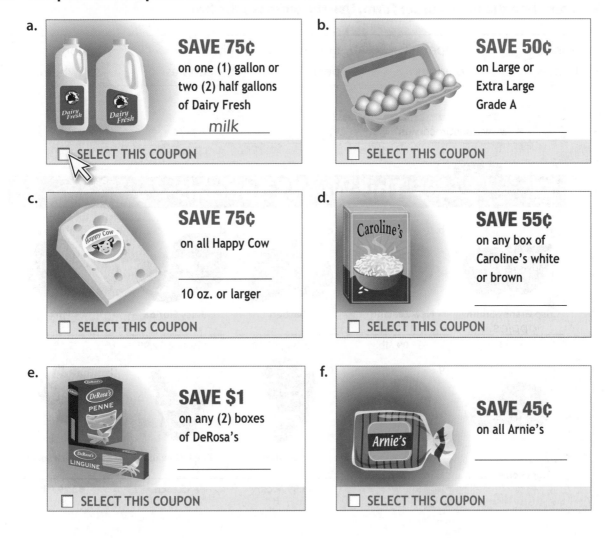

a. **SAVE 75¢**
on one (1) gallon or
two (2) half gallons
of Dairy Fresh
_____*milk*_____
☐ SELECT THIS COUPON

b. **SAVE 50¢**
on Large or
Extra Large
Grade A
_____
☐ SELECT THIS COUPON

c. **SAVE 75¢**
on all Happy Cow
_____
10 oz. or larger
☐ SELECT THIS COUPON

d. **SAVE 55¢**
on any box of
Caroline's white
or brown
_____
☐ SELECT THIS COUPON

e. **SAVE $1**
on any (2) boxes
of DeRosa's
_____
☐ SELECT THIS COUPON

f. **SAVE 45¢**
on all Arnie's
_____
☐ SELECT THIS COUPON

6. What about you? Do you use store coupons?

☐ Yes   ☐ No   If *yes*, for what items? _____

CHALLENGE   Look in your dictionary. Which foods do you like? Make a list. Compare lists with
a classmate. Do you and your classmate like the same things?

1. **Look in your dictionary. Write the name of the fruit.**

   a. They're to the right of the figs.   _____dates_____

   b. They're to the left of the tangerines.   _____

   c. They're below the peaches.   _____

   d. They're above the mangoes.   _____

   e. They're to the right of the raspberries.   _____

   f. One is ripe, one is unripe, and one is rotten. _____

2. **Complete the online order form. Use the words in the box.**

~~apples~~	grapefruit	grapes	kiwi	lemons
limes	oranges	pears	pineapples	strawberries

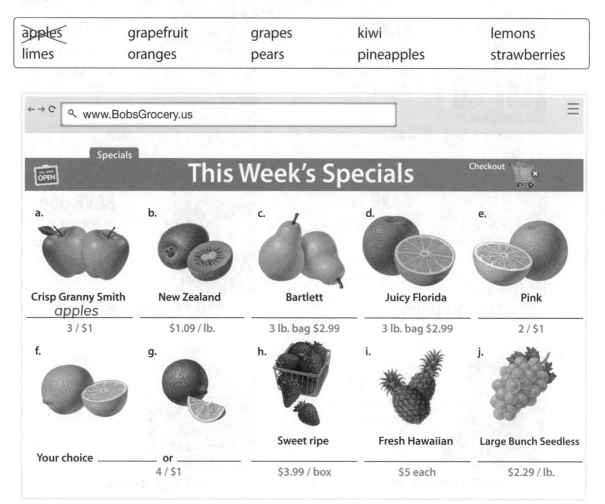

← → C   🔍 www.BobsGrocery.us

Specials

This Week's Specials   Checkout

a. Crisp Granny Smith
   apples
   3 / $1

b. New Zealand
   _____
   $1.09 / lb.

c. Bartlett
   _____
   3 lb. bag $2.99

d. Juicy Florida
   _____
   3 lb. bag $2.99

e. Pink
   _____
   2 / $1

f. / g. Your choice _____ or _____
   4 / $1

h. Sweet ripe
   _____
   $3.99 / box

i. Fresh Hawaiian
   _____
   $5 each

j. Large Bunch Seedless
   _____
   $2.29 / lb.

3. **What about you? Make a shopping list using the fruit in Exercise 2. How much or how many will you buy? How much will it cost?**

   Example: *6 apples—$2.00*

   CHALLENGE Make a list of fruit from your native country.

1. Look in your dictionary. Which vegetables are . . . ? Put them in the correct columns.

Yellow / Orange	Green		Red
sweet potatoes	_____	_____	_____
_____	_____	_____	_____
_____	_____	_____	_____
_____	_____	_____	_____
_____	_____	_____	_____
	_____	_____	
	_____	_____	
	_____	_____	

2. Look at the chart. Which has more vitamin A? Circle the correct answer.

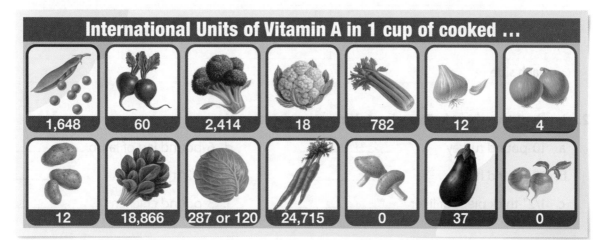

International Units of Vitamin A in 1 cup of cooked ...

1,648	60	2,414	18	782	12	4
12	18,866	287 or 120	24,715	0	37	0

Based on information from: U.S. Department of Agriculture, Agricultural Research Service. 2015. USDA National Nutrient Database for Standard Reference, Release 28.

a. cabbage / (spinach)   **d.** carrots / celery   **g.** broccoli / cauliflower

b. beets / turnips   **e.** onions / potatoes   **h.** spinach / celery

c. mushrooms / garlic   **f.** turnips / eggplant   **i.** beets / peas

3. What about you? How often do you eat these vegetables in a week? Circle the numbers.

carrots	0	1	2	3	4	more than 4 times a week
broccoli	0	1	2	3	4	more than 4 times a week
spinach	0	1	2	3	4	more than 4 times a week

[CHALLENGE]   Make a list of vegetables from your native country.

Meat and Poultry

1. **Look in your dictionary. Label the foods in the chart.**

		Size	Cooking time	Method
	a. ___*lamb*___	5–8 pounds	30 min./pound	oven
	b. _____	1/2" thick	3 min.*	broiler
	c. _____	1 1/2" thick	10 min.*	broiler
	d. _____	8–20 pounds	20 min./pound	oven
	e. _____	8–12 pounds	3–4 hours	oven
	f. _____	2 1/2 –3 pounds	1 1/4 hours	oven

*each side

2. **Look at the chart in Exercise 1. Write the cooking times.**

a. 10-pound turkey ___*3–4 hours*___

b. 10-pound ham _____

c. 1/2"-thick piece of liver _____

d. 6-pound leg of lamb _____

e. 1-1/2" thick steak _____

f. 3-pound chicken _____

3. **Label the chicken parts.**

a. ___*breast*___ ·············>

b. _____ ·············>

c. _____ ·············>

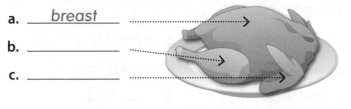

4. **What about you? Check (✓) the meat and poultry you eat.**

☐ veal cutlets   ☐ bacon   ☐ duck   ☐ lamb chops

☐ tripe   ☐ beef ribs   ☐ pork chops   ☐ sausage

[CHALLENGE] Take a survey. Ask five people which meats and poultry they eat.

1. **Look in your dictionary. Write the names of the seafood.**

a. _____halibut steak_____   e. _____   i. _____

b. _____   f. _____   j. _____

c. _____   g. _____   k. _____

d. _____   h. _____   l. _____

2. **Look at the sandwich. Complete the order form. Check (✓) the correct boxes.**

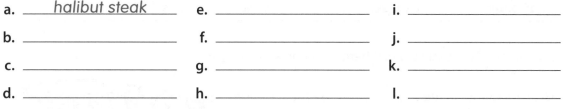

Sandwich Order		
Meat	**Cheese**	**Bread**
✓ smoked turkey	☐ American	☐ white
☐ roast beef	☐ mozzarella	☐ wheat
☐ corned beef	☐ Swiss	☐ rye
☐ salami	☐ cheddar	
☐ pastrami		

3. **What about you? Complete your order with the food on the form in Exercise 2.**

I'd like a _____ sandwich with _____ cheese on _____ bread.

[CHALLENGE] Ask five classmates what they want from the deli. Write their orders.

A Grocery Store

1. Look in your dictionary. *True* or *False*?

a. The stocker is in the pet food section. _____*true*_____

b. The manager is in aisle 3A. _____

c. The grocery clerk is in the produce section. _____

d. There's a scale in the dairy section. _____

e. There are five customers in line. _____

f. You can get frozen vegetables in aisle 2B. _____

g. The bagger is near the cashier. _____

h. The self-checkout doesn't have a cash register. _____

2. Complete the conversations. Use the words in the box.

~~Bagger~~	dairy	cart	checkstands
~~Customer~~	manager	scale	self-checkout

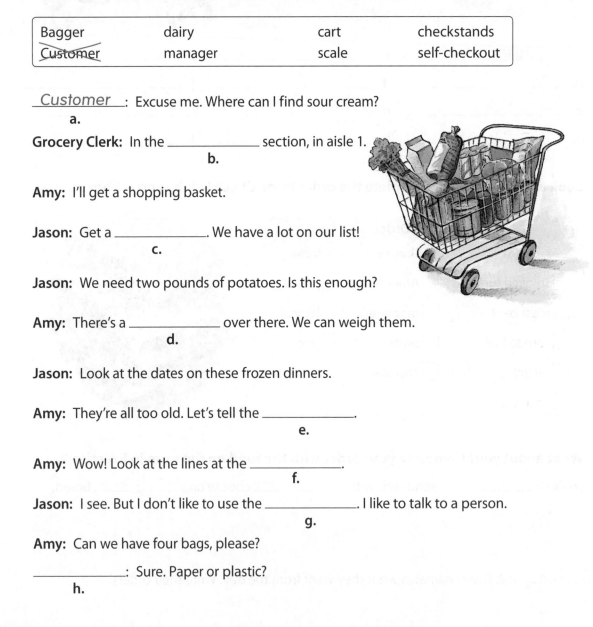

_____*Customer*_____ : Excuse me. Where can I find sour cream?
       a.

Grocery Clerk: In the _____ section, in aisle 1.
                              b.

Amy: I'll get a shopping basket.

Jason: Get a _____. We have a lot on our list!
                   c.

Jason: We need two pounds of potatoes. Is this enough?

Amy: There's a _____ over there. We can weigh them.
                    d.

Jason: Look at the dates on these frozen dinners.

Amy: They're all too old. Let's tell the _____.
                                            e.

Amy: Wow! Look at the lines at the _____.
                                        f.

Jason: I see. But I don't like to use the _____. I like to talk to a person.
                                              g.

Amy: Can we have four bags, please?

_____: Sure. Paper or plastic?
       h.

3. Look at the things Amy and Jason bought. Check (✓) the items on the shopping list.

Grocery List

☑ potatoes	☐ soup	☐ plastic wrap
☐ tuna	☐ cookies	☐ apple juice
☐ aluminum foil	☐ nuts	☐ sour cream
☐ bagels	☐ margarine	☐ coffee
☐ yogurt	☐ sugar	☐ cake
☐ potato chips	☐ ice cream	☐ candy bars
☐ beans	☐ oil	

4. Put the items from the list in Exercise 3 in the correct category. Use your dictionary for help.

Canned Foods	Dairy	Snack Foods
_____	_____	_____
_____	_____	_____
_____	_____	

Baking Products	Beverages	Baked Goods
_____	_____	_____
_____	_____	_____
		_____

Grocery Products	Produce	Frozen Foods
_____	*potatoes*	_____
_____		

CHALLENGE   Make a shopping list for yourself. Write the section for each item.
Example: *scallops—seafood section*

Containers and Packaging

1. Look at <u>pages 72 and 73</u> in your dictionary. What is the container or packaging for . . . ?

a. pinto beans _____can_____   **c.** sour cream _____

b. plastic storage bags _____   **d.** potato chips _____

2. Complete these coupons. Use the words in the box.

bag	bottle	carton	loaf
six-pack	package	roll	~~tube~~

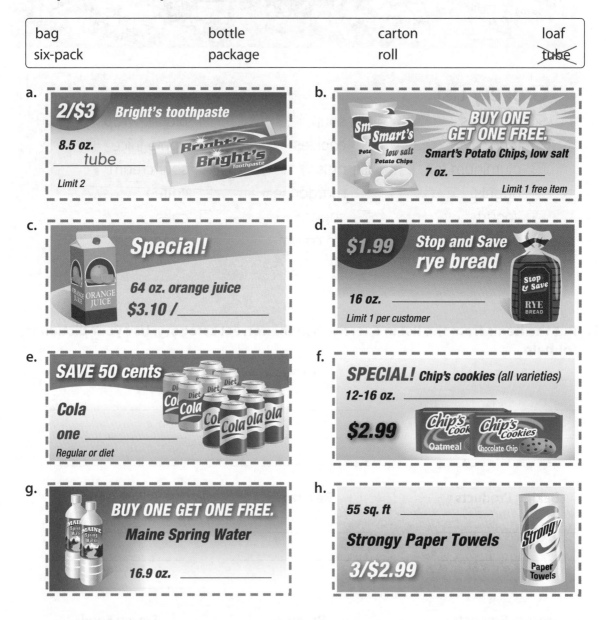

a.
2/$3 **Bright's toothpaste**
8.5 oz.
_____tube_____
Limit 2

b.
BUY ONE GET ONE FREE.
Smart's Potato Chips, low salt
7 oz. _____
Limit 1 free item

c.
Special!
64 oz. orange juice
$3.10 / _____

d.
$1.99 **Stop and Save rye bread**
16 oz. _____
Limit 1 per customer

e.
SAVE 50 cents
Cola
one _____
Regular or diet

f.
SPECIAL! Chip's cookies (all varieties)
12-16 oz. _____
$2.99

g.
BUY ONE GET ONE FREE.
Maine Spring Water
16.9 oz. _____

h.
55 sq. ft _____
Strongy Paper Towels
3/$2.99

3. Write a shopping list. Use all the coupons in Exercise 2.

Example: *2 tubes of toothpaste*

CHALLENGE Which foods do you think are in your refrigerator? Make a list. Then check your answers at home. **Example:** *a bottle of soda*

74

1. Look in your dictionary. Write the words.

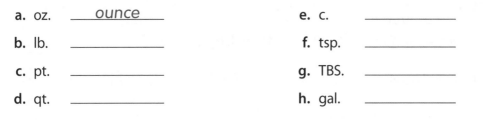

a. oz. ____ounce____

b. lb. _____

c. pt. _____

d. qt. _____

e. c. _____

f. tsp. _____

g. TBS. _____

h. gal. _____

2. Write the weight or measurement.

a. ____1 1/2 pounds of potatoes____

b. _____

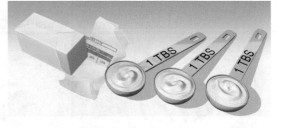

c. _____

d. _____

e. _____

f. _____

3. What about you? How much . . . do you eat or drink every week?

a. cheese _____

b. water _____

c. fish _____

d. sugar _____

CHALLENGE Look at page 260 in this book. Follow the instructions.

Food Preparation and Safety

1. **Look in your dictionary.** *True* or *False*? **Correct the <u>underlined</u> words in the false sentences.**

   counters

   a. Clean the kitchen <s>windows</s>.   _false_   d. Cook <u>meat</u> to 165°.   _____

   b. Separate carrots and <u>meat</u>.   _____   e. Chill leftovers in the <u>refrigerator</u>. _____

   c. Cook <u>chicken</u> to 160°.   _____

2. **Look at the pictures. Which preparation has the most calories? Number them in order.
   (1 = the most calories)**

   Calories in 3 oz. Chicken Breast

   150   161   222

   172   168   175

   ___ a. boiled   ___ c. grilled   _1_ e. fried

   ___ b. broiled   ___ d. roasted   ___ f. stir-fried

3. **What about you? Label the preparations and check (✓) the ways you like to eat eggs.**

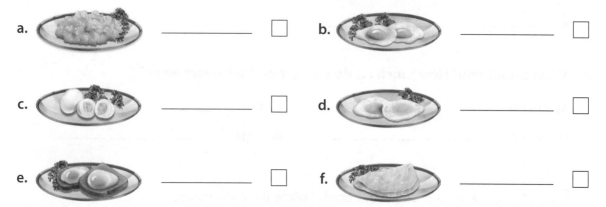

   a. _____ ☐   b. _____ ☐

   c. _____ ☐   d. _____ ☐

   e. _____ ☐   f. _____ ☐

4. Look in your dictionary. Read the recipe. <u>Underline</u> all the food preparation words.

🎩 Baked Carrots   email ✉   print 🖨   ★★★★

Ingredients:
1 lb. (450 g.) carrots
3 TBS. butter
1 small onion
salt and pepper
1/8 tsp. nutmeg
1 tsp. sugar
1/2 cup water

Method:
<u>Preheat</u> the oven to 350°F (180°C). Dice the onion. Peel and grate the carrots. Grease a small pan. Add the onion and sauté until soft. Stir in the carrots. Add the sugar, salt, pepper, nutmeg, and water. Bake in a covered casserole until soft, about 30–40 minutes, or microwave on high for 7–10 minutes. Stir after half the cooking time.

5. Look at the recipe in Exercise 4. Number the pictures in order.

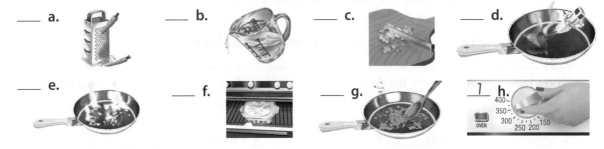

___ a.   ___ b.   ___ c.   ___ d.

___ e.   ___ f.   ___ g.   ___ h.

6. Look at the pictures. Circle the words to complete the recipe.

Potatoes and Sautéed Onions   Ingredients: potatoes, onions, butter, salt, pepper

a.
Step 1: (Boil) / Beat the potatoes until soft.

b.
Step 2: Slice / Dice the cool potatoes.

c.
Step 3: Grate / Chop the onion.

d.
Step 4: Sauté / Bake the onion in butter until brown. Add the potatoes.

e.
Step 5: Stir / Simmer the ingredients.

f.
Step 6: Sauté / Steam until potatoes are brown. Add salt.

[CHALLENGE] Write the recipe for one of your favorite foods. Share it with a classmate.

Kitchen Utensils

1. Look in your dictionary. *True* or *False*?

   a. The grater is below the steamer and the storage container.   *false*

   b. The eggbeater is between the spatula and the whisk.   _____

   c. The vegetable peeler, tongs, strainer, and saucepan are on the wall.   _____

   d. The ladle and the wooden spoon are in the pot.   _____

   e. There are lids on the double boiler and casserole dish.   _____

   f. The frying pan is next to the roasting pan.   _____

   g. The kitchen timer is near the colander and the paring knife.   _____

2. Complete the two-part words. Use the words in the box.

bowl	holders	knife	opener
~~pan~~	pin	press	sheet

   a. cake   _____*pan*_____   e. rolling   _____

   b. mixing   _____   f. cookie   _____

   c. garlic   _____   g. can   _____

   d. pot   _____   h. carving   _____

3. Which kitchen utensils do you need? Use words from Exercise 2.

   a.   *garlic press*   b. _____   c. _____

   d. _____   e. _____   f. _____

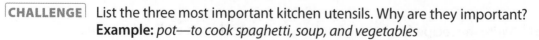

> **CHALLENGE** List the three most important kitchen utensils. Why are they important?
> **Example:** *pot—to cook spaghetti, soup, and vegetables*

78

1. **Look in your dictionary.** *True* or *False*? **Correct the underlined words in the false sentences.**

    a. There are muffins and ~~onion rings~~ on the counter.   *false*
       donuts

    b. The restaurant has <u>pizza</u>.   _____

    c. The <u>counterperson</u> is talking to a woman.   _____

    d. The <u>plastic utensils</u> are next to the salad bar.   _____

    e. A woman is drinking <u>a milkshake</u> with a straw.   _____

    f. A man is using <u>sugar substitute</u>.   _____

2. **Look at the orders. Write the food.**

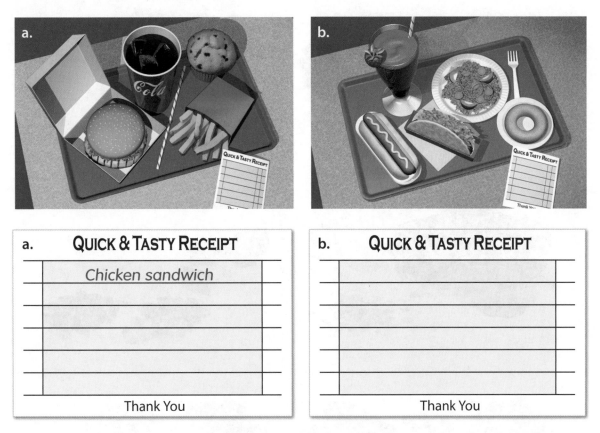

a.	QUICK & TASTY RECEIPT	
	Chicken sandwich	
	Thank You	

b.	QUICK & TASTY RECEIPT	
	Thank You	

3. **What about you? Look at the fast food in your dictionary. Tell a classmate your order.**

    Example: *I'd like a cheeseburger.*

    CHALLENGE   Look at the fast food in your dictionary. Which foods are the most healthy?
    Make a list.

A Coffee Shop Menu

1. **Look in your dictionary. Complete the chart. Do not include sandwiches or salads.**

meat	vegetables	breads	hot beverages
bacon			

2. **Look at the ingredients. Write the food.**

a. _____club sandwich_____

b. _____

c. _____

d. _____

e. _____

f. _____

3. **Cross out the word that doesn't belong.**

   a. Potatoes   baked potato   hash browns   mashed potatoes   ~~rice~~

   b. Breads   garlic bread   roll   pie   toast

   c. Beverages   soup   coffee   low-fat milk   tea

   d. Breakfast food   biscuits   layer cake   pancakes   waffles

   e. Side salads   chef's salad   coleslaw   pasta salad   potato salad

   f. Desserts   cheesecake   layer cake   pie   hot cereal

4. **Look at the food. Complete the orders.**

a. **FOOD ORDER FORM**

roast chicken

_____

_____

_____

_____

Thank You!

b. **FOOD ORDER FORM**

_____

_____

_____

_____

_____

_____

Thank You!

5. **What about you? What's your favorite . . . ?**

   soup _____   dessert _____   hot beverage _____

CHALLENGE   Show five people the coffee shop menu in your dictionary. Write their orders.

1. Look in your dictionary. Who . . . ?

   a. washes dishes   *dishwasher*

   b. leaves a tip   _____

   c. takes the orders   _____

   d. cooks food   _____

   e. seats the customers   _____

   f. orders from the menu   _____

2. Look in your dictionary. Circle the answers.

   a. The patrons are in the <u>dish room</u> / (dining room)

   b. The baby is in the <u>booth / high chair</u>.

   c. The chef is in the <u>dish room / kitchen</u>.

   d. The hostess is in the <u>dining room / kitchen</u>.

   e. The server pours the water in the <u>dish room / dining room</u>.

3. Look at the order and the place setting. Check (✓) the items the diner needs.

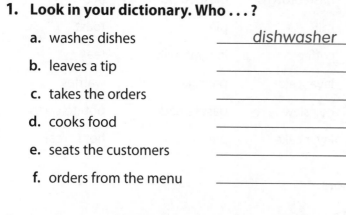

```
        GUEST CHECK
Date  Table  Guests  Server
                            410121

    onion soup
    house salad
    steak
    broccoli
    mashed potatoes
    garlic bread
    half bottle of red wine
    coffee


_____
                    Total
Thank you! Please come again.
```

☐ dinner plate	☐ wine glass	☐ dinner fork
✓ salad plate	☐ cup	☐ steak knife
☐ soup bowl	☐ saucer	☐ knife
☐ bread-and-butter plate	☐ napkin	☐ teaspoon
☐ water glass	☐ salad fork	☐ soup spoon

4. Look at the menu. Complete the check.

The Bistro
MENU

Soup of the day	$4.50
House salad	$3.50
Fish of the day	$15.50
Chicken á l'orange	$12.50
Sirloin steak	$19.00
Vegetables	$2.50
Potatoes	$2.50
Cherry pie	$4.00
with ice cream	$5.00
Coconut cake	$4.50
Coffee or tea	$1.50

The Bistro
242 West Street   555-0700
GUEST CHECK

832000

black bean soup	$4.50
house salad	_____
grilled salmon	_____
peas	_____
french fries	_____
cherry pie w/vanilla ice cream	_____
coffee	_____
Subtotal	_____
Tax (5%)	_____
Total	_____

THANK YOU!

5. In the United States, most restaurant patrons leave a tip for the server when they pay the check. The tip is often 20% of the subtotal. Look at the check in Exercise 4. Circle the answers and complete the sentences.

a. The subtotal is ___$35.00___ .   ($35.00) $36.75 $40.25

b. A 20% tip is _____ . $1.75 $5.25 $7.00

c. Diners leave the tip on the _____ .   menu   table   dinner plate

6. What about you? Do restaurant patrons leave tips for the server in your

native country? _____

If *yes*, how much? _____

Where do they leave it? _____

CHALLENGE   Look at the menu in Exercise 4. Order a meal. Figure out the subtotal, 5% tax, the total, and a 20% tip.

Go to page 251 for Another Look (Unit 4).

The Farmers' Market

1. Look in your dictionary. *True* or *False*?

a. There's live music at the farmers' market. _____*true*_____

b. The avocados are with the fruit. _____

c. A vendor is counting watermelons. _____

d. You can find the herb *dill* at the farmers' market. _____

e. There are free samples of vegetables. _____

f. The avocados are organic. _____

g. The lemonade is sweet. _____

2. Look at the signs. Match.

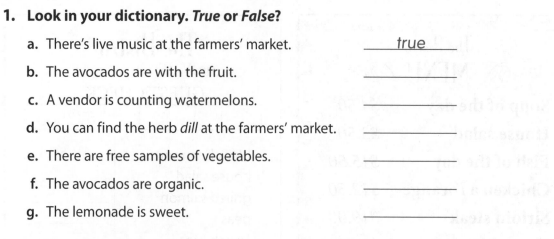

1. Sweet!
2. TAKE ONE!
3. USDA
4. FRESH!
5. Basil

_____ **a.** herb _____ **c.** samples _____ **e.** vegetables

_____ **b.** organic _1_ **d.** strawberries

3. Complete the chart. Use the words in the box.

| ~~avocados~~ | dill | Herbs | lemonade | Vegetables | Vendors | watermelon | zucchini |

Fruit			Beverages			
avocados	peppers			Green Farms	parsley
strawberries			soda	Cara's Bakery	
	onions		milk	Hot Food	basil

84

4. Look in your dictionary. Circle the words to complete the flyer.

Welcome to
Greenview (Farmers') / Fish *Market*
a.

Right now we have fresh:
- vegetables (tomatoes / turnips, lettuce, zucchini)
  b.
- fruits (avocados / apples, strawberries, apricots,
  c.
  peaches / pineapples)
  d.
- fish / herbs (basil, dill, parsley, chives)
  e.
- local cheese / ice cream (Swiss, cheddar, mozzarella)
  f.

We also have USDA organic / sour produce.
g.

Free samples / vendors of many items! (Take one, you'll like it!)
h.

Some of our samples / vendors:
i.
- Green Farms (fresh fruits / vegetables)
  j.
- The Lemonade / Live Music Stand (sweet / sour, but good!)
  k. **l.**
- Cara's Bakery (freshly baked apple pies / pancakes, donuts, and
  m.
  cupcakes: sweet / sour and delicious!)
  n.
- Hot Food (sandwiches / tacos and much more!)
  o.
Listen to live music / vendors (featuring The Two-Step Band)!
p.

Time: Saturdays 8:00 a.m. – 2:00 p.m.
Place: Union Square, 4th and Park

5. What about you? Imagine you are at the farmers' market. Check (✓) the things you will do there. Then, compare answers with a classmate.

- ☐ listen to live music
- ☐ have lunch
- ☐ buy sweets
- ☐ buy organic vegetables
- ☐ speak to the vendors
- ☐ meet friends
- ☐ drink lemonade
- ☐ eat samples

CHALLENGE   Make a shopping list for the farmers' market in your dictionary.

1. Look in your dictionary. Which clothing items are . . . ?

a. green _____dress_____ and _____

b. dark blue _____, _____, and _____

c. red _____

d. yellow _____ and _____

e. white _____, _____, _____, _____, and _____

f. pink _____

g. orange _____

h. beige _____

2. Look at the picture of Courtney and Nicholas. Read the school clothing rules. Complete the sentences.

Courtney

Nicholas

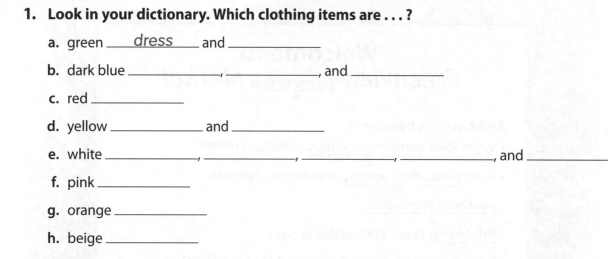

CLOTHING RULES

Wear...	Don't wear...
shirts	T-shirts
blouses	jeans
slacks	baseball caps
skirts	sneakers
dresses	
socks	

What's OK?

a. Courtney is wearing a _____blouse_____.

b. Nicholas is wearing _____.

c. He's also wearing _____.

What's NOT OK?

d. Courtney is wearing _____ and _____.

e. Nicholas is wearing a _____ and a _____.

3. What about you? What are you wearing today?

_____

4. Look in your dictionary. _True_ or _False_?

   a. The man in the blue shirt is wearing jeans.   _true_

   b. The woman with white shoes is wearing socks.   _____

   c. The girl with the baseball cap is tying her shoes.   _____

   d. The woman in the skirt is putting on a sweater.   _____

   e. The woman with the sweater has a handbag.   _____

   f. The man in the green shirt and slacks has tickets.   _____

5. Look in your dictionary. Circle the words to complete the conversation.

Nina: Clio? I'm in front of the theater. Where are you? It's 7:45!

Clio: Sorry. I'm still getting dressed. What are you wearing?

Nina: A blue (blouse)/ T-shirt and a white baseball cap / skirt.
                   a.   **b.**

Clio: Is it cold out? Do I need a handbag / sweater?
                         c.

Nina: Maybe. It _is_ a little cool. What are you wearing?

Clio: Right now I'm wearing a dress / pants, but maybe I'll put on slacks / socks.
                        d.   **e.**

Nina: OK. But hurry! The concert starts at 8:15!

6. Cross out the word that doesn't belong.

   a. **You wear it on top.**   ~~handbag~~   T-shirt   sweater

   b. **They're for your feet.**   shoes   socks   pants

   c. **It's only for women.**   dress   blouse   suit

   d. **You wear it on bottom.**   jeans   shirt   slacks

7. What about you? Complete the checklist. Do you wear . . . ?

	Yes	No	If _yes_, where?
jeans	☐	☐	_____
sneakers	☐	☐	_____
a T-shirt	☐	☐	_____
a suit	☐	☐	_____
a sweater	☐	☐	_____
a baseball cap	☐	☐	_____

CHALLENGE   Look in your dictionary. Imagine you have tickets for the concert. What are you going to wear? Tell a partner.

Casual, Work, and Formal Clothes

1. Look in your dictionary. Circle the words to complete the sentences.

a. The woman's ~~business suit~~ / briefcase is purple.

b. The <u>cardigan / pullover</u> sweater is green.

c. The <u>evening gown / uniform</u> is turquoise.

d. The <u>tank top / sweatshirt</u> is gray.

e. The <u>overalls / sweatpants</u> are red.

f. The <u>knit top / sport shirt</u> is blue and white.

g. The <u>cocktail / maternity</u> dress is orange.

2. Which clothes do women or men usually wear? Which clothes can both wear? Put the words from the box in the correct spaces in the circles.

~~business suit~~	vest	shorts	cardigan sweater
uniform	tie	evening gown	sweatpants
pullover sweater	sandals	sport jacket	tuxedo
maternity dress	tank top	cocktail dress	capris

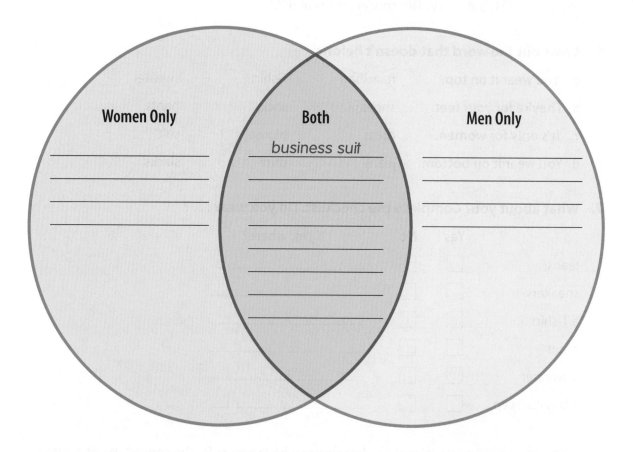

Women Only

Both

business suit

Men Only

3. **Look at the picture. Write the names of the clothing items on the list. Write the color, too.**

Packing Log

to pack for *Chicago Wedding*

a. ___yellow tank top___
   and _____

b. _____
   and _____

c. _____
   and _____

d. _____
   and _____

4. **Match the activity with the clothes from Exercise 3.**

SATURDAY

HOTEL CHICAGO
ALEXANDRA PLACE
CHICAGO

___c__ 1. Meet Nina in exercise room   7:30 a.m.

_____ 2. Lunch near swimming pool   12:00 p.m.

_____ 3. Formal dinner at the Grill   6:00 p.m.

_____ 4. Wedding party at the   9:00 p.m.
        Grand Hotel Ballroom

5. **What about you? Where do you wear these clothes? Check (✓) the columns.**

	At School	At Work	At Home	At a Party	Never
pullover sweater					
vest					
sweatpants					
tuxedo or gown					
uniform					
cap					

CHALLENGE   What casual clothes do you have? Work clothes? Formal clothes? Exercise wear? Give two examples for each type of clothes.

1. Look in your dictionary. *True* or *False*?

a. The man with the headwrap is wearing a jacket. _____*true*_____

b. The man with the down jacket is wearing earmuffs. _____

c. The woman in the poncho is wearing yellow rain boots. _____

d. The man with sunglasses is wearing a trench coat. _____

2. Look at the ad. Circle the words to complete the sentences.

Dress for the Snow

Jessica is wearing a dark green <u>down vest</u> / <u>parka,</u>
        a.

white <u>earmuffs</u> / <u>headband</u>, and green
        b.

<u>gloves</u> / <u>mittens</u>. Justin is wearing a blue
   c.

<u>down jacket</u> / <u>coat</u>, black <u>ski hat</u> / <u>ski mask</u>, and
     d.   **e.**

a light blue <u>winter scarf</u> / <u>hat</u>.
       f.

DRESS FOR THE SUN

Kimberly is wearing a <u>headwrap</u> / <u>straw hat</u>,
        g.

black <u>swimming trunks</u> / <u>swimsuit</u>, and a white
       h.

<u>cover-up</u> / <u>windbreaker</u>. Her <u>raincoat</u> / <u>umbrella</u>
  i.   **j.**

and <u>leggings</u> / <u>sunglasses</u> protect her from the sun.
     k.

3. What about you? Circle the words to complete the sentences.

a. I <u>am</u> / <u>am not</u> wearing a jacket or coat today.

b. I <u>wear</u> / <u>don't wear</u> sunglasses.

c. I <u>sometimes</u> / <u>never</u> wear a hat.

CHALLENGE   Look at the clothes in your dictionary. List eight items you have. When do you wear them? **Example:** *gloves—for cold weather*

1. Look in your dictionary. Circle the words to complete the sentences.

a. The (pajamas) / tights are pink.

b. The slippers / crew socks are gray.

c. The thermal undershirt / blanket sleeper is yellow.

d. The robe / nightshirt is blue and white.

e. The body shaper / nightgown is beige.

2. Look at the ad. Complete the bill.

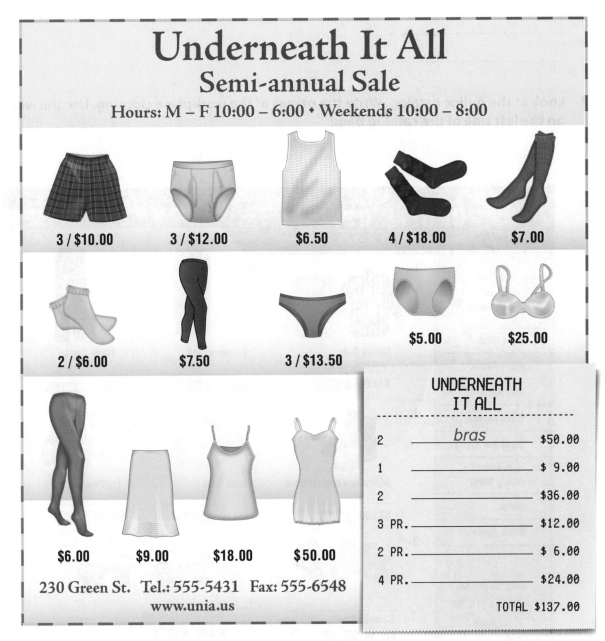

Underneath It All
Semi-annual Sale
Hours: M – F 10:00 – 6:00 ◆ Weekends 10:00 – 8:00

3 / $10.00	3 / $12.00	$6.50	4 / $18.00	$7.00
2 / $6.00	$7.50	3 / $13.50	$5.00	$25.00
$6.00	$9.00	$18.00	$50.00	

230 Green St. Tel.: 555-5431 Fax: 555-6548
www.unia.us

UNDERNEATH IT ALL

2	_bras_	$50.00
1	_____	$ 9.00
2	_____	$36.00
3 PR.	_____	$12.00
2 PR.	_____	$ 6.00
4 PR.	_____	$24.00
	TOTAL	$137.00

CHALLENGE Choose clothes from the ad in Exercise 2. Write a bill. Figure out the total.

1. Look in your dictionary. Put the words in the correct column.

For Your Head	For Your Face	For Your Hands
hard hat		
		For Your Feet

2. Look at the online catalog. Write the names of the workplace clothing. Use the words on the left side of the catalog page.

www.onsite.us

ONSITE.US
Your First Stop for Workplace Clothes

Best Sellers

Shop Online

Hard Hats
~~Work Shirts~~
Tool Belts
Work Gloves
Steel Toe Boots
High Visibility Safety Vests
Jeans
Work Pants

FREE SHIPPING
on orders of $150
or more

a. Heavy Duty *work shirts* $18.00 Buy Now!

b. Stonewashed $30.00 Buy Now!

c. 100% Cotton $80.00 Buy Now!

d. Warm and comfortable $75.00 Buy Now!

e. Rain brim $10.00 Buy Now!

f. Lightweight $20.00 Buy Now!

g. 12 pairs/box $25.00 Buy Now!

h. High quality nylon $32.00 Buy Now!

3. **Look in your dictionary.** *True* or *False*? **Correct the <u>underlined</u> words in the false sentences.**

a. The construction worker is wearing a ~~polo~~ work shirt. ___false___

b. The road worker is wearing <u>jeans</u>. _____

c. The farmworker is wearing <u>work gloves</u>. _____

d. The salesperson is wearing a <u>badge</u>. _____

e. The manager is wearing a <u>blazer</u>. _____

f. The counterperson is wearing a <u>chef's hat</u>. _____

g. The nurse is wearing <u>scrubs</u>. _____

h. The security guard has a <u>name tag</u>. _____

i. The medical technician is wearing a <u>lab coat</u>. _____

j. The surgeon is wearing a <u>surgical scrub cap</u>. _____

4. **Look at the online catalog in Exercise 2. What items will people buy? Complete the chart.**

Job	Quantity	Item	Item Price	Total
a. road worker	2 pairs	steel toe boots	$75	$150
	1 pair	_____	$80	_____
b. construction worker	1	_____	$32	_____
	2	safety vests	_____	_____
	1 box	_____	_____	_____

5. **What about you? Check (✓) the clothing you have. Do you wear the clothing for work?**

	For Work	Not for Work
☐ safety glasses	☐	☐
☐ waist apron	☐	☐
☐ blazer	☐	☐
☐ polo shirt	☐	☐
☐ work gloves	☐	☐
☐ helmet	☐	☐
☐ hairnet	☐	☐

CHALLENGE Look at <u>pages 170 and 171</u> in your dictionary. List three people's work clothing.
Example: *the dental assistant—a face mask and disposable gloves*

1. Look at the top picture in your dictionary. How many . . . can you see?

a. salesclerks   _3_

b. customers waiting in line   ___

c. hats   ___

d. customers trying on shoes   ___

e. customers purchasing jewelry   ___

f. display cases   ___

2. Look at the pictures. Label the items. Use the words in the box.

backpack	bracelet	pin	change purse	earrings	~~wallet~~
locket	cell phone case	ring	shoulder bag	tote bag	watch

a. _____wallet_____   b. _____   c. _____   d. _____

e. _____   f. _____   g. _____   h. _____

i. _____   j. _____   k. _____   l. _____

3. Look at the answers in Exercise 2. Put the words in the correct columns.

Jewelry Department		Other Accessories	
_____	_____	_____wallet_____	_____
_____	_____	_____	_____
_____	_____	_____	_____

4. **Cross out the word that doesn't belong.**

   a. Things you wear around your neck   necklace   ~~belt~~   scarf   locket

   b. Types of necklaces   beads   buckles   chain   string of pearls

   c. Things you keep a change purse in   backpack   handbag   wallet   tote bag

   d. Types of shoes   oxfords   boots   pumps   shoelaces

   e. Parts of a shoe   sole   suspenders   heel   toe

5. **Complete the ad. Use the words in the box.**

   ~~pumps~~   flats   boots   hiking boots   loafers   oxfords   tennis shoes   high heels

   SALE

   The Good Sole

   Save 20% on men's and women's shoes!

   a. ___pumps___

   b. _____

   c. _____

   d. _____

   e. _____

   f. _____

   g. _____

   h. _____

   Located at the Lincoln Mall.
   Route 65

6. **What about you? Check (✓) the items you have.**

   ☐ chain   ☐ watch   ☐ pierced earrings

   ☐ clip-on earrings   ☐ belt buckle   ☐ cell phone case

   CHALLENGE List the kinds of shoes you have. When do you wear them?
   Example: *boots—I wear them in cold or wet weather.*

Describing Clothes

1. Look at the T-shirts in your dictionary. *True* or *False*?

   a. They come in six sizes.   __*true*__   **d.** They are short-sleeved.   _____

   b. They have a V-neck.   _____   **e.** They are checked.   _____

   c. They are solid blue.   _____   **f.** They are stained.   _____

2. Look in your dictionary. Match the opposites.

   __5__ **a.** big   **1.** plain

   ____ **b.** fancy   **2.** wide

   ____ **c.** heavy   **3.** long

   ____ **d.** loose   **4.** tight

   ____ **e.** narrow   **5.** small

   ____ **f.** high   **6.** print

   ____ **g.** short   **7.** low

   ____ **h.** solid   **8.** light

3. Look at the picture. Describe the problems.

   a. His jeans are too ___*baggy*___ and too _____.

   b. His sweater is too _____ and the sleeves are _____.

   c. His jacket sleeve is _____ and a button _____.

4. Look at the order form. Circle the words to complete the statements.

ITEM #	PAGE #	DESCRIPTION	SIZE	COLOR	QUANTITY	ITEM PRICE	TOTAL
563218	3	CREWNECK SWEATER	S	RED AND BLACK STRIPED	3	$15.00	$45.00
962143	12	JACKET	M	BLACK	1	$62.00	$62.00
583614	8	3/4-SLEEVED SHIRT	L	PAISLEY	1	$18.00	$18.00
769304	15	MINI-SKIRT	S	RED	1	$50.00	$50.00
216983	10	LOOSE JEANS	8	DARK BLUE	1	$98.00	$98.00

Clothes Town — THE CATALOG STORE — toll free 1-800-000-4627 www.clothestown.us

a. The customer wants extra-small / (small) crewneck sweaters.

b. She's ordering a long / large paisley shirt.

c. It's a 3/4-sleeved / sleeveless shirt.

d. She also wants a plaid / medium jacket.

e. The skirt is short / long.

f. The jeans are expensive / tight.

5. What about you? Look at the ad. Choose two items to order. Add them to the order form in Exercise 4.

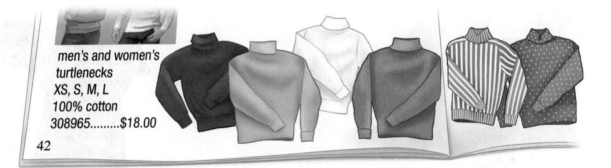

men's and women's
turtlenecks
XS, S, M, L
100% cotton
308965.........$18.00

42

6. What about you? Describe a problem you have or had with your clothes.

Example: *My jacket zipper is broken.*

_____

CHALLENGE Describe the clothes you are wearing today. Include the color, style, and pattern. **Example:** *I'm wearing tight black jeans, a red and white striped shirt, and a light jacket.*

Making Clothes

1. **Look at the garment factory in your dictionary. How many . . . are there?**

    a. women sewing by hand   _1_

    b. women sewing by machine   ___

    c. bolts of fabric   ___

    d. shirts on the rack   ___

    e. sewing machine needles   ___

2. **Write the name of the material. Use the words in the box.**

    | cotton | ~~cashmere~~ | leather | linen | silk | wool |

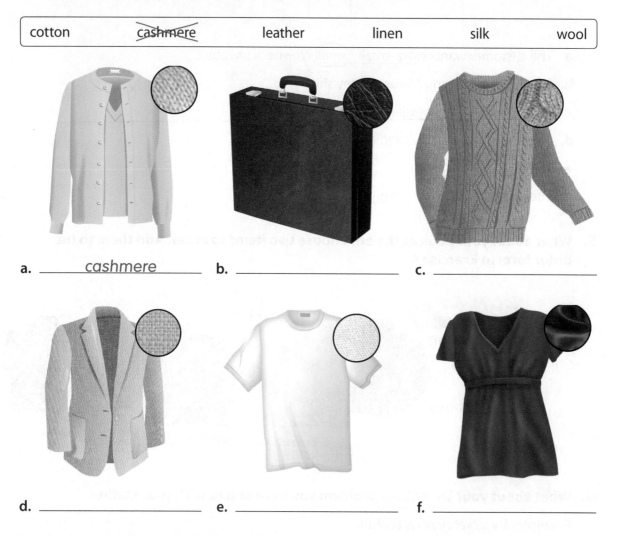

    a. _cashmere_   b. _____   c. _____

    d. _____   e. _____   f. _____

3. **What about you? What materials are you wearing today? Write three sentences.**

    Example: *I'm wearing a cotton sweater.*

    _____

    _____

    _____

4. **Look in your dictionary. Cross out the word that doesn't belong.**

    a. Closures   zipper   snap   buckle   ~~ribbon~~

    b. Trim   thread   sequins   fringe   beads

    c. Material   cashmere   pattern   leather   nylon

    d. Sewing machine parts   bobbin   rack   needle   feed dog

5. **Look at the picture. Circle the words to complete the sentences.**

Vilma is wearing a (denim) / wool jacket with <u>buttons / snaps</u>. Her jacket has beautiful
                      a.   **b.**

<u>appliqués / sequins</u> on it. Her husband, Enrique, is wearing a <u>corduroy / suede</u> jacket with
      c.   **d.**

<u>fringe / ribbon</u>. It's cold outside, but his jacket <u>buckle / zipper</u> is open. Their daughter,
    e.   **f.**

Rosa, is wearing a <u>lace / velvet</u> jacket with <u>beads / thread</u>. Her jacket is closed with
              g.   **h.**

<u>hooks and eyes / buttons</u>.
      i.

6. **What about you? What type of closures do your clothes have?**

    Example: *My shirt has buttons. My jeans have a zipper.*

[CHALLENGE] Look at <u>pages 86 and 87</u> in your dictionary. Describe two people's clothing. Include
the fabric, material, closures, and trim. **Example:** *One man is wearing blue denim jeans
with a zipper and button, a light blue cotton shirt with buttons, and brown leather loafers.*

Making Alterations

1. Look in your dictionary. Who is . . . ? Check (✓) the answers.

	Dressmaker	Tailor
a. working in the alterations shop	✓	✓
b. working on a dress	☐	☐
c. using a sewing machine	☐	☐
d. using a dummy	☐	☐
e. using a tape measure	☐	☐
f. using thread	☐	☐

2. Look at the pictures. Check (✓) the alterations the tailor made.

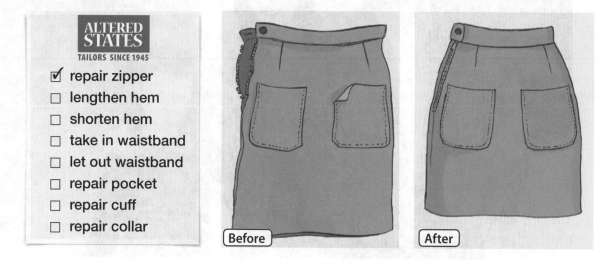

ALTERED STATES
TAILORS SINCE 1945

- ☑ repair zipper
- ☐ lengthen hem
- ☐ shorten hem
- ☐ take in waistband
- ☐ let out waistband
- ☐ repair pocket
- ☐ repair cuff
- ☐ repair collar

Before   After

3. List the items in the sewing basket.

tape measure _____

_____ _____

_____ _____

_____ _____

_____

CHALLENGE Look at the boy on page 96 of this workbook. What alterations do his clothes need? Discuss them with a classmate. **Example:** *He needs to shorten his pants.*

1. Look in your dictionary. Where is the . . . ? Use *in* or *on* in your answers.

a. iron   *on the ironing board*

b. fabric softener   _____

c. spray starch   _____

d. wet polo shirt   _____

e. laundry   _____

f. clothespins   _____

2. Look at the pictures. Write the instructions. Use the sentences in the box.

Clean the lint trap.	Fold the laundry.	Unload the washer.
~~Sort the laundry.~~	Load the washer.	Add the detergent.

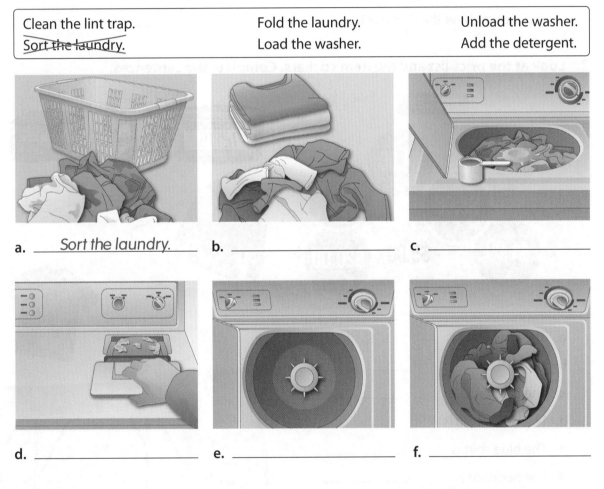

a. *Sort the laundry.*   b. _____   c. _____

d. _____   e. _____   f. _____

3. What about you? Do you do the laundry in your family? Check (✓) the items you use.

☐ iron   ☐ hanger   ☐ clothespins

☐ ironing board   ☐ spray starch   ☐ dryer sheets

☐ clothesline   ☐ fabric softener   ☐ bleach

CHALLENGE Which clothes do you iron? Which clothes do you hang up?

A Garage Sale

1. **Look in your dictionary.** *True* or *False*?

   a. You can buy new clothing at the garage sale.   _____false_____

   b. The flyer has information about the prices.   _____

   c. A woman is bargaining for an orange sweatshirt.   _____

   d. The sweatshirt has a blue sticker on it.   _____

   e. She buys the sweatshirt for $.75.   _____

   f. Some customers are browsing.   _____

   g. You can buy the folding card table and folding chair.   _____

   h. The CD / cassette player is new.   _____

   i. A customer buys the clock radio.   _____

2. **Look at the price list and the item stickers. Complete the sentences.**

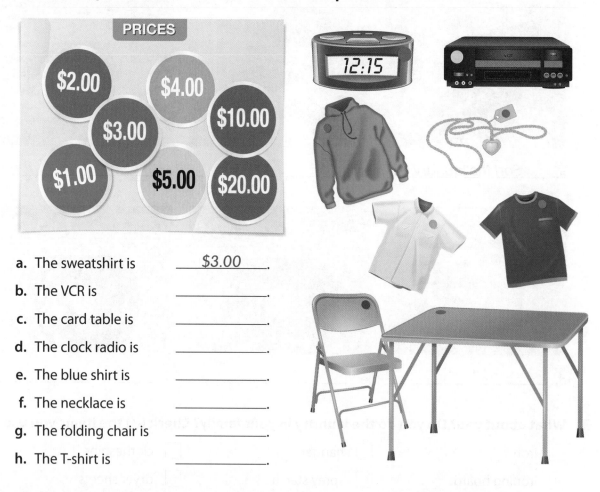

   a. The sweatshirt is _____$3.00_____.

   b. The VCR is _____.

   c. The card table is _____.

   d. The clock radio is _____.

   e. The blue shirt is _____.

   f. The necklace is _____.

   g. The folding chair is _____.

   h. The T-shirt is _____.

3. **What about you? Look in your dictionary. Imagine you are at the garage sale. What will you buy? What price do you want to pay for it? Tell a partner.**

4. **Look in your dictionary. Check (✓) the items you can buy at the garage sale.**

☐ belt	☐ socks	☐ necklace
✓ books	☐ sport jacket	☐ sewing machine
☐ bracelet	☐ straw hat	☐ shoes
☐ briefcase	☐ necklace	☐ sweatshirt
☐ clock radio	☐ hard hat	☐ T-shirt
☐ folding card table	☐ ironing board	☐ VCR
☐ purse	☐ jeans	☐ pin cushion

5. **Complete the flyer. Use the words in the box.**

bargain	browse	clock radios	folding card tables	folding chairs
~~Garage Sale~~	sweatshirts	CD / cassette player	Used Clothing	sticker

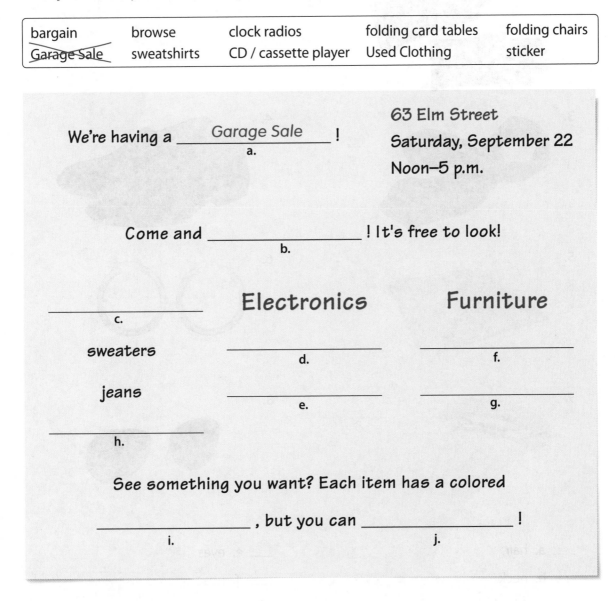

We're having a _____Garage Sale_____ !
a.

63 Elm Street
Saturday, September 22
Noon–5 p.m.

Come and _____ ! It's free to look!
b.

_____   **Electronics**   **Furniture**
c.

sweaters   _____   _____
d.   f.

jeans   _____   _____
e.   g.

_____
h.

See something you want? Each item has a colored

_____ , but you can _____ !
i.   j.

CHALLENGE Work with a partner. Imagine you are going to have a garage sale. What items will you sell? Make a flyer. Use the flyer in Exercise 5 as an example.

103

The Body

1. Look in your dictionary. How many . . . do you see?

a. heads   _11_

b. feet   ___

c. hands   ___

d. backs   ___

e. eyes   ___

f. ears   ___

g. shoulders   ___

2. Look at the pictures. Where on the body do you find them? Match.

1.

2.

3.

4.

5.

6.

7.

8.

___ **a.** hair

___ **b.** neck

___ **c.** feet

___ **d.** ears

___ **e.** eyes

___ **f.** nose

_1_ **g.** hands

___ **h.** finger

3. **How many . . . do people usually have? Put the words in the correct column.**

One	Two	Ten
head		

4. **Look at the medical chart.** *True* **or** *False***?**

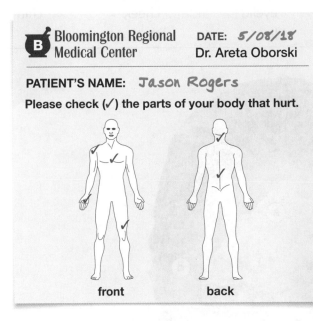

a. Jason's head hurts.   *false*

b. His right hand hurts.   _____

c. His left shoulder hurts.   _____

d. He has a pain in his neck.   _____

e. His leg hurts.   _____

f. He has a pain in his chest.   _____

g. His back hurts.   _____

CHALLENGE   Which parts of the body do these doctors help? Look online or ask a classmate.

podiatrist _____   ophthalmologist _____   chiropractor _____

Inside and Outside the Body

1. **Look in your dictionary. Cross out the word that doesn't belong.**

a. The face	forehead	jaw	chin	~~toe~~
b. Inside the body	liver	intestines	abdomen	stomach
c. The leg and foot	knee	heel	ankle	tongue
d. The skeleton	pelvis	brain	skull	rib cage
e. The hand	thumb	shin	palm	wrist
f. The senses	taste	hear	lip	smell

2. **Label the parts of the face. Use the words in the box.**

eyebrow	eyelashes	eyelid	cheek	chin
~~forehead~~	jaw	lip	teeth	

a. _forehead_

b. _____

c. _____

d. _____

e. _____

f. _____

g. _____

h. _____

i. _____

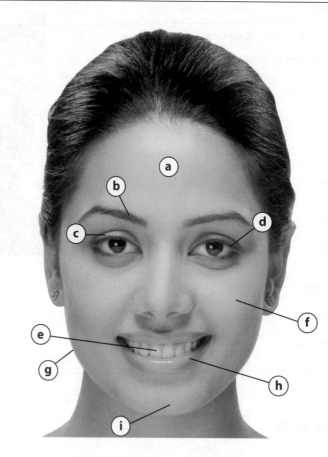

3. **Look at the picture. Check (✓) the parts of the body that are NOT covered by clothes.**

✓	arms	☐	buttocks
☐	calves	☐	hip
☐	elbows	☐	fingers
☐	feet	☐	forearms
☐	hands	☐	head
☐	knees	☐	legs
☐	lower back	☐	shins
☐	shoulder blades	☐	jaw

4. **Match.**

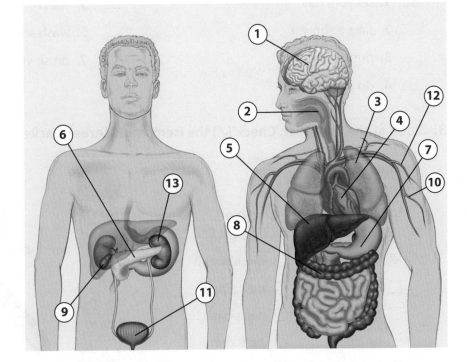

_4_ **a.** heart

___ **b.** kidney

___ **c.** lung

___ **d.** liver

___ **e.** gallbladder

___ **f.** bladder

___ **g.** throat

___ **h.** stomach

___ **i.** pancreas

___ **j.** brain

___ **k.** intestines

___ **l.** artery

___ **m.** vein

5. **What about you? <u>Underline</u> the words for parts of the body that are NOT OK for men to show on the street in your native country. Circle the words for parts of the body that are NOT OK for women to show.**

arms	abdomen	elbows	face	mouth
ankles	chest	knees	calves	feet

CHALLENGE Choose five parts of the body. What are their functions?
Example: _brain—We use it to think._

1. Look in your dictionary. Cross out the word that doesn't belong.

a. shower cap	soap	~~hair spray~~	bath powder
b. electric shaver	razorblades	aftershave	sunscreen
c. hair clip	emery board	nail polish	nail clipper
d. barrettes	eyebrow pencil	bobby pins	hair gel
e. blush	foundation	eyeliner	deodorant
f. body lotion	shampoo	blow dryer	conditioner
g. toothbrush	comb	dental floss	toothpaste

2. Look at Exercise 1. Write the letter of the items that you need for these activities.

_d_ **1.** do your hair

___ **2.** take a shower

___ **3.** put on makeup

___ **4.** do your nails

___ **5.** shave

___ **6.** wash and dry your hair

___ **7.** brush your teeth

3. Look at the checklist. Check (✓) the items that Teresa packed.

Travel Packing List

to pack for **San Diego**

- ☑ bath powder
- ☐ blow dryer
- ☐ bobby pins
- ☐ brush
- ☐ comb
- ☐ conditioner
- ☐ curling iron
- ☐ dental floss
- ☐ deodorant
- ☐ emery board
- ☐ lipstick
- ☐ mascara
- ☐ mouthwash
- ☐ nail clipper
- ☐ nail polish
- ☐ perfume
- ☐ razor
- ☐ shampoo
- ☐ shaving cream
- ☐ shower cap
- ☐ soap
- ☐ sunscreen
- ☐ toothbrush
- ☐ toothpaste

4. Teresa is at the hotel. Go back to the checklist in Exercise 3. Check (✓) the additional items that Teresa has now.

5. What does Teresa still need from the checklist in Exercise 3? Complete her shopping list.

HOTEL KENT

TO BUY

bobby pins

_____

_____

_____

_____

6. What about you? How often do you use . . . ? Check (✓) the columns.

	Every Day	Sometimes	Never
sunblock			
shower gel			
perfume or cologne			
hair spray			
dental floss			
body lotion or moisturizer			
mouthwash			
Other: _____			

CHALLENGE List the personal hygiene items you take with you when you travel.

Symptoms and Injuries

1. **Look in your dictionary. *True* or *False*?**

   a. The man in picture 10 has an insect bite on his right arm.   *true*

   b. The man in picture 12 has a cut on his thumb.   _____

   c. The man in picture 17 has a blister on his hand.   _____

   d. The woman in picture 16 has a swollen toe.   _____

   e. The woman in picture 14 has a sprained ankle.   _____

2. **Look at Tania's medicine. Complete the form. Look at <u>page 115</u> in your dictionary for help.**

   DATE: *3/5/18*

   PATIENT'S NAME: *Tania Zobor*

   Please check (✓) all your symptoms.

   I OFTEN GET. . . .

☐ headaches	☐ sore throats
☑ earaches	☐ a cough
☐ toothaches	☐ fevers
☐ stomachaches	☐ bruises
☐ backaches	☐ sunburns
☐ bloody noses	☐ chills

   I OFTEN. . . .

   ☐ feel dizzy   ☐ feel nauseous   ☐ vomit

3. **What about you? Complete the form. Use your own information or information about someone you know.**

   PATIENT'S NAME: _____   Please check (✓) all your symptoms.

I OFTEN GET. . . .			I OFTEN. . . .
☐ headaches	☐ backaches	☐ fevers	☐ feel dizzy
☐ earaches	☐ bloody noses	☐ bruises	☐ feel nauseous
☐ toothaches	☐ sore throats	☐ sunburns	☐ vomit
☐ stomachaches	☐ a cough	☐ chills	

   CHALLENGE Choose four health problems in Exercise 3. What can you do for them? Look at <u>page 115</u> in your dictionary for help. **Example:** *headaches—Take pain reliever.*

1. **Look in your dictionary. Who . . . ? Check (✓) the columns.**

	Patient	Receptionist	Doctor	Nurse
a. has an appointment	✓			
b. checks blood pressure				
c. has a thermometer				
d. examines the throat				
e. has a health insurance card				
f. is on the examination table				
g. is holding a health history form				
h. has a stethoscope				

2. **Look at the doctor's notes. Which medical instrument did the doctor use? Match.**

MEDICAL CENTER

Dr. D. Ngoc Huynh

DATE: 3/5/18

PATIENT'S NAME: Carla Vega

1. checked BP—120/80
2. took temp.—98.6°
3. listened to lungs—clear
4. drew blood

_4_ **a.** syringe

___ **b.** thermometer

___ **c.** blood pressure gauge

___ **d.** stethoscope

3. **What about you? Think of the last time you saw the doctor. How long were you . . . ?**

in the waiting room _____

in the examining room _____

on the examination table _____

Did the doctor or nurse . . . ? Check (✓) the answers.

☐ check your blood pressure   ☐ draw blood

☐ examine your eyes   ☐ take your temperature

CHALLENGE   Find out about health insurance in other countries. Which countries have national health insurance? Who can get it?

1. Look in your dictionary. Match the problem with the illness or condition.

_6_ **a.** My skin and eyes look yellow.

____ **b.** I can't eat peanuts.

____ **c.** I have a rash on my neck. It hurts.

____ **d.** I have red spots on my face.

____ **e.** My forehead feels very hot.

____ **f.** My nose is red and I'm coughing.

1. allergy

2. flu

3. measles

4. cold

5. shingles

6. hepatitis

2. Look at photos of Mehmet when he was a child. Complete the medical history form.

Nov 1999   Jan 2001   Dec 2006   May 2008

FHC FAMILY HEALTH CENTER	NAME: *Mehmet Caner*	DATE OF BIRTH: *April 18, 1993*
CHECK (✓) THE ILLNESSES OR CONDITIONS YOU HAD AS A CHILD.		
☐ DIABETES	☐ CHICKEN POX	☐ MUMPS
☐ INTESTINAL PARASITES	☐ ASTHMA	☐ ALLERGIES
☑ EAR INFECTIONS	☐ STREP THROAT	☐ PNEUMONIA

3. What about you? Complete the medical history form. Use your own information or information about someone you know.

FHC FAMILY HEALTH CENTER	NAME:	DATE OF BIRTH:
CHECK (✓) THE ILLNESSES OR CONDITIONS YOU HAD AS A CHILD.		
☐ DIABETES	☐ CHICKEN POX	☐ MUMPS
☐ INTESTINAL PARASITES	☐ ASTHMA	☐ ALLERGIES
☐ EAR INFECTIONS	☐ STREP THROAT	☐ PNEUMONIA

CHALLENGE List the things you do when you have a cold or flu.
Example: *drink hot water with lemon*

4. **Look at the bottom picture on page 113 in your dictionary. Write the illness or medical condition.**

   a. intestines   _intestinal parasites_

   b. brain   _____

   c. breast   _____

   d. neck and shoulder   _____

   e. lungs   _____

   f. pancreas   _____

5. **Circle the words to complete the sentences. Use your dictionary and the index in the back of your book for help with new words.**

   a. Sneezing / Shellfish is an allergic reaction.

   b. Some people are allergic to animals / asthma.

   c. You can get malaria / TB from a mosquito bite.

   d. AIDS / anaphylaxis can result from HIV.

   e. Anaphylaxis includes difficulty breathing and swelling / sneezing.

   f. You can get a rash from measles / dementia.

   g. Breathing is difficult when you have nasal congestion / an ear infection.

   h. You sometimes need injections of insulin when you have diabetes / HIV.

   i. You need to measure your blood pressure when you have hypertension / dementia.

6. **What about you? What do you do when you have…?**

   a rash   _____

   swelling   _____

   nasal congestion   _____

   the flu   _____

   a cold   _____

   strep throat   _____

   hives   _____

CHALLENGE   What are the differences between a cold and the flu? Research the answer online. Discuss your answer with a partner.

1. **Look in your dictionary.** *True* or *False*? **Correct the <u>underlined</u> words in the false sentences.**

   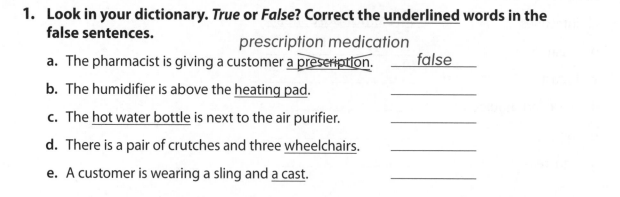

   prescription medication

   a. The pharmacist is giving a customer a <u>~~prescription~~</u>.   _false_

   b. The humidifier is above the <u>heating pad</u>.   _____

   c. The <u>hot water bottle</u> is next to the air purifier.   _____

   d. There is a pair of crutches and three <u>wheelchairs</u>.   _____

   e. A customer is wearing a sling and <u>a cast</u>.   _____

2. **Complete the medical warning labels. Use the sentences in the box.**

Take with dairy products.	Do not take with dairy products.	Finish all medication.
~~Do not drive or operate heavy machinery~~	Take with food or milk.	Do not drink alcohol

   a.

   Do not drive or operate heavy machinery **when taking this medicine**

   b.

   c.

   d. **IMPORTANT**

   e.

   f. when taking this medicine

3. **Look at the picture. Circle the words to complete the sentences.**

a. Brian got over-the-counter /(prescription) medication.

b. The name of the <u>pharmacist / pharmacy</u> is Duggen Drugs.

c. The bottle contains <u>capsules / tablets</u>.

d. The prescription number is <u>20 / 639180</u>.

e. The <u>prescription / warning</u> label says, "Do not take with dairy products."

f. Brian can't <u>drink water / eat cheese</u> with this medicine.

g. The medicine isn't good after <u>September 2018 / March 2020</u>.

h. The dosage is <u>two / four</u> capsules every day.

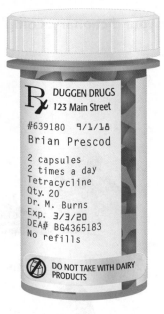

4. **What about you? Check (✓) the items you think are in your medicine cabinet. Then check your answers at home.**

☐ pain reliever
☐ cold tablets
☐ antacid
☐ cream
☐ cough syrup
☐ throat lozenges
☐ nasal spray
☐ ointment
☐ eye drops
☐ vitamins

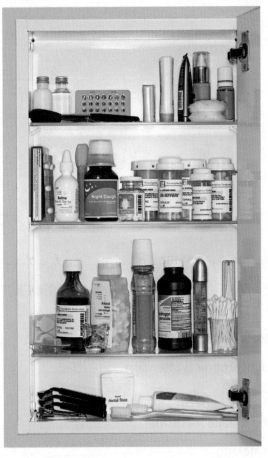

CHALLENGE Look at some prescription or over-the-counter medication in your medicine cabinet. What's the dosage? The expiration date? Is there a warning label? Make a list.

1. Look in your dictionary. Complete the poster.

For Good Health...

a. _____Eat_____ a healthy diet.

b. _____ lots of fluids.

c. _____ fit.

d. _____

e. _____ immunized.

f. _____ regular checkups.

2. Look at the doctor's notes. *True* or *False*?

a. The patient sought* medical attention. _____true_____

b. The patient should get bed rest. _____

c. She doesn't need to take medicine. _____

d. She must stop smoking. _____

e. She should drink more fluids. _____

*sought = past tense of *seek*

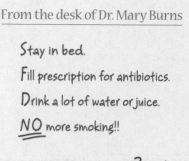

From the desk of Dr. Mary Burns

Stay in bed.

Fill prescription for antibiotics.

Drink a lot of water or juice.

<u>NO</u> more smoking!!

Call for Appointment in __2 weeks__

3. **Look in your dictionary. Complete the chart.**

Problem	Doctor	Help
a. *vision problems*		glasses or *contact lenses*
b.		hearing aid
c. stress or		talk therapy or
d. knee pain		

4. **Match.**

   _7_ **a.** I see my doctor every January.

   ____ **b.** I'd like some more vegetables, please.

   ____ **c.** I exercise every day.

   ____ **d.** No cigarettes for me, thanks.

   ____ **e.** I always get a flu vaccination.

   ____ **f.** I'll have another glass of water, please.

   ____ **g.** I need to see the doctor today.

   ____ **h.** It's time for my pills.

1. Eat a healthy diet.

2. Seek medical attention.

3. Get immunized.

4. Don't smoke.

5. Take medicine

6. Drink fluids.

7. Have regular checkups.

8. Stay fit.

5. **What about you? Check (✓) the things you do. Explain.**

Example: *stay fit—I exercise four times a week.*

- ☐ stay fit   _____
- ☐ eat a healthy diet   _____
- ☐ get immunized   _____
- ☐ drink fluids   _____
- ☐ have regular checkups   _____
- ☐ follow medical advice   _____
- ☐ Other: _____

CHALLENGE   List three other kinds of doctors. What problems do they treat?
        Example: *orthopedist—for problems with bones*

1. **Look in your dictionary. *True* or *False*?**

   a. A paramedic is helping an unconscious woman.   *true*

   b. The woman in the red sweater is in shock.   _____

   c. The man near the bookcase is hurt.   _____

   d. The boy in the dark blue shirt is having an allergic reaction.   _____

   e. The child in the swimming pool is getting frostbite.   _____

   f. The woman at the table is choking.   _____

   g. The boy in the doctor's office broke a leg.   _____

   h. The man holding his chest is having a heart attack.   _____

2. **Circle the words to complete the sentences.**

   a. Millions of people <u>have an allergic reaction</u> /(fall) on the stairs each year.

   b. Many people cut themselves and <u>bleed / can't breathe</u> when they use a knife.

   c. Riding a bike can be dangerous. People often <u>fall / overdose</u> and break a bone.

   d. Don't put the fork in the toaster! You can get <u>frostbite / an electric shock</u>.

   e. A lot of people <u>choke / burn themselves</u> when they use a stove or oven.

   f. Teach your children to swim. Many children <u>drown / swallow poison</u> each year.

3. **Look in your dictionary. What's the problem? Match the sentences on the left with the medical emergency.**

   <u>4</u> a. Help! I can't swim!   1. He's having a heart attack.

   ___ b. I have chest pain!   2. He's bleeding.

   ___ c. Ow! This pot is hot!   3. He burned himself.

   ___ d. I can't feel my fingers!   4. He's drowning.

   ___ e. Look! I cut myself!   5. She has frostbite.

4. **What about you? Check (✓) the emergencies that have happened to you. When or where did they happen?**

   Emergency   When or Where

   ☐ I had an allergic reaction to _____.   _____

   ☐ I fell.   _____

   ☐ I broke my _____.   _____

   ☐ Other: _____.   _____

   CHALLENGE   Write a paragraph about an emergency in Exercise 3. What treatment did you (or someone you know) get? Look at <u>page 119</u> in your dictionary for help.

1. Look in your dictionary. Write the first aid item for these conditions.

   a. rash on hand   <u>antihistamine cream</u>

   b. broken finger   _____

   c. swollen foot   _____ or _____

   d. infected cut   _____ or _____

2. Look at Chen's first aid kit. Check (✓) the items he has.

FAMILY FIRST AID AND EMERGENCY PREPAREDNESS

✓ adhesive bandages	☐ first aid manual
☐ antihistamine cream	☐ antibacterial ointment
☐ elastic bandage	☐ hydrogen peroxide
☐ splint	☐ ice pack
☐ sterile pad	☐ sterile tape
☐ gauze	☐ tweezers

3. What about you? Check (✓) the first aid items you have at home. Then check (✓) the things you can do.

At home I have . . .	
☐ adhesive bandages	☐ first aid manual
☐ antihistamine cream	☐ antibacterial ointment
☐ elastic bandages	☐ hydrogen peroxide
☐ splints	☐ ice packs
☐ sterile pads	☐ sterile tape
☐ gauze	☐ tweezers

I can do . . .
☐ CPR
☐ rescue breathing
☐ the Heimlich maneuver

CHALLENGE   Look at the items in Exercise 3. What can you use them for?
           Example: _adhesive bandages—cuts_

Dental Care

1. **Circle the words to complete the sentences.**

   a. A dental assistant / orthodontist helps the dentist.

   b. A dental hygienist uses <u>dental instruments / fillings</u> to clean teeth.

   c. <u>An orthodontist / A dentist</u> gives people braces.

   d. <u>A crown / Plaque</u> causes gum disease.

   e. The dentist takes X-rays to help find <u>cavities / dentures</u>.

   f. The dentist uses a syringe to <u>drill a tooth / numb the mouth</u>.

   g. The dentist numbs your mouth before <u>taking X-rays / pulling a tooth</u>.

2. **Label the pictures. Use the words in the box.**

   | clean teeth | ~~drill a tooth~~ | fill a cavity | numb the mouth | pull a tooth | take X-rays |

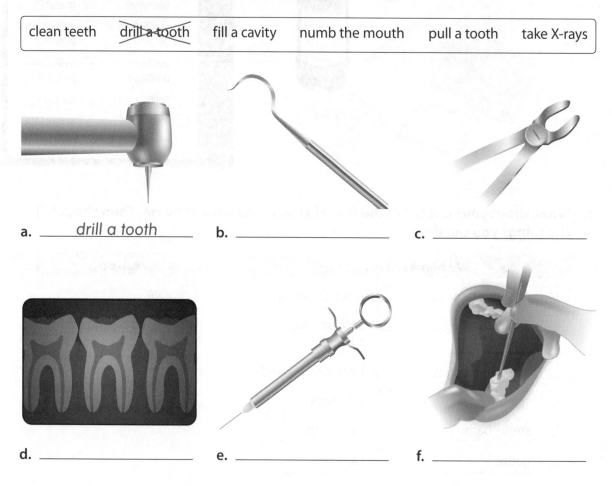

   a. ___*drill a tooth*___   b. _____   c. _____

   d. _____   e. _____   f. _____

CHALLENGE How can you try to prevent gum disease? Write three sentences.
Example: *Go to the dentist two times a year.*

1. Look in your dictionary. Match.

_3_ **a.** $35   1. carrier

____ **b.** the children   2. policyholder

____ **c.** $834   3. co-pay

____ **d.** the man   4. insurance plan

____ **e.** Bronze   5. premium

____ **f.** BeWell Health Insurance   6. dependents

2. Circle the words to complete the phone conversation.

A: Hello. I'd like to make an appointment. I need an X-ray of my right hand.

B: OK. Who is your (carrier) / policyholder?
          a.

A: BeWell.

B: That's good. ABC Radiology is <u>in network / out of network</u>.
          b.

A: Great. And how much is an X-ray?

B: Which <u>insurance plan / EOB</u> do you have?
          c.

A: Bronze.

B: OK. For an X-ray, your <u>co-pay / premium</u> is $35.00.
          d.

3. Look in your dictionary. Who . . . ? Check (✓) the answers.

	The Policyholder	BeWell	ABC Radiology
a. compared plans	✓	☐	☐
b. got a check from BeWell	☐	☐	☐
c. has an insurance policy	☐	☐	☐
d. paid a co-pay	☐	☐	☐
e. is in network	☐	☐	☐
f. receives benefits	☐	☐	☐
g. paid a claim	☐	☐	☐

CHALLENGE Find out the names of some health insurance carriers in your city, state, or country. How much are the monthly premiums?

1. Look in your dictionary. Match.

_5_ **a.** general health problems

___ **b.** heart

___ **c.** cancer

___ **d.** depression

___ **e.** eyes

___ **f.** children

___ **g.** pregnant women

___ **h.** X-rays

1. radiologist

2. oncologist

3. ophthalmologist

4. psychiatrist

5. internist

6. pediatrician

7. cardiologist

8. obstetrician

2. Circle the words to complete the sentences. Use your dictionary for help.

a. The <u>internist</u> / (surgical nurse) helps the surgeon during an operation.

b. The <u>anesthesiologist / radiologist</u> makes the patient "sleep" on the operating table.

c. The <u>emergency medical technician / pediatrician</u> takes the patient out of the ambulance.

d. The <u>oncologist / phlebotomist</u> takes the patient's blood for blood tests.

e. The <u>admissions clerk / volunteer</u> works in the hospital for no pay.

f. The <u>certified nursing assistant / dietician</u> plans the patient's food.

g. The <u>administrator / orderly</u> takes the patient from place to place.

h. The <u>registered nurse / surgical nurse</u> checks the patient's IV.

i. The <u>licensed practical nurse / phlebotomist</u> takes the patient's blood pressure.

3. Write the full forms. Use your dictionary for help.

a. IV ___*intravenous drip*___

b. EMT _____

c. CNA _____

d. LPN _____

e. RN _____

4. Look at the hospital room in your dictionary. *True* or *False*?

a. The patient is on a stretcher.   _*false*_

b. There's a bedpan near the bed.   _____

c. The volunteer is carrying medication.   _____

d. The nurse is wearing a hospital gown.   _____

e. There's medication on the bed table.   _____

f. The vital signs monitor is near the hospital bed. _____

g. The patient is using the call button now.   _____

5. Look at the picture and the supply list. Match.

Supplies

a. _3_ intravenous drip

b. ____ surgical gloves

c. ____ medical charts

d. ____ medical waste disposal

e. ____ surgical caps

f. ____ surgical gowns

CHALLENGE Find out the names of an internist, an ophthalmologist, and a pediatrician in your community. Make a list.

Go to page 253 for Another Look (Unit 6).   123

A Health Fair

1. Look in your dictionary. How many people are . . . ? Write the number.

a. doing aerobic exercise ___4___

b. doing yoga now _____

c. getting acupuncture _____

d. waiting to get a free eye exam _____

e. listening to the nutrition lecture _____

f. taking people's blood pressure _____

g. watching the Healthy Cooking demonstration _____

h. getting a low-cost exam _____

2. Look in your dictionary. Match the people with the booths.

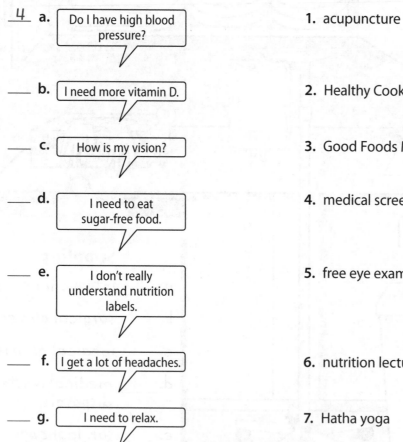

Booth

___4___ a. [Do I have high blood pressure?]   1. acupuncture

_____ b. [I need more vitamin D.]   2. Healthy Cooking

_____ c. [How is my vision?]   3. Good Foods Market

_____ d. [I need to eat sugar-free food.]   4. medical screenings

_____ e. [I don't really understand nutrition labels.]   5. free eye exam

_____ f. [I get a lot of headaches.]   6. nutrition lecture

_____ g. [I need to relax.]   7. Hatha yoga

3. What about you? Look in your dictionary. Imagine you are at the health fair. Where will you go? Why? Tell a partner.

4. **Look in your dictionary.** *True* or *False*? **Correct the <u>underlined</u> words in the false sentences.**

a. The health fair is at a ~~hospital~~. *clinic*   _____false_____

b. A nurse is checking a woman's <u>temperature</u>.   _____

c. People pay $5.00 for <u>a medical screening</u>.   _____

d. Four people are doing <u>yoga</u>.   _____

e. They sell <u>sugar-free</u> food at Healthy Cooking.   _____

f. The woman in line at the eye exam booth uses a <u>walker</u>.   _____

g. The acupuncture doctor is going to put a needle in the man's <u>hand</u>.   _____

5. **Complete the flyer. Use the words in the box.**

Acupuncture	aerobic exercise	demonstration	Health Clinic	Free
~~Health Fair~~	lecture	Low-cost	nurse	
nutrition label	pulse	Sugar-free	yoga	

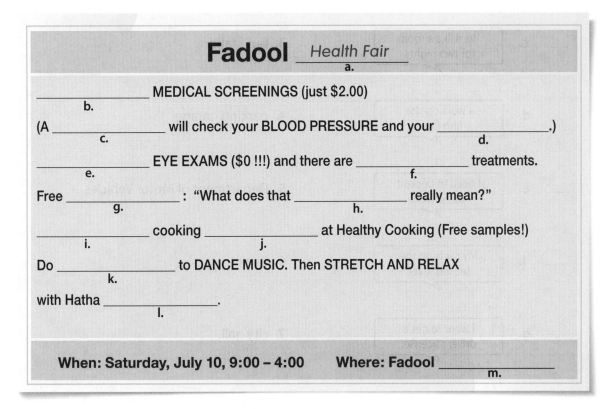

Fadool _Health Fair_
                  a.

_____ MEDICAL SCREENINGS (just $2.00)
    b.

(A _____ will check your BLOOD PRESSURE and your _____.)
      c.   d.

_____ EYE EXAMS ($0 !!!) and there are _____ treatments.
    e.   f.

Free _____: "What does that _____ really mean?"
      g.   h.

_____ cooking _____ at Healthy Cooking (Free samples!)
    i.   j.

Do _____ to DANCE MUSIC. Then STRETCH AND RELAX
      k.

with Hatha _____.
         l.

When: Saturday, July 10, 9:00 – 4:00   **Where: Fadool _____**
                                                                    m.

CHALLENGE Look at three nutrition labels. How much sugar does the food have? How much salt?
Example: *La Rosa spaghetti sauce has 6 grams of sugar and 310 milligrams of salt in a half cup serving.*

Downtown

1. **Look at page 126 in your dictionary. *True* or *False*?**

   a. The parking garage is next to the office building.   _____true_____

   b. The bank is on the corner of Main and Grand.   _____

   c. The Department of Motor Vehicles is on 5th Street.   _____

   d. There's a bus station across from the hotel.   _____

   e. There's a clock on the city hall building.   _____

2. **Match.**

   _3_ a. [I'm taking the 5:10 to Boston.]   1. hotel

   ____ b. [We need to get a marriage license.]   2. office building

   ____ c. [We'd like a room for two nights.]   3. bus station

   ____ d. [I work on the fifth floor.]   4. parking garage

   ____ e. [I need to deposit this check.]   5. Department of Motor Vehicles

   ____ f. [My car is on the second level.]   6. bank

   ____ g. [I want to get a driver's license.]   7. city hall

3. **What about you? Write the street locations for these places in your community.**

   bus station   _____Broadway and West 10th Street_____

   bank   _____

   office building   _____

   city hall   _____

4. **Look in your dictionary. Complete the sentences.**

   a. The _____hospital_____ is on 6th Street.

   b. The _____ is next to the fire station.

   c. There's a Chinese _____ on Main Street.

   d. The _____ is on the corner of Main and Grand Avenue.

   e. The _____ is to the right of the restaurant.

   f. There's a _____ across from the hospital.

5. **Look at the pictures. Where should the people go? Use the words in the box.**

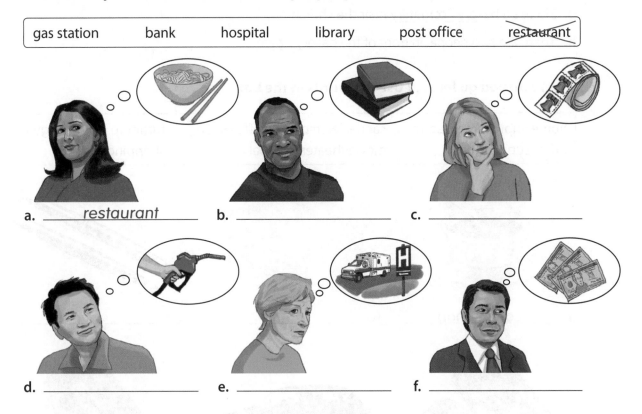

| gas station | bank | hospital | library | post office | ~~restaurant~~ |

   a. ____restaurant____   b. _____   c. _____

   d. _____   e. _____   f. _____

6. **What about you? How often do you go to the . . . ? Check (✓) the columns.**

	Often	**Sometimes**	**Never**
gas station			
library			
post office			
hospital			
courthouse			

CHALLENGE   Look in your dictionary. Choose four places. Why do you go there? Write
sentences. **Example:** *I go to the post office to buy stamps.*

1. **Look in your dictionary. Circle the words to complete the sentences.**

   a. There's a (furniture store)/ coffee shop on Second and Oak.

   b. There's a <u>school / factory</u> on Third near Elm.

   c. The <u>mosque / synagogue</u> is on Second and Oak.

   d. There's a <u>car dealership / construction site</u> on Oak and First.

   e. The garbage truck is in front of the <u>home improvement store / office supply store</u>.

   f. The shopping mall is next to the <u>movie theater / theater</u>.

   g. There's a <u>bakery / cemetery</u> near the church.

   h. There are two people in front of the <u>bakery / gym</u>.

2. **Where do you go for . . . ? Use the words in the box.**

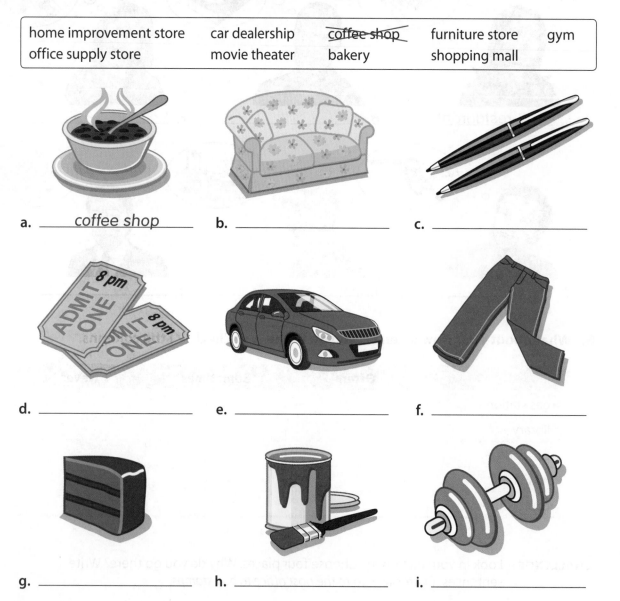

| home improvement store | car dealership | ~~coffee shop~~ | furniture store | gym |
| office supply store | movie theater | bakery | shopping mall | |

a.   coffee shop

b. _____

c. _____

d. _____

e. _____

f. _____

g. _____

h. _____

i. _____

3. Look at the map. Complete the notes.

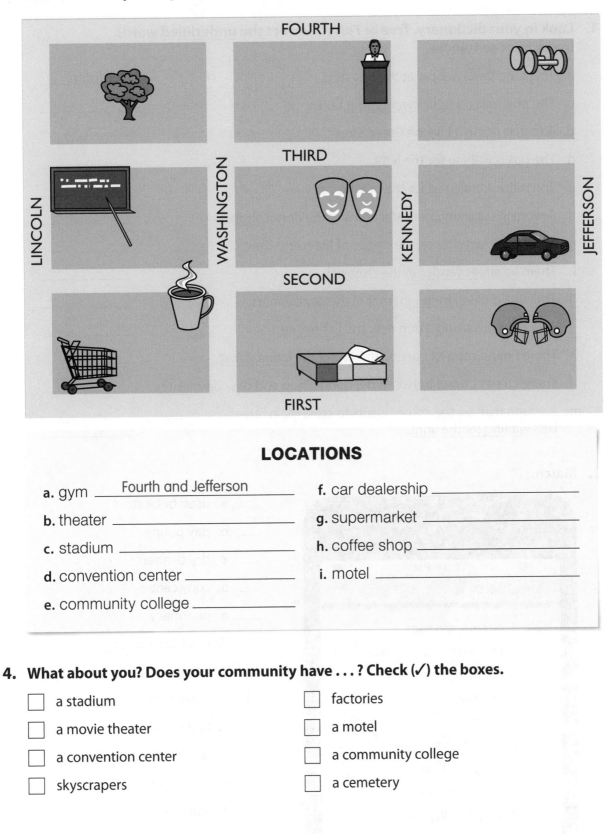

LOCATIONS

a. gym ___Fourth and Jefferson___

b. theater _____

c. stadium _____

d. convention center _____

e. community college _____

f. car dealership _____

g. supermarket _____

h. coffee shop _____

i. motel _____

4. What about you? Does your community have . . . ? Check (✓) the boxes.

☐ a stadium

☐ a movie theater

☐ a convention center

☐ skyscrapers

☐ factories

☐ a motel

☐ a community college

☐ a cemetery

[CHALLENGE] Draw a street map of an area you know. Use some of the places in Exercises 2, 3, and 4.

An Intersection

1. **Look in your dictionary.** *True* or *False*? **Correct the underlined words in the false sentences.**

             two

   a. There are ~~three~~ people at the bus stop.   *false*

   b. The pharmacy is open <u>twenty-four</u> hours.   _____

   c. A man is riding a bike on <u>Green Street</u>.   _____

   d. The <u>bus</u> is waiting for the light.   _____

   e. The traffic light is <u>red</u> for the orange car.   _____

   f. A woman is parking her car in front of the <u>donut shop</u>.   _____

   g. There's a <u>street sign</u> on the corner of Main and Green.   _____

   h. There's a <u>street vendor</u> in the crosswalk.   _____

   i. There's a parking <u>meter</u> in front of the dry cleaners.   _____

   j. A woman is walking a dog near the <u>fire hydrant</u>.   _____

   k. There's handicapped parking in front of the <u>laundromat</u>.   _____

   l. There's a pay phone between the donut shop and the <u>copy center</u>.   _____

   m. A young man on the corner wants to cross Main Street. He's <u>waiting for the light</u>.   _____

2. **Match.**

   Reminders

1. buy milk and eggs	
2. pick up headache medicine	
3. buy newspaper	
4. mail rent	
5. get hair cut	
6. meet Meng for lunch	
7. pick up raincoat	
8. buy a dictionary	
9. copy English paper	
10. wash sheets and towels	
11. pick up Olga's daughter at 5:00	
12. call Olga	

   ___ **a.** used book store

   ___ **b.** pay phone

   ___ **c.** dry cleaners

   ___ **d.** copy center

   ___ **e.** pharmacy

   ___ **f.** childcare center

   ___ **g.** laundromat

   _1_ **h.** convenience store

   ___ **i.** barbershop

   ___ **j.** fast food restaurant

   ___ **k.** newsstand

   ___ **l.** mailbox

3. Cross out the word that doesn't belong.

a. **People**   pedestrian   street vendor   ~~corner~~

b. **Stores**   donut shop   mailbox   pharmacy

c. **Services for clothes**   street sign   laundromat   dry cleaners

d. **Transportation**   drive-thru window   bus   bike

e. **Parts of the street**   curb   sidewalk   cart

f. **Things you put coins in**   pay phone   parking meter   fire hydrant

g. **Things that move**   bus   cart   crosswalk

4. Write the location of these signs.

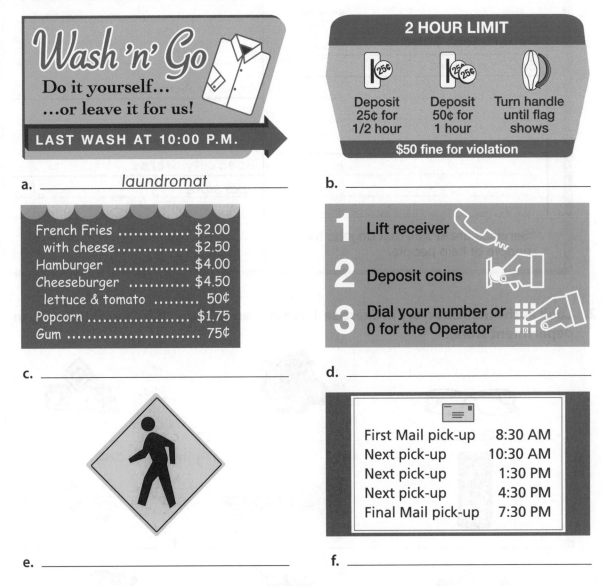

a. _____laundromat_____

b. _____

c. _____

d. _____

e. _____

f. _____

CHALLENGE   Look in your dictionary. Write the locations of five stores. **Example:** *The donut shop is on the corner of Main and Green.*

131

1. **Look in your dictionary. Complete the mall directory. Use the words in the box.**

florist	jewelry store	nail salon	food court
travel agency	maternity store	hair salon	candy store
~~kiosk~~	ice cream shop	optician	~~pet store~~
toy store	electronics store	music store	shoe store

MALL DIRECTORY

	Floor
Department Store	1, 2
Entertainment / Music	
Food	

*Services are stores that do jobs for people or help people.

Services*	Floor
kiosk	1
Shoes / Accessories	
Specialty Stores	
pet store	1

2. **Look at the mall directory in Exercise 1. Where can you buy these items (other than a department store)?**

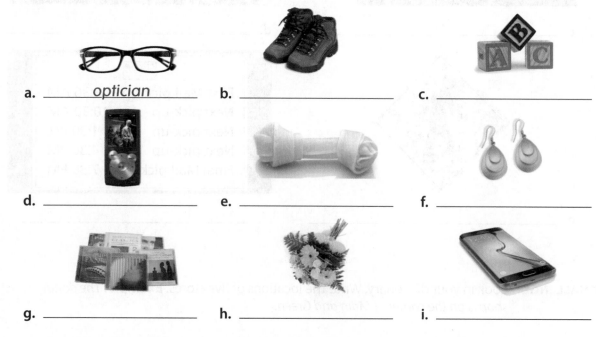

a. _____optician_____   b. _____   c. _____

d. _____   e. _____   f. _____

g. _____   h. _____   i. _____

3. **Look at this mall directory and map. Circle the words to complete the conversations.**

NEWPORT MALL

DIRECTORY—SECOND FLOOR

Books / Cards
The Book Market   6
Cards Galore   8

Department Store
L.R. Nickel's—See Map

Entertainment / Music
Music World   9
Eli's Electronics   3

Food / Restaurants
Candy Corner   2
The Ice Cream Cart   12
Food Court—See Map

Services
Eye Shop   13
Hair's Where   1
Nan's Nails   14
Travel Smart   10

Shoes
Walkrite   7

Specialty Shop
The New Mom   4
Flower Bud   5
Toy with Us   11

(?) Guest Services
Escalator
Restrooms
Telephone
Play area

L.R. Nickel's

Food Court

Customer 1:	Excuse me. Where's the card store?
Guest Services:	It's next to the nail salon / <u>shoe store</u>.
	a.
Customer 2:	Can you tell me where the hair salon is?
Guest Services:	Sure. It's across from <u>the department store / guest services</u>.
	b.
Customer 3:	I'm looking for the <u>elevator / escalator</u>.
	c.
Guest Services:	It's next to Nickel's.
Customer 4:	Hi. Where's the travel agency, please?
Guest Services:	It's right over there. Next to the <u>toy / music</u> store.
	d.
Customer 5:	Excuse me. I'm looking for the candy store.
Guest Services:	It's between the <u>music / electronics</u> store and the
	e.
	<u>hair salon / maternity store</u>.
	f.
Customer 6:	Excuse me. Is there an optician in this mall?
Guest Services:	Yes. There's one across from the <u>florist / bookstore</u>.
	g.

CHALLENGE   Look at the map in Exercise 3. Write the locations of Flower Bud, The Ice Cream Cart, and Guest Services.

133

1. Look in your dictionary. Circle the words to complete the sentences.

a. The <u>security guard</u> / (teller) is speaking to a customer.

b. The customer is <u>making a deposit / withdrawing cash</u>.

c. The <u>ATM / vault</u> is near the security guard.

d. The <u>account manager / customer</u> is holding a form.

e. The two customers on the right are <u>cashing a check / opening a new account</u>.

2. Look at the ATM receipt. *True* or *False*?

a. This is a bank statement. *false*

b. The customer made a deposit. _____

c. Her ATM card ends in 6434. _____

d. She withdrew cash. _____

e. She withdrew $100 from her checking account. _____

f. Her savings account number is 056588734. _____

g. Her balance is $623.40. _____

```
------------------------------------------
                FIRST BANK
             54 CHURCH STREET
             LIBERTYVILLE, IL
------------------------------------------

DATE: 05/06/18          TIME: 11:51
ATM: 045-3
CARD NUMBER:      ************6434

TRANSACTION:            WITHDRAWAL
SERIAL NUM.:                   345
AMOUNT:                       $100
FROM SAVINGS:            056588734
BALANCE:                    $6,234
```

3. How do you use an ATM? Number these steps in order. (1 = the first thing you do)

_____ **a.** enter your PIN

_____ **b.** withdraw cash

_____ **c.** remove your card

_1_ **d.** insert your ATM card

4. What about you? Check (✓) the things you did last month.

☐ cash a check ☐ make a deposit

☐ use an ATM ☐ open an account

☐ withdraw cash ☐ read a bank statement

☐ Other: _____ ☐ Other: _____

CHALLENGE Which documents and valuables do people keep in a safety deposit box? Make a list.

1. Look in your dictionary. Where can you find . . . ?

    a. titles and locations of library books   _online catalog_

    b. magazines and newspapers   _____

    c. maps   _____

    d. DVDs, e-books, and audiobooks   _____

    e. the library clerk   _____

2. Circle the words to complete the sentences.

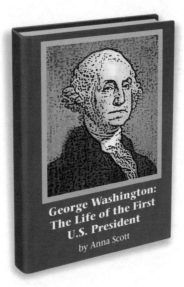

JEFFERSON PUBLIC LIBRARY
CENTRAL BRANCH

CHECK OUT DATE: APRIL 15
DUE DATE: MAY 06
----
1 GEORGE WASHINGTON:
THE LIFE OF THE FIRST
U.S. PRESIDENT

LATE FINE: $.10 A DAY

TOTAL ITEMS: 1

    a. The (author)/ reference librarian is Anna Scott.

    b. The headline / title of the book is _George Washington: The Life of the First U.S. President_.

    c. This book is a biography / novel.

    d. You need a library card to check out / return the book.

    e. You return the book on May 16. The book is / is not late.

    f. The book is ten days late. The late fine is $.10 / $1.00.

3. What about you? Check (✓) the items you would like to borrow from a library.

    ☐ novels   ☐ e-books

    ☐ DVDs   ☐ picture books

    ☐ audiobooks   ☐ Other: _____

CHALLENGE   Find out about your school library or a public library in your community. For how long can you borrow the items in Exercise 3? Ask at the library or check online.

1. **Look in your dictionary. Match.**

_6_ **a.** Certified Mail™
b. airmail
c. Express Mail®
d. ground post
e. Media Mail®
f. Priority Mail®

1. for delivery tomorrow
2. for packages
3. for CDs
4. for two- to three-day delivery
5. for mail to other countries
6. for very important mail

2. **Circle the words to complete the sentences.**

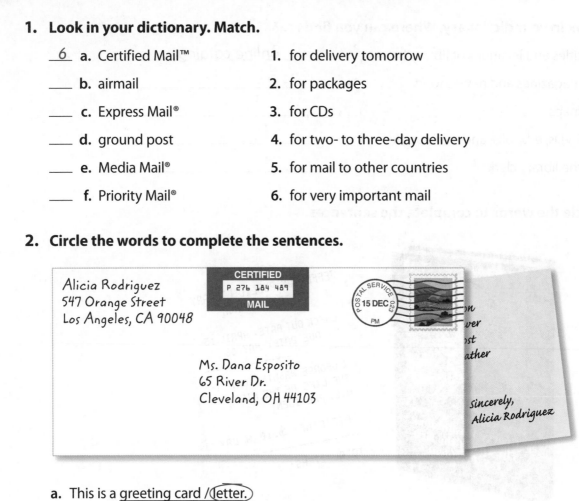

Alicia Rodriguez
547 Orange Street
Los Angeles, CA 90048

CERTIFIED
P 276 184 489
MAIL

POSTAL SERVICE
15 DEC 023
PM

Ms. Dana Esposito
65 River Dr.
Cleveland, OH 44103

...on
...ver
...ost
...ather

sincerely,
Alicia Rodriguez

a. This is a greeting card /letter.

b. The envelope / letter is white.

c. The mailing / return address is 65 River Dr., Cleveland, OH 44103.

d. The postal form / postmark is December 15.

e. Alicia sent this Priority Mail® / Certified Mail™.

3. **What about you? Address this envelope to your teacher. Use your school's address. Don't forget your return address.**

4. **Look in your dictionary.** *True* or *False*?

   a. A postal clerk is using a scale. _____true_____

   b. Letter carriers deliver packages and letters. _____

   c. You can mail a letter in a PO box. _____

   d. A postal clerk is using the automated postal center. _____

   e. A United States mailbox is yellow. _____

   f. Sonya wrote her return address on the envelope. _____

   g. Cindy received a postcard from Sonya. _____

5. **Put the sentences in order. Use your dictionary for help. (1 = the first thing you do)**

   ____ a. Write a note in the card.

   ____ b. Put on a stamp.

   ____ c. Go to the APC.

   ____ d. Find the mailbox.

   _1_ e. Buy a greeting card.

   ____ f. Buy a book of stamps.

   ____ g. Mail the card.

   ____ h. Go to the post office.

   ____ i. Address the envelope.

6. **What about you? Check (✓) the things you did last month.**

   ☐ go to the post office   ☐ buy stamps

   ☐ receive a card   ☐ speak to a postal clerk

   ☐ address an envelope   ☐ read a letter from a friend

   ☐ mail a postcard   ☐ write back to a friend

   ☐ speak to the letter carrier ☐ receive a package

   ☐ complete a postal form   ☐ use an APC

   CHALLENGE Find out how much it costs to send a Priority Mail® letter.

Department of Motor Vehicles (DMV)

1. **Look at page 138 in your dictionary. How many . . . do you see?**

   a. people in the testing area   __3__

   b. DMV clerks   ____

   c. DMV handbooks   ____

   d. open windows   ____

   e. closed windows   ____

   f. people taking a vision exam   ____

2. **Circle the words to complete the sentences.**

   a. This is a (driver's license) / license plate.

   b. The driver's license number is
      020589 / 832643436.

   c. There's a fingerprint / photo
      of Luisa Rodriguez.

   d. The expiration date is 12-27-17 / 02-05-27.

   e. This is a driver's license / license plate.

   f. It has two driver's license numbers /
      registration tags.

   g. The expiration date / license number
      is August 2020.

3. **What about you? Check (✓) the things you have.**

   ☐ driver's license

   ☐ license plate

   ☐ registration tags

   ☐ proof of insurance

4. Look at page 139 in your dictionary. *True* or *False*?

a. Miguel wants to get a driver's license.   _____*true*_____

b. He needs a learner's permit to take a driver's training course.   _____

c. He takes two tests.   _____

d. He takes three courses.   _____

e. He shows two forms of identification.   _____

f. He pays the application fee with cash.   _____

g. He passes the written test.   _____

h. He studies the DMV handbook.   _____

i. He passes the driving test.   _____

5. Which happens first? Bubble in the first event.

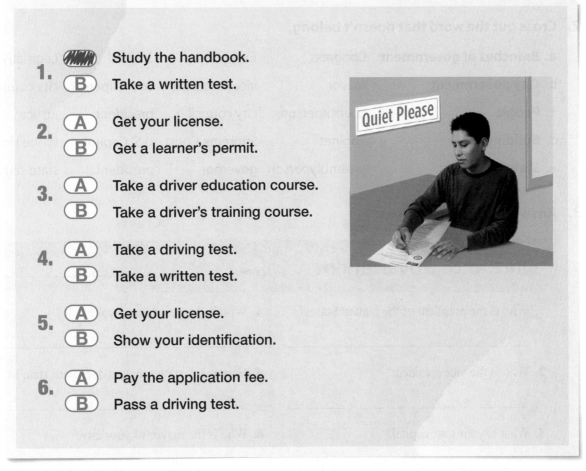

1. (A) Study the handbook.
   (B) Take a written test.

2. (A) Get your license.
   (B) Get a learner's permit.

3. (A) Take a driver education course.
   (B) Take a driver's training course.

4. (A) Take a driving test.
   (B) Take a written test.

5. (A) Get your license.
   (B) Show your identification.

6. (A) Pay the application fee.
   (B) Pass a driving test.

CHALLENGE   Answer these questions about your community.

a. Where is the DMV?   _____

b. How much is the application fee?   _____

Government and Military Service

1. Look at page 140 in your dictionary. Put the words in the box in the correct column.

Cabinet	chief justice	Congress	congressperson
House of Representatives	justices	president	Senate
Supreme Court	U.S. Capitol	vice president	White House

Executive Branch	Legislative Branch	Judicial Branch
Cabinet	_____	_____
_____	_____	_____
_____	_____	_____
_____	_____	
	_____	

2. Cross out the word that doesn't belong.

a. **Branches of government**   ~~Congress~~   Executive   Judicial   Legislative

b. **City government**   mayor   vice president   councilperson   city council

c. **People**   councilperson   city council   president   justice

d. **Buildings**   Cabinet   Supreme Court   U.S. Capitol   White House

e. **State officials**   assemblyperson   governor   president   state senator

3. Answer the quiz questions.

Quiz: U.S. Government   Name: _____

1. Who is the president of the United States?

_____

2. Who is the vice president?

_____

3. What is your state capital?

_____

4. Who is the governor of your state?

_____

5. How many state senators does your state have?

_____

6. Who is the mayor of your city?

_____

4. Look at page 141 in your dictionary. *True* or *False*?

a. The Pentagon has five sides. _____true_____

b. The man on reserve always wears a uniform. _____

c. All veterans are old. _____

d. Some veterans have injuries. _____

e. Recruits are new soldiers. _____

f. All recruits are men. _____

g. The general and admiral are standing. _____

5. Where do the branches of the military work? Check (✓) the answers.

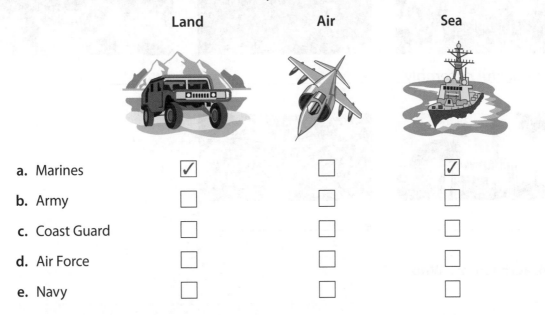

	Land	Air	Sea
a. Marines	✓	☐	✓
b. Army	☐	☐	☐
c. Coast Guard	☐	☐	☐
d. Air Force	☐	☐	☐
e. Navy	☐	☐	☐

6. Look in your dictionary. Complete the chart.

Branch	Person
Air Force	airman
	soldier
	national guardsman
Navy	
	coast guardsman
Marines	

CHALLENGE How long can the president of the U.S. serve? The chief justice of the Supreme Court? The governor of Texas? The Secretary of Defense? A U.S. Senator? Search the Internet for the answers.

Civic Engagement

1. **Look in your dictionary. Check (✓) the civic responsibilities.**

- ✓ pay taxes
- ☐ free speech
- ☐ serve on a jury
- ☐ obey the law
- ☐ vote
- ☐ peaceful assembly

2. **Label the pictures. Use the words in the box.**

> fair trial   free speech   freedom of the press   freedom of religion   ~~peaceful assembly~~

a. _peaceful assembly_   b. _____   c. _____

d. _____   e. _____

3. **Look at the forms. Who . . . ?**

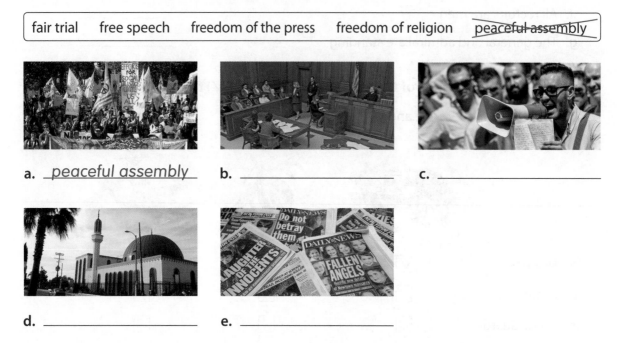

Name: Hassan Al Bahraini   **Date of Birth:** 8/13/07
Address: 25 Colony St.   **Lived there** 8 years
Houston, Texas 77036   **Gender: M** ☑   **F** ☐

Name: Yoko Tanaka   **Date of Birth:** 2/9/91
Address: 209 Gorham St.   **Lived there** 4 years
Los Angeles, CA 90049   **Gender: M** ☐   **F** ☑

Name: Ana Suarez   **Date of Birth:** 5/6/92
Address: 38 Opechee Dr.   **Lived there** 10 years
Miami, Florida 33133   **Gender: M** ☐   **F** ☑

Name: Chen Lu   **Date of Birth:** 11/11/99
Address: 47 Bleecker St.   **Lived there** 3 years
New York, N.Y. 10005   **Gender: M** ☑   **F** ☐

a. lived in the U.S. for five or more years   _Hassan_ and _Ana_

b. is 18 years or older   _____, _____, and _____

c. can take a U.S. citizenship test   _____

d. must register with the Selective Service   _____

[CHALLENGE] List the ways people can be informed. **Example:** *read the paper*

4. **Look at page 143 in your dictionary. Who . . . ? Check (✓) name or names.**

	Chen	Larson
a. is a candidate	✓	✓
b. runs for office	☐	☐
c. doesn't get elected	☐	☐
d. serves on the city council	☐	☐
e. debates the issues	☐	☐
f. has a rally	☐	☐

5. **Look at page 143 in your dictionary. Circle the words to complete the newspaper headlines.**

   a. Chen (Gets Elected) / Runs for Office with 100,000 Votes

   b. Chen is New Opponent / Elected Official on City Council

   c. Chen's Candidate / Opponent Receives Only 65,000 Votes

   d. Chen Runs Very Good Ballot / Campaign

   e. 100,000 People Vote for Chen at Polling Booths / Ballots

   f. Chen Will Debate / Serve for Four Years on City Council

6. **What about you? Did you ever . . . ? Check (✓) the answers.**

   If *yes*, when?

   ☐ watch a debate _____

   ☐ go to a rally _____

   ☐ watch or listen to election results _____

   ☐ go to a voting booth _____

CHALLENGE Search online for election results in a country or city you know. Who ran for office? Who got elected? How many votes did he or she get? How many votes did his or her opponent get?

The Legal System

1. Look in your dictionary. Circle the words to complete the sentences.

a. The guard /(police officer) arrested the suspect.

b. The suspect / witness wears handcuffs.

c. The defense attorney / prosecuting attorney is a man.

d. The court reporter / judge says, "Guilty."

e. There are ten / twelve people on the jury.

f. The judge is in the courtroom / prison.

g. The convict / bailiff is in prison.

2. Complete the sentences with the words in the box. Then number the events in order. (1 = the first event)

court	defendant	~~jail~~	lawyer	released	suspect	trial	verdict

____ a. The defendant goes to _____jail_____.

____ b. The defendant stands _____.

____ c. The judge sentences the _____.

____ d. The defendant appears in _____.

____ e. The convict is _____.

____ f. The judge reads the _____.

_1_ g. The police officer arrests a _____.

____ h. The suspect hires a _____.

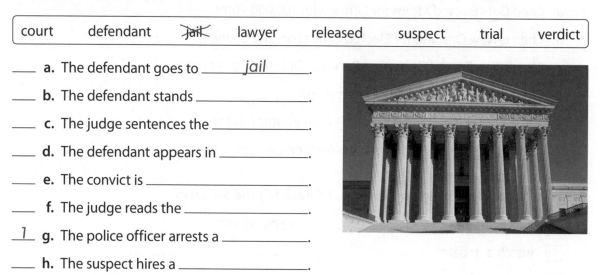

3. Label the pictures. Use the words in the box.

bail	evidence	handcuffs

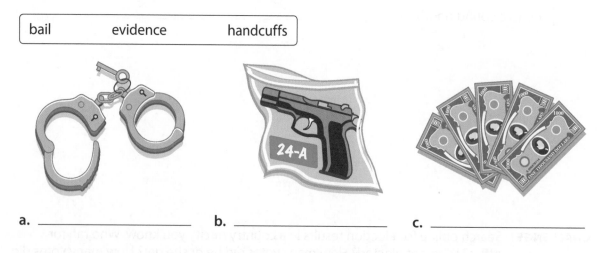

a. _____   b. _____   c. _____

CHALLENGE Look in your dictionary. Tell the story. Begin: *The police officer arrested the suspect . . . .*

1. Look in your dictionary. Read the TV movie descriptions. Circle the crime words.

8:00 P.M.	**TELEVISION GUIDE**
2	**UNDER THE INFLUENCE** ('15) (Drunk driving) destroys two families.
4	**THE BREAK-IN** ('12) A burglary changes life in a small, quiet town.
5	**CRIMES AGAINST PROPERTY** ('19) Teenage boys commit vandalism.
7	**THE VICTIM** ('10) A man fights back after a mugging.
9	**THE FIVE-FINGER DISCOUNT** ('17) A young woman can't stop shoplifting.
11	**IT'S MY LIFE!** ('19) Identity theft causes big problems.
13	**KEEP THE CHANGE** ('15) An assault changes a man's life.
28	**EAST SIDE SAGA** ('19) A story of gang violence.
41	**WITH HIS GUN** ('09) A doctor tries to hide her husband's murder.

2. Match the TV movies with the descriptions in Exercise 1. Write the channel numbers.

a. _____28_____

b. _____

c. _____

d. _____

e. _____

f. _____

g. _____

h. _____

i. _____

CHALLENGE Look at the movies in Exercise 1. Which do you want to see? Which don't you want to see? Why?

Public Safety

1. **Look in your dictionary. Put the public safety tips in the correct columns.**

At Home

Lock your doors.

_____

_____

_____

_____

On the Street

_____

_____

_____

_____

_____

At the Airport

_____

At the Bank

_____

2. **Give these people advice. Use the information from Exercise 1.**

a. _Be aware of your_
   surroundings.

b. _____

   _____

c. _____

   _____

d. _____

   _____

e. _____

   _____

f. _____

   _____

CHALLENGE   Make a list of things you do to be safe in public.

1. **Look in your dictionary. Match the online danger with the safety solution.**

   _a_ 1. cyberbullying

   ___ 2. phishing

   ___ 3. inappropriate material

   ___ 4. hacking an email account

   ___ 5. old security software

   a. monitor children's Internet use

   b. update software

   c. delete suspicious emails

   d. turn on parental controls

   e. create secure passwords

2. **Look in your dictionary. *True* or *False*?**

   1. The boy in picture 1 is cyberbullying.   _false_

   2. The girl in picture 2 is an online predator.   _____

   3. The boy in picture 3 is getting inappropriate material.   _____

   4. The man in picture 5 is blocking an inappropriate website. _____

   5. The email in picture 4 is an example of suspicious email. _____

   6. The website in picture F is secure.   _____

3. **Read about Ana. What should she do?**

   1. Her password is Ana1234.

      create a secure password

   2. She is going to pay for a sweater at http://www.sweaters.com.

      _____

   3. She got an email from her bank. It asked for her password and account number.

      _____

   4. Her little girl can look at websites with inappropriate content.

      _____

   5. Her security software is five years old.

      _____

4. **What about you? What do you do to be safe online? Discuss your answers with a partner.**

CHALLENGE   Research the rules for creating a safe password. Write an example of a good and a bad password. Discuss your examples with a partner. Do not use your real passwords!

Emergencies and Natural Disasters

1. **Look in your dictionary. Circle the emergency or disaster.**

a.
| It covered almost half the house! |

earthquake / mudslide

b.
| It's going to hit the farm! |

tornado / volcanic eruption

c.
| We need rain. |

drought / famine

d.
| Don't move. We're coming to get you! |

flood / forest fire

e.
| The light was red! You didn't stop. |

airplane crash / car accident

f.
| There's almost a foot of snow! |

blizzard / explosion

2. **Match.**

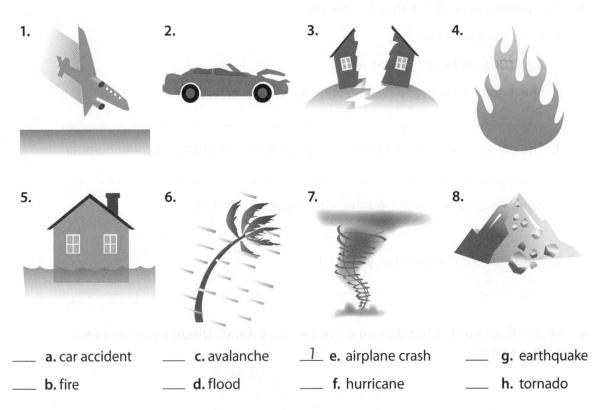

1. 2. 3. 4.

5. 6. 7. 8.

____ **a.** car accident   ____ **c.** avalanche   _1_ **e.** airplane crash   ____ **g.** earthquake

____ **b.** fire   ____ **d.** flood   ____ **f.** hurricane   ____ **h.** tornado

3. Match.

a. _____3_____   b. _____   c. _____

d. _____   e. _____   f. _____

1. **EXTRA**
   EXPLOSION ROCKS CITY CENTER

2. **Strongville Chronicle**
   SEARCH AND RESCUE TEAM SAVES FLOOD VICTIMS

3. **SUNDAY EDITION**
   TIDAL WAVE HITS JAPAN

4. **Boston Global**
   Lost Child Home Safe

5. **Town Spirit**
   Firefighters Fight Forest Fires

6. **EARTH MAGAZINE**
   VOLCANIC ERUPTION AT MT. ST. HELENS

4. What about you? Check (✓) the natural disasters your state has experienced. Complete the chart.

Disaster	Which city?	When?
earthquake		
blizzard		
hurricane		
tornado		
flood		
Other: _____		

CHALLENGE Find information about a natural disaster. Look online or in an almanac, encyclopedia, or newspaper. What kind of disaster was it? Where and when was it?

1. Look in your dictionary. Match.

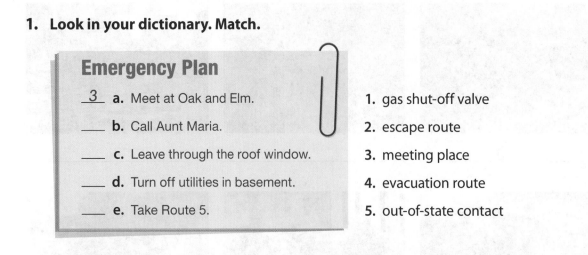

Emergency Plan

_3_ **a.** Meet at Oak and Elm.

___ **b.** Call Aunt Maria.

___ **c.** Leave through the roof window.

___ **d.** Turn off utilities in basement.

___ **e.** Take Route 5.

1. gas shut-off valve
2. escape route
3. meeting place
4. evacuation route
5. out-of-state contact

2. Carlos is starting a disaster kit. Check (✓) the items he has.

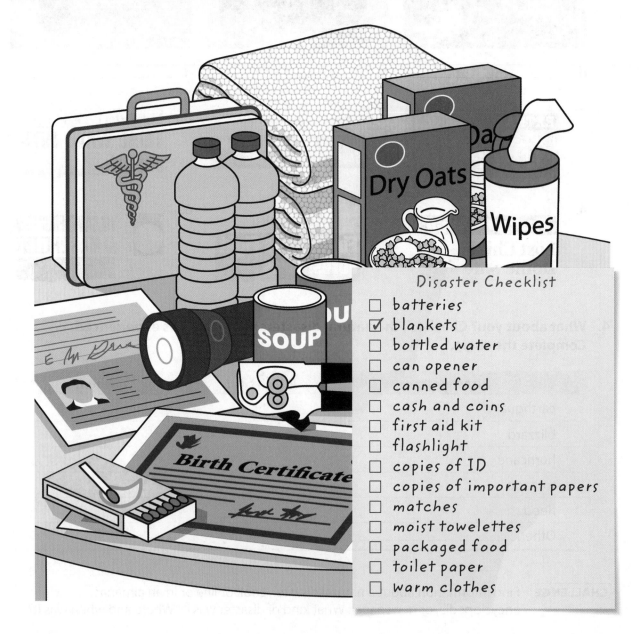

Disaster Checklist

- ☐ batteries
- ☑ blankets
- ☐ bottled water
- ☐ can opener
- ☐ canned food
- ☐ cash and coins
- ☐ first aid kit
- ☐ flashlight
- ☐ copies of ID
- ☐ copies of important papers
- ☐ matches
- ☐ moist towelettes
- ☐ packaged food
- ☐ toilet paper
- ☐ warm clothes

3. Look in your dictionary. Circle the answers.

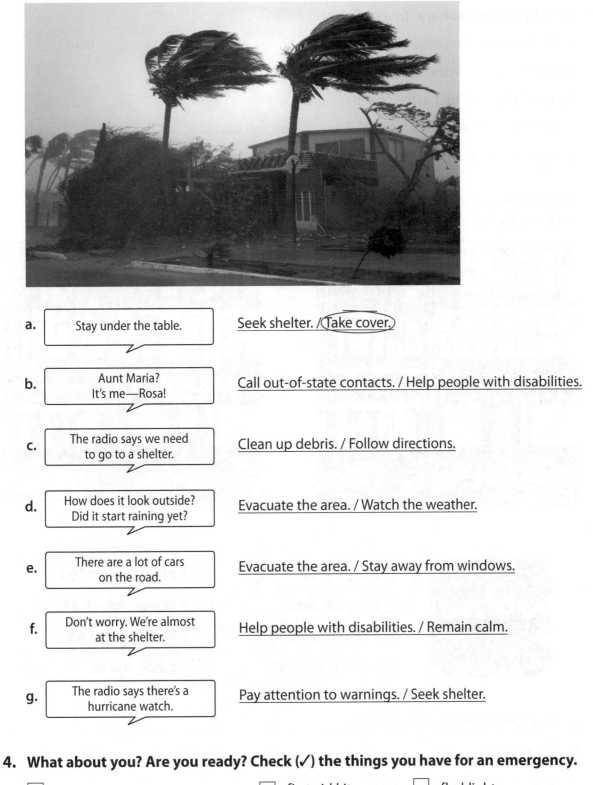

a. | Stay under the table. | Seek shelter. / (Take cover.)

b. | Aunt Maria? It's me—Rosa! | Call out-of-state contacts. / Help people with disabilities.

c. | The radio says we need to go to a shelter. | Clean up debris. / Follow directions.

d. | How does it look outside? Did it start raining yet? | Evacuate the area. / Watch the weather.

e. | There are a lot of cars on the road. | Evacuate the area. / Stay away from windows.

f. | Don't worry. We're almost at the shelter. | Help people with disabilities. / Remain calm.

g. | The radio says there's a hurricane watch. | Pay attention to warnings. / Seek shelter.

4. What about you? Are you ready? Check (✓) the things you have for an emergency.

☐ can opener ☐ first aid kit ☐ flashlight

☐ copies of important papers ☐ batteries ☐ Other: _____

CHALLENGE Make a list of other items for a disaster kit. **Example:** *medicine*

Go to page 254 for Another Look (Unit 7).

1. Look in your dictionary. *True* or *False*?

a. Marta's street has problems. _____*true*_____

b. There's graffiti on the stores. _____

c. There's litter in front of the pharmacy. _____

d. The hardware store is between the donut shop and the florist. _____

e. The man in the hardware store is upset. _____

2. Look at the pictures. Check (✓) the changes. Then write sentences about each item on the list.

OAK STREET ASSOCIATION	✓ repair street sign	☐ clean up graffiti
	☐ repair curb	☐ repair streetlight
	☐ repair sidewalk	☐ repair windows
	☐ clean up litter	☐ paint stores

a. *They repaired the street sign.*   e. _____

b. *They didn't* _____   f. _____

c. _____   g. _____

d. _____   h. _____

3. Look in your dictionary. Who . . . ? Check (✓) the columns.

	Marta Lopez	City Council	Volunteers	Citizens of City Center	Hardware store manager
a. is upset	✓				✓
b. gives a speech					
c. signs the petition					
d. applauds Marta					
e. votes *yes*					
f. cleans up the street					
g. donates donuts					
h. donates paint					
i. changes Main Street					

4. Complete the letter to the City Center city council. Use the words in the box.

street	change	~~hardware store~~	graffiti	litter	volunteers

5/6/18

Dear Councilperson:

I live in City Center, and I am the owner of Hammers & More ____hardware store____.
 a.
I am very upset about the problems on my _____. There is _____
 b. **c.**
on the buildings and _____ in the street. The streetlight in front of my store
 d.
is broken, too. We have many _____ ready to help clean up the street, but
 e.
we need your help. Please repair the streetlights. Together we can _____
 f.
Main Street.

Sincerely yours,

Tom Lee

Tom Lee

5. What about you? Imagine you live in City Center. How can you volunteer to help Main Street?

CHALLENGE Imagine you own the florist on Main Street. Write a letter to the City Center city council about the problems on your street.

Basic Transportation

1. **Look in your dictionary. How many . . . do you see?**

a. cars   _2_

b. bicycles   ___

c. trucks   ___

d. airplanes   ___

e. helicopters   ___

f. motorcycles   ___

g. people at the bus stop   ___

h. passengers leaving the subway station   ___

2. **Look at the graph. Complete the sentences.**

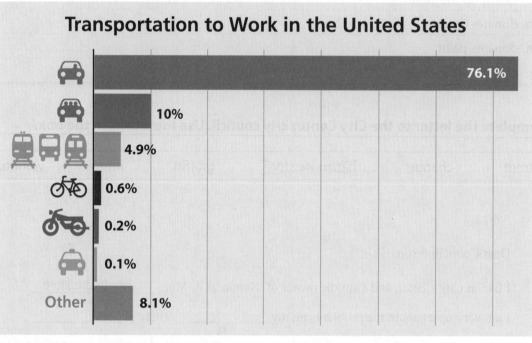

Transportation to Work in the United States

- 76.1%
- 10%
- 4.9%
- 0.6%
- 0.2%
- 0.1%
- Other 8.1%

Based on information from: *2009 American Community Survey,* U.S. Census Bureau.

a. More than 75% of Americans get to work alone in a _____ car _____.

b. Exactly 10% go to work in a _____ with other people.

c. Only 0.1% take a _____.

d. Only 0.2% ride a _____ to work.

e. Only 0.6% ride a _____ to work.

f. Almost 5% take a _____, _____, or _____ to work.

3. **What about you? How do you get to . . . ?**

a. school   _____

b. work   _____

c. the supermarket   _____

d. Other: _____   _____

4. Look in your dictionary. *True* or *False*?

a. A passenger is getting into a taxi.　　　　___true___

b. There is a bus at the bus stop.　　　　_____

c. Two people are entering the subway station.　_____

d. There's a train near the airport.　　　　_____

e. There's a helicopter over the bus.　　　　_____

f. There are bicycles on the street.　　　　_____

g. The motorcycle is with the bicycles.　　　_____

h. The bus stop is in front of Mario's Italian Deli.　_____

5. Look at the pictures. Match.

____ **a.** car　　___1___ **b.** plane　　____ **c.** taxi　　____ **d.** train　　____ **e.** subway

6. What about you? How often do you take or ride a . . . ? Check (✓) the columns.

	Often	Sometimes	Never
car			
taxi			
motorcycle			
truck			
train			
plane			
subway			
bus			
bicycle			

CHALLENGE　Take a survey. How do your classmates come to school? **Example:** *Five students take the bus, two students . . . .*

Public Transportation

1. Look in your dictionary. Circle the words to complete the sentences.

a. There are three conductors /(riders)on the bus.

b. The girl on the bus has the <u>fare / transfer</u> in her hand.

c. The man at the subway vending machine is buying a <u>fare card / token</u>.

d. The woman <u>at the subway turnstile / in the subway car</u> is paying the fare.

e. The ticket to St. Louis is for a <u>one-way trip / round trip</u>.

f. The woman on the <u>platform / track</u> in the train station has a ticket.

g. The airport <u>shuttle / town car</u> is bright blue.

h. The taxi license has a photo of the <u>taxi driver / meter</u>.

2. Cross out the word that doesn't belong.

a. Types of transportation	bus	shuttle	subway	~~track~~
b. People	rider	driver	transfer	conductor
c. Forms of payment	fare	track	token	fare card
d. Places to wait for transportation	subway car	platform	bus stop	taxi stand
e. Things with words	schedule	turnstile	transfer	fare card
f. Things with numbers	taxi license	ticket	meter	rider

3. Look at the ticket. *True* or *False*?

a. This is a train ticket. _____*true*_____

b. It shows the fare. _____

c. It's for a one-way trip. _____

d. It shows the track number. _____

YORK RAIL			
CLASS	**TICKET TYPE**	**ADULT**	**CHILD**
COACH	ROUND TRIP	ONE	NONE
START DATE	**NAME OF PASSENGER**		**PRICE**
02 NOV 17	FOX/STEVE MR.		$16.88
FROM	**VALID UNTIL**		**BAGGAGE**
19TH AVE	10 NOV17		
TO	**DATE OF PURCHASE**		
SHEPPARD/YOUNG	10 AUG17		

ROUND TRIP/SPECIAL FARE
PASSENGER RECEIPT 13303 1226058975

4. What about you? Check (✓) the items you have or use.

☐ bus transfer   ☐ train ticket   ☐ taxi license

☐ token   ☐ train schedule   ☐ Other: _____

☐ fare card   ☐ bus schedule

CHALLENGE What public transportation can you take to the nearest airport? How much does it cost?

156

1. **Look in your dictionary.** *True* or *False*?

   a. A man is going under the bridge.   *false*

   b. There are two people walking down the steps.   _____

   c. A woman is getting into a taxi.   _____

   d. A man is getting out of a taxi.   _____

   e. A red car is getting on the highway.   _____

   f. A yellow car is getting off the highway.   _____

   g. A taxi is driving through the tunnel.   _____

2. **Look at the map. Circle the words to complete the directions.**

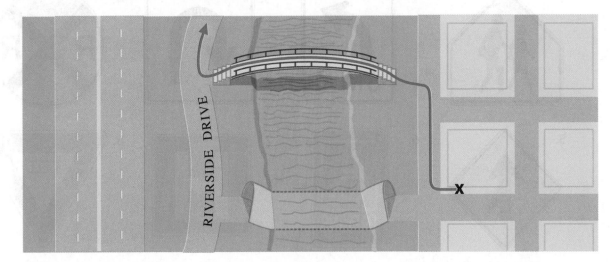

   Man: Excuse me. How do I get to Riverside Drive?

   Woman: Riverside Drive? Go around the (corner) / tunnel. Then go <u>down</u> / up the steps and
                                            a.   **b.**

             <u>over</u> / under the <u>bridge</u> / highway. Go <u>down</u> / up the steps and you'll be right on
                  c.   **d.**   **e.**
             Riverside Drive.

   Man: Oh, so I have to go <u>across</u> / around the bridge?
                                            f.

   Woman: That's right.

3. **Read the conversation in Exercise 2 again. Circle the answer.**

   The man is <u>driving / on a bus / walking</u>.

CHALLENGE   Write directions from your home to school.

Traffic Signs

1. **Look at the intersection on <u>pages 130 and 131</u> in your dictionary. *True* or *False*?**

a. There's a stop sign at the intersection. _____*false*_____

b. There's a no parking sign near the fire hydrant. _____

c. There's a pedestrian crossing sign at Main and Green Streets. _____

d. The bus is on a one-way street. _____

e. There's handicapped parking in front of Al's Mini Mart. _____

f. There are no speed limit signs. _____

2. **Look at the traffic signs. Match.**

_____ **a.** yield

_____ **b.** road work

_____ **c.** U-turn OK

_____ **d.** hospital

_____ **e.** do not enter

_____ **f.** pedestrian crossing

_____ **g.** railroad crossing

_____ **h.** no left turn

_*1*_ **i.** school crossing

_____ **j.** right turn only

_____ **k.** merge

_____ **l.** handicapped parking

CHALLENGE Draw three more traffic signs. Work with a partner. What do they mean?

1. **Look at pages 130 and 131 in your dictionary. Circle the words to complete the sentences.**

   a. The bicycle is going east / (west) on Green Street.

   b. It just went past Mel's / Print Quick.

   c. The orange car is going north / south.

   d. To get to the bus stop, the bus must turn right / left at the intersection.

   e. Dan's Drugstore is on the northwest / northeast corner.

2. **Look at the map. Use your pen or pencil to follow the directions to a shoe store. Put an X on the shoe store.**

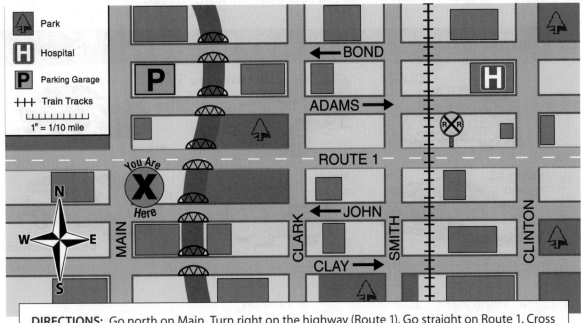

   DIRECTIONS: Go north on Main. Turn right on the highway (Route 1). Go straight on Route 1. Cross the tracks and continue to Clinton. Turn left. The store is on the left side of Clinton, but you can't make a U-turn there. So, continue north on Clinton. Go past the hospital. Turn left on Bond, left on Smith, and left again on Adams. Then turn right on Clinton. The shoe store is in the middle of the block, on the west side.

3. **Look at the map in Exercise 2.** *True* or *False*?

   a. This is an Internet map.   _____false_____

   b. The map has a key.   _____

   c. There is a symbol for schools.   _____

   d. One inch equals 1/10 of a mile.   _____

[CHALLENGE] Give directions to a place near your school. Draw a map.

Cars and Trucks

1. Look in your dictionary. Circle the words to complete the sentences.

a. The <u>convertible</u> / (sports car) is black.

b. The <u>tank truck / cargo van</u> is light brown.

c. The <u>dump truck / tow truck</u> is white.

d. The <u>moving van / tractor trailer</u> has a red cab.

e. The <u>camper / school bus</u> is yellow.

f. The <u>limo / cargo van</u> is white.

g. The <u>hybrid / RV</u> uses gas and electricity.

2. Look at the chart. Match the car models with the kinds of car.

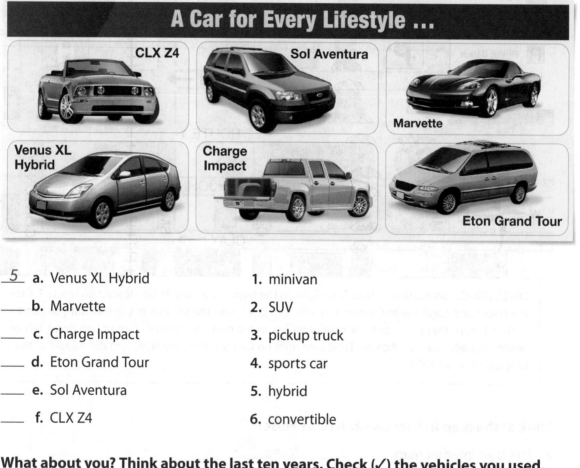

A Car for Every Lifestyle ...

CLX Z4   Sol Aventura   Marvette

Venus XL Hybrid   Charge Impact   Eton Grand Tour

<u>5</u>   a. Venus XL Hybrid   1. minivan

_____ b. Marvette   2. SUV

_____ c. Charge Impact   3. pickup truck

_____ d. Eton Grand Tour   4. sports car

_____ e. Sol Aventura   5. hybrid

_____ f. CLX Z4   6. convertible

3. What about you? Think about the last ten years. Check (✓) the vehicles you used.

☐ cargo van   ☐ tow truck   ☐ moving van

☐ dump truck   ☐ school bus   ☐ tractor trailer

CHALLENGE Look at Exercise 2. Which car do you like? Why?
Example: *I like the minivan because I have a big family.*

1. Look in your dictionary. *True* or *False*?

a. Juan is looking at car ads on the Internet and in the newspaper. _____*true*_____

b. He buys the car. Then he takes the car to a mechanic. _____

c. He asks the mechanic, "How many miles does it have?" _____

d. He negotiates a price with the seller. _____

e. He registers the car. Then he gets the title. _____

f. He gets the title in the registration office. _____

2. Match.

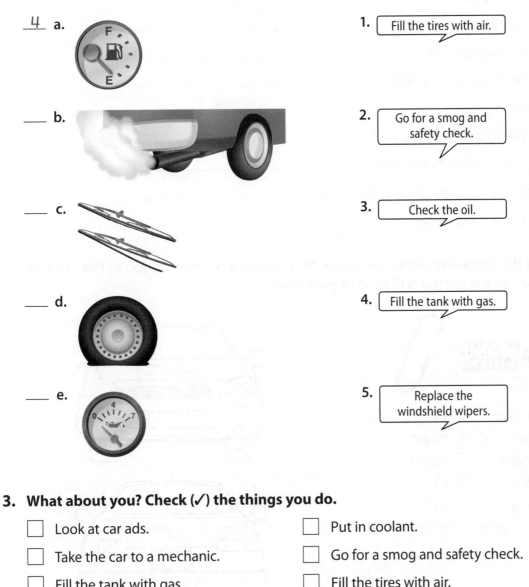

__4__ a.

__ b.

__ c.

__ d.

__ e.

1. Fill the tires with air.

2. Go for a smog and safety check.

3. Check the oil.

4. Fill the tank with gas.

5. Replace the windshield wipers.

3. What about you? Check (✓) the things you do.

☐ Look at car ads.

☐ Take the car to a mechanic.

☐ Fill the tank with gas.

☐ Put in coolant.

☐ Go for a smog and safety check.

☐ Fill the tires with air.

[CHALLENGE] What are other ways to buy a used car? **Example:** *from a friend*

Parts of a Car

1. **Look in your dictionary. What does the person need to use or check?**

   Page 162

   a. Turn left!   *turn signal*

   b. It's raining. _____

   c. The battery is dead. _____

   d. It's getting dark outside. _____

   Page 163

   e. It's hot in here. _____

   f. Do we need gas? _____

   g. That car doesn't see us! _____

   h. You're going too slow. _____

   i. Stop at the next traffic light. _____

   j. It's cold in here. _____

   k. Let's listen to some music, OK? _____

   l. I forgot to charge my cell phone. _____

   m. What's the weather report for tomorrow? _____

   n. How fast are you going? _____

2. **Look at the diagrams of the rental car. An X shows a problem. Look at the list and check (✓) all the car parts that have problems.**

- ✓ brake light
- ☐ bumper
- ☐ headlight
- ☐ hood
- ☐ hubcap
- ☐ license plate
- ☐ sideview mirror
- ☐ tail light
- ☐ tail pipe
- ☐ tire
- ☐ trunk
- ☐ windshield

3. **Put the words in the correct column. Use your dictionary for help.**

| accelerator | brake pedal | clutch | gear shift | horn |
| ignition | seat belt | steering wheel | stick shift | |

Things you use with your hands

_____

_____

_____

_____

_____

_____

Things you use with your feet

_____ *accelerator* _____

_____

_____

4. **Cross out the word that doesn't belong.**

a. **For problems**   lug wrench   jack   spare tire   ~~gas tank~~

b. **For safety**   airbag   hazard lights   front seat   seat belt

c. **To measure things**   oil gauge   speedometer   engine   temperature gauge

d. **To see other cars**   rearview mirror   windshield   muffler   sideview mirror

5. **Circle the words to complete the sentences.**

a. You can keep maps in the (glove compartment) / power outlet.

b. The key is in the ignition / muffler.

c. You should always wear a clutch / seat belt in the car.

d. It's important to have a spare tire / steering wheel in the trunk.

e. The radiator is inside the trunk / under the hood.

f. Small children should sit in the front seat / backseat.

6. **What about you? Check (✓) the items that are important to you in a car.**

☐ air conditioning

☐ child safety seat

☐ touch screen

☐ stick shift

☐ Other: _____

CHALLENGE   Explain your answers in Exercise 6. **Example:** *I think air conditioning is important because it's more comfortable.*

1. Look in your dictionary. Who . . . ?

a. works at the check-in kiosk   *ticket agent*

b. goes through security   _____

c. examines your luggage in the screening area   _____

d. helps passengers carry their baggage   _____

e. is in the cockpit   _____

f. helps passengers on the airplane   _____

g. looks at your declaration form   _____

2. Circle the words to complete the conversations. Then write where the people are. Use the words in the box.

~~airplane~~	airplane	baggage carousel	boarding area	cockpit	customs

Passenger 1: Where's your carry-on bag?

Passenger 2: Up there, (in the overhead compartment)/ on the tray table.   *airplane*
                              a.

Passenger 3: Is our flight still on time?

Passenger 4: Let's check the arrival and departure monitors / turbulence.   _____
                                    b.

Customs Officer: Do you have anything to declare?

Passenger 1: Yes. Here's my declaration form / e-ticket.   _____
                                c.

Flight Attendant: You have a mobile boarding pass / life vest under
                                    d.
                     your seat in case of emergency. Please look for the

                     nearest emergency exit / reclined seat now.   _____
                                        e.

Passenger 5: I don't see my e-ticket / luggage.
                            f.

Passenger 6: Don't worry. More bags are still coming out.   _____

Pilot: I hope you enjoyed your flight. We will land / take off in about ten minutes,
                                                     g.
         and we will be at the check-in kiosk / gate in about twenty minutes.   _____
                                        h.

3. Look at page 164 in your dictionary. Match.

_3_ **a.** I just have this one bag.

___ **b.** Is this 14F?

___ **c.** Can I walk through now?

___ **d.** Now I just press PRINT.

___ **e.** OK. I'm pressing ON for airplane mode.

___ **f.** Here's my driver's license.

___ **g.** Here it is! The large red one.

___ **h.** I think I ate too much! It's a little too tight.

___ **i.** Oh, good. It fits in the overhead compartment.

1. Stow your carry-on bag.

2. Claim your baggage.

3. Check your bags.

4. Find your seat.

5. Check in electronically.

6. Go through security.

7. Show your ID.

8. Put your cell phone in airplane mode.

9. Fasten your seatbelt.

4. Look at the picture. Check (✓) the things the passenger did.

- ✓ got her boarding pass
- ☐ stowed her carry-on bag
- ☐ fastened her seat belt
- ☐ found her seat
- ☐ read the emergency card
- ☐ boarded the plane
- ☐ landed
- ☐ took off
- ☐ checked in

CHALLENGE List the things you can do to make a plane trip more comfortable.
Example: *wear comfortable clothing*

Go to page 255 for Another Look (Unit 8).

A Road Trip

1. Look in your dictionary. *True* or *False*?

a. Joe packs his bags near the car.   _____true_____

b. The ranger talks about stars.   _____

c. Joe and Rob are lost in Yellowstone National Park.   _____

d. They see beautiful scenery and wildlife.   _____

e. They get a ticket in New York.   _____

f. They arrive at their destination by car.   _____

2. Look at the pictures. Match.

1.

2.

3.

4.

5.

6.

7.

8.

_____ **a.** They get a ticket.

_____ **b.** The car breaks down.

_1_ **c.** They pack their car.

_____ **d.** They arrive at their destination.

_____ **e.** They see beautiful scenery.

_____ **f.** They run out of gas.

_____ **g.** They have a flat tire.

_____ **h.** They are lost.

166

3. **Look in your dictionary. Circle the words to complete the sentences about Joe and Rob.**

   a. Their destination is Texas /(New York).

   b. They put their bags in the trunk / on the back seat of the car.

   c. One night they sleep in the car / under the stars.

   d. Joe gives the police officer / tow truck driver his automobile club card.

   e. There is a flat / spare tire in the trunk.

4. **Look at the pictures in Exercise 2. Complete the online post with the words in the box.**

automobile club card	broke down	destination	got
had	packed	ran out	~~were~~

   ## A Road Trip

   The trip was TERRIBLE. We had a lot of problems. After only two hours on the

   road, our GPS broke. We _____were_____ lost! Then we _____
   a.   b.

   a ticket — $120.00. Next, we _____ a flat tire. Then we
                                          c.

   _____ of gas. Finally, the car _____ ! It was a good
   d.   e.

   thing I had my _____ with me. We called a tow truck and the driver
                        f.

   towed us to the nearest city. Two days later, we _____ our bags and
                                                                              g.

   continued to our _____ —by taxi and two days late! I'm REALLY
                            h.

   happy to be home now.

5. **What about you? Did you ever . . . ? Check (✓) the answers.**

   If *yes*, where?

   ☐ have a flat tire   _____

   ☐ run out of gas   _____

   ☐ get a speeding ticket   _____

   ☐ see beautiful scenery   _____

   ☐ use an automobile club card _____

CHALLENGE Work with a partner. Plan a trip. What's your starting point? How will you travel?
           What will you pack? What's your destination? Compare your answers.

1. Look in your dictionary. Complete Dan King's job application.

EMPLOYMENT APPLICATION

S & K GROCERY, INC.

Name: Dan King

Job applying for: _____

1. How did you hear about this job? (Please check (✓) all appropriate boxes.)

☐ friends ☐ employment website ☐ help wanted sign

2. Hours: ☐ part-time ✓ full-time

3. Have you had any experience? ☐ Yes ☐ No

If yes, how long? _____

4. References: Jack Martin, manager

FOR OFFICE USE ONLY

Resume received: 9/17 **Interviewed by:** Ron Hill 9/21

Hired? ☐ Yes ☐ No **Starting date:** 9/26

---

2. Match.

__5__ **a.** Excuse me, sir. Where are the supplies? | 1. Be hired.

____ **b.** I'm going to find a summer job. | 2. Set up an interview.

____ **c.** Is it OK for me to give them your phone number? | 3. Set a goal.

____ **d.** Tom, I'm looking for a job. Is S & K hiring? | 4. Go on an interview.

____ **e.** Please come at 9:00. Bring your resume. | 5. Start a new job.

____ **f.** I have a lot of experience. | 6. Contact references.

____ **g.** Congratulations! You can start next Monday. | 7. Talk to friends.

3. **Look in your dictionary and at Exercise 1.** *True* or *False*?

a. Dan set two goals. _____false_____

b. He researched the number one grocery company. _____

c. He completed an application. _____

d. He wrote a resume by hand. _____

e. He had four years' experience as a grocery clerk. _____

f. He wrote a cover letter. _____

g. He read magazines and websites. _____

h. He submitted his application after the interview. _____

i. He got a job at ABC Employment. _____

4. **Which comes first? Number the steps in the correct order (1 and 2).**

a. start a new job _2_   be hired _1_

b. set up an interview ___   apply for a job ___

c. complete an application ___   submit an application ___

d. research companies ___   apply for a job ___

e. go on an interview ___   set up an interview ___

f. set a goal ___   network ___

g. write a cover letter ___   write a resume ___

h. get a job ___   contact references ___

5. **What about you? What do you think are the best ways to find a job? Number them in order. (1 = the best)**

____ research local companies

____ look for help wanted signs

____ network

____ check employment websites

____ go to an employment agency

____ Other: _____

[CHALLENGE] Survey four classmates. How did they find their jobs?

1. **Look in your dictionary. Who is . . . ?**

   a. putting together computer parts   _assembler_

   b. making bread   _____

   c. repairing a refrigerator   _____

   d. working in a theater   _____

   e. planning a building   _____

   f. reading stories to children   _____

   g. taking notes at a meeting   _____

   h. using a computer on a plane   _____

   i. standing in front of a store   _____

   j. working at a table with children   _____

2. **Match.**

   _4_ a. baker

   ____ b. accountant

   ____ c. mechanic

   ____ d. butcher

   ____ e. carpenter

   ____ f. artist

   ____ g. cashier

   1.

   2.

   3.

   4.

   5.

   6.

   7.

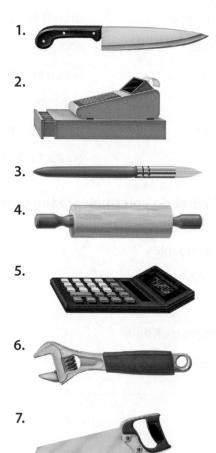

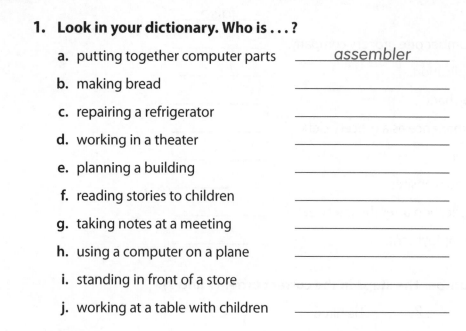

CHALLENGE   Look in your dictionary. Choose one job. Would you like that job?
Why or why not? Write three sentences.

1. **Look in your dictionary. Where do they work? Check (✓) the columns.**

	Inside	Outside
a. gardener		✓
b. electronics repairperson		
c. customer service representative		
d. dockworker		
e. delivery person		
f. home healthcare aide		
g. graphic designer		
h. dental assistant		
i. hairdresser		

2. **Look at the bar graph. Who works more hours? Circle the job.**

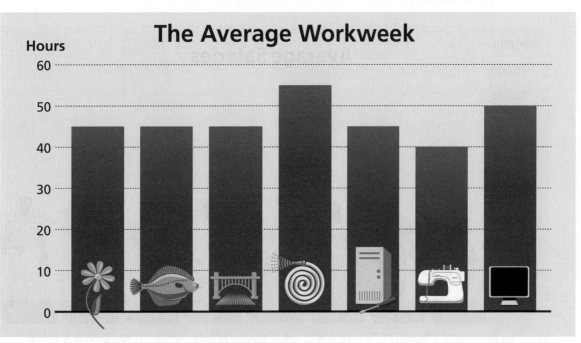

Based on information from: Krantz, L. *Jobs Rated Almanac*. (NJ: Barricade Books, 2002)

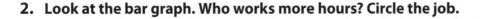

a. a computer technician or a (computer software engineer)

b. a commercial fisher or a firefighter

c. an engineer or a computer software engineer

d. a garment worker or a commercial fisher

e. a florist or a garment worker

CHALLENGE   Go to page 260 in this book. Follow the instructions.

1. Look in your dictionary. *True* or *False*? **Write a question mark (?) if you don't know.**

a. The interpreter can speak Spanish. _____?_____

b. The manicurist is painting the woman's toenails. _____

c. The occupational therapist is helping a woman use a microwave. _____

d. The homemaker is in the kitchen. _____

e. The lawyer is in court. _____

f. The movers are carrying a table. _____

g. The physician assistant is talking to a patient. _____

h. The messenger rides a bicycle. _____

i. The medical records technician works in a hospital. _____

2. Look at the bar graph. Number the jobs in order of how much money people make. (1 = the most money)

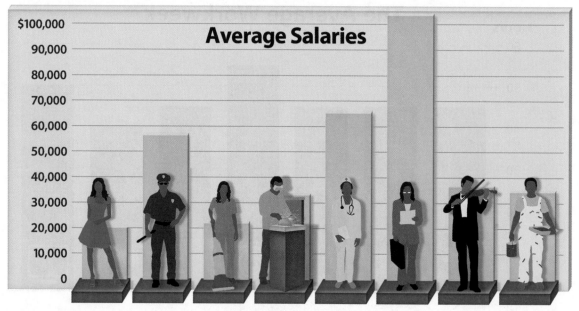

Based on information from: *U.S. Department of Labor, Bureau of Labor Statistics Occupational Outlook Handbook, 2012*

_____ a. house painter

_____ b. police officer

_____ c. musician

_____ d. model

__1__ e. lawyer

_____ f. housekeeper

_____ g. nurse

_____ h. machine operator

CHALLENGE What are the differences between a homemaker and a housekeeper? Write three sentences.

1. **Look in your dictionary. Circle the words to complete the sentences.**

   a. The (receptionist) / server sits at a desk all day.

   b. The <u>sanitation worker / security guard</u> works outside.

   c. The <u>stock clerk / writer</u> uses a computer.

   d. The <u>postal worker / printer</u> wears a uniform.

   e. The <u>truck driver / veterinarian</u> travels from place to place.

2. **Look at the job preference chart. Choose a job for each person.**

Likes to . . .	Ari	Luisa	Tom	Chris	Mia	Dave
work with people				✓		
speak on the phone	✓					
be inside	✓	✓	✓	✓		✓
be outside		✓	✓		✓	
sell things	✓					✓
be on TV			✓			
travel			✓		✓	
repair things		✓				
help people				✓		
wear a uniform					✓	
do physical work					✓	

   a. telemarketer _____*Ari*_____   d. welder _____

   b. social worker _____   e. retail clerk _____

   c. soldier _____   f. reporter _____

3. **What about you? Look at <u>pages 170–173</u> in your dictionary. Write two jobs on each line.**

   Jobs I can do now: _____

   Jobs I can't do now: _____

   Jobs I would like to do: _____

   Jobs I wouldn't like to do: _____

CHALLENGE Look at your answers in Exercise 3. Explain your choices.

1. **Look at page 174 in your dictionary. Check the things that Alma does.**

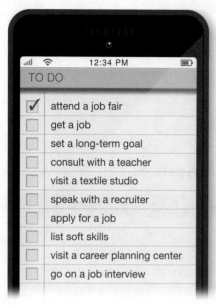

2. **What are the people doing? Circle the answers.**

a. [Cooking and reading.]

She is <u>exploring career options</u> / <u>(taking an interest inventory)</u>

b. [I want to become a nurse and work in a hospital.]

He is setting a <u>short-term</u> / <u>long-term</u> goal.

c. [ABC corporation is a great place to work. The salary is good, too.]

She is <u>consulting with a career counselor</u> / <u>speaking with a recruiter</u>.

d. [I am a very patient and honest person.]

He is <u>listing his soft skills</u> / <u>identifying his technical skills</u>.

e. [With my skills, can I get a job in the fashion industry?]

She is <u>consulting with a career counselor</u> / <u>attending a job fair</u>.

3. **What about you?**

List two of your soft skills: _____   _____

Identify one of your technical skills: _____

Set a short-term goal: I want to _____

4. Look at page 175 in your dictionary. Complete the sentences.

a. You can get a(n) _____basic education_____ at Valley High.

b. *Medical Transcription* is the name of a(n) _____.

c. *The Future of Textiles* is the name of a(n) _____.

d. *Nursing Assistant Class 306* gives you _____.

e. You can get a(n) _____ at Valley Community College.

f. You can learn about electricity if you have a(n) _____.

g. *What's New in Textiles?* is a(n) _____ class.

5. Look at page 175 in your dictionary. Circle the words to complete these two online posts.

I got <u>an entry-level job</u> /(<u>a new job</u>) I'm now a sewing machinist. This is the fourth
    a.
step on my career path to becoming a fashion designer. At first, I had <u>an</u>

<u>entry-level job</u> / <u>on-the-job training</u>. I took clothes from place to place. Then I took
    b.
a <u>basic education</u> / <u>continuing education</u> class in textiles. Very interesting! Soon, I hope
    c.
to get a <u>workshop</u> / <u>promotion</u>. Then I'll be an assistant fashion designer!
    d.

I got <u>a new job</u> / <u>on-the-job training</u>, too! I'm now a nursing assistant at the hospital.
    e.
Next, I plan to get a <u>promotion</u> / <u>college degree</u> at the community college.
    f.
<u>Career advancement</u> / <u>An apprenticeship</u> is very important to me. I really want to
    g.
become a nurse. That is my <u>short-term</u> / <u>long-term</u> goal.
    h.

6. What about you? What is the best way to learn these jobs? Check (✓) the type of training.

	On-the-job	Vocational training	Online course	Apprenticeship	Continuing education	College
Car mechanic	☐	☐	☐	☐	☐	☐
Florist	☐	☐	☐	☐	☐	☐
Cashier	☐	☐	☐	☐	☐	☐
Hair stylist	☐	☐	☐	☐	☐	☐
Computer technician	☐	☐	☐	☐	☐	☐
Engineer	☐	☐	☐	☐	☐	☐

[CHALLENGE] Interview a classmate, friend, or relative about his or her job. Write about that person's career path. **Example:** *Lisa is an accountant. First, she studied math in college. Then she …*

1. **Look in your dictionary. Circle the job skills in the job ads below. Then, write the name of the job. Use the words in the box.**

| Administrative Assistant | Assembler | Carpenter | Chef | Childcare Worker |
| Home Healthcare Aide | Manager | ~~Salesperson~~ | Server | Garment Worker |

Job Title and Description	Company
a. _Salesperson_ needed part-time to (sell cars) at our new Route 29 location. Must have experience and be able to work weekends.	Herb Rupert
b. _____ wanted to take care of small children. Part-time. Must speak English and Spanish. Experience and references required.	ChildCare
c. _____ wanted to assist medical patients. Good income. Experience required.	Medical Homecare
d. _____ needed to assemble telephone components in midtown factory. Immediate full-time employment.	Top Telecom
e. _____ wanted to make tables and chairs in our small shop.	Woodwork Corner
f. _____ wanted to supervise staff full-time at our small, friendly architecture company.	Nicolas Pyle, Inc.
g. _____ needed for busy law office. Must type 50 words per minute.	DeLucca, Smith, & Rotelli
h. _____ wanted to sew clothes in our downtown factory. Experience necessary.	L & H Clothing, Inc.
i. _____ wanted to cook everything from hamburgers to duck à l'orange at our small neighborhood restaurant.	The Corner Bistro
j. _____ needed to wait on customers at a busy downtown coffee shop. Part-time only. Experience preferred.	Kim's

2. **What about you? Check (✓) the job skills you have. Circle the skills you want to learn.**

- ☐ assemble components
- ☐ cook
- ☐ do manual labor
- ☐ drive a truck
- ☐ fly a plane
- ☐ make furniture
- ☐ operate heavy machinery
- ☐ program computers
- ☐ repair appliances
- ☐ sew clothes
- ☐ solve math problems
- ☐ speak another language
- ☐ supervise people
- ☐ teach
- ☐ use a cash register
- ☐ take care of children
- ☐ Other: _____
- ☐ Other: _____

CHALLENGE Choose two job ads from Exercise 1. Can you do the jobs? Why or why not?

1. **Look in your dictionary. For which skills do the employees need . . . ?**
   Put the words in the correct columns.

   A Computer

   type a letter

   _____

   _____

   _____

   _____

   _____

   _____

   Paper

   type a letter

   _____

   _____

   _____

   _____

   _____

   _____

   _____

   _____

2. **Match.**

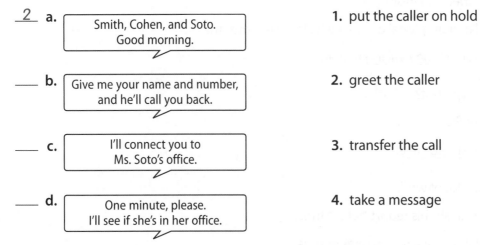

   __2__ **a.** | Smith, Cohen, and Soto. Good morning.

   _____ **b.** | Give me your name and number, and he'll call you back.

   _____ **c.** | I'll connect you to Ms. Soto's office.

   _____ **d.** | One minute, please. I'll see if she's in her office.

   1. put the caller on hold

   2. greet the caller

   3. transfer the call

   4. take a message

3. **What about you? Check (✓) the office skills you have.**

   ☐ type a letter

   ☐ enter data

   ☐ transcribe notes

   ☐ take notes

   ☐ organize materials

   ☐ make copies

   ☐ collate papers

   ☐ staple

   ☐ scan a document

   ☐ fax a document

   ☐ print a document

   ☐ take a message

CHALLENGE Work with a partner. Role-play a phone call. Student A is a caller. Student B is a receptionist. Leave a message and take a message.

1. Look in your dictionary. Match the sentences with the skills.

___4___ **a.** Sorry. I'll fix that now.

_____ **b.** But *why* is Plan B better for us?

_____ **c.** The solution is online training!

_____ **d.** Let's choose Plan B.

_____ **e.** We're starting on line 15. Right?

1. solve problems

2. clarify instructions

3. make decisions

4. respond well to feedback

5. think critically

2. Read the conversations. Circle the words to complete the sentences.

Ana: I'm sorry, but Mr. Rodriguez is on the phone.

Ben: That's OK. I can wait.

a. Ben is honest / patient.

Leo: Can you speak Spanish?

Eva: No, but I'm going to take a Spanish class next month.

b. Eva is managing time / willing to learn.

Bao: Can you type fast?

Feng: No, not really.

c. Feng is honest / positive.

Jan: We have a lot of work!

Tom: Yes. Let's finish this report before lunch.

d. Tom is thinking critically / managing time.

3. What about you? How often are these statements true for you? Check (✓) the columns.

	Always	Often	Sometimes	Never
a. I am patient.				
b. I manage my time well.				
c. I am a positive person.				
d. I communicate clearly.				
e. I cooperate with other people.				

CHALLENGE   Think about a job. Which soft skills are important for that job? Why?

1. Look in your dictionary. When did Mr. Ortiz . . . ? Check (✓) the columns.

	Before the Interview	During the Interview	After the Interview
a. ask questions		✓	
b. dress appropriately			
c. prepare			
d. talk about his experience			
e. shake hands			
f. greet the interviewer			
g. write a thank-you note			

2. Look at the picture. Check (✓) Amy's interview skills.

> How long were you at your last job?

> I was a graphic designer at ABC. I was very happy there.

Interview Skills Checklist

- ☑ be on time
- ☐ dress appropriately
- ☐ be neat
- ☐ bring resume
- ☐ bring ID
- ☐ turn off cell phone
- ☐ make eye contact
- ☐ listen carefully
- ☐ talk about job experience

3. What about you? Check (✓) the things you do on a job interview.

Interview Skills Checklist

- ☐ be on time
- ☐ dress appropriately
- ☐ be neat
- ☐ bring resume
- ☐ bring ID
- ☐ turn off cell phone
- ☐ make eye contact
- ☐ listen carefully
- ☐ talk about job experience

CHALLENGE Make a list of questions to ask on a job interview. **Example:** *What are the hours?*

Go to page 256 for Another Look (Unit 9).

First Day on the Job

1. **Look in your dictionary. Who . . . ? Check (✓) the people.**

	Leo	Nurse Castro	Resident(s)	Co-Worker(s)
a. is a CNA	✓			✓
b. has a day shift				
c. directs Leo to room 10D				
d. sleeps in a hospital bed				
e. makes mistakes				
f. yells at Leo				
g. wears a uniform				
h. talks about past jobs				
i. distributes snacks				
j. asks about Leo's first day				

2. **Look in your dictionary. _True_ or _False_? Correct the <u>underlined</u> words in the false sentences.**

                     first

a. Leo works the ~~second~~ shift.   *false*

b. The third shift <u>ends</u> at 11:00 p.m.   _____

c. A <u>co-worker</u> says, "Not so fast!"   _____

d. A <u>social worker</u> says, "He doesn't know anything."   _____

e. A <u>resident</u> says, "I was an actor."   _____

f. Leo told Nurse Castro, "I made <u>mistakes</u>."   _____

3. **Cross out the word or phrase that doesn't belong.**

a. **People**	~~shift~~	resident	co-worker
b. **Places**	room	facility	staff
c. **Jobs**	social worker	receptionist	team player
d. **Job Skills**	cook	answer phones	complain
e. **Soft Skills**	make a mistake	be positive	be on time
f. **Problems**	go to the wrong room	distribute snacks	make mistakes

4. Look in your dictionary. Check (✓) Leo's job duties.

- [✓] Distribute snacks
- [ ] Drive an ambulance
- [ ] Cook
- [ ] Give physical therapy
- [ ] Drive the van
- [ ] Take blood pressures
- [ ] Play on the Lakeview team
- [ ] Assist the residents
- [ ] Distribute medicine
- [ ] Supervise co-workers

5. Circle the words to complete Leo's blog entry.

Today was my first day as (a CNA) / an RN at Lakeview. It's a nice
_a._

factory / facility. There are trees outside, and the building is modern and clean.
_b._

The shift / staff is friendly and helpful. The nurse / team player, Ms. Castro,
_c._   _d._

introduced me to the other employees / engineers. But then things got a little
_e._

difficult. I tried to help a resident / doctor, and he yelled at me. I also took a
_f._

resident to the wrong room / mall. Then another co-worker / resident
_g._   _h._

complained, "He doesn't know anything." That was about me! But the day

wasn't all bad. I listened to people's stories, I directed / distributed snacks,
_i._

and I drove some people to the mall / hospital. Nurse Castro said it was a
_j._

good first day. She said I have a positive attitude. She also said I am a

resident / team player. I think I'm going to like it here!
_k._

CHALLENGE Would you like to work at the Lakeview Nursing and Rehabilitation Center?
Why or why not? Discuss your answers with a partner.

The Workplace

1. Look in your dictionary. *True* or *False*?

a. Irina Sarkov is the receptionist. _____false_____

b. The receptionist sits across from the entrance. _____

c. The time clock shows 9:15. _____

d. The safety regulations are in the office. _____

e. There are two employees in the office. _____

f. The employer is writing paychecks now. _____

g. A customer is at the entrance. _____

h. The employer is also the owner. _____

2. Who said . . . ? Use the words in the box.

| employee | ~~employer~~ | payroll clerk | receptionist | customer | supervisor |

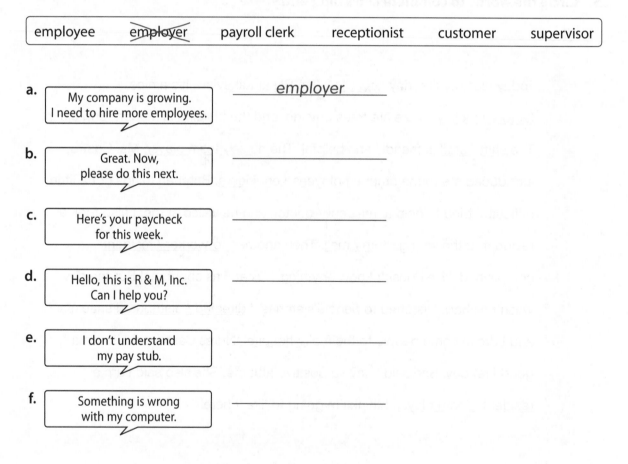

a. My company is growing.
I need to hire more employees. _____employer_____

b. Great. Now,
please do this next. _____

c. Here's your paycheck
for this week. _____

d. Hello, this is R & M, Inc.
Can I help you? _____

e. I don't understand
my pay stub. _____

f. Something is wrong
with my computer. _____

3. Look in your dictionary. Circle the answers to complete the sentences.

a. (An employee)/ The boss is fixing a computer.

b. Kate Babic is talking to the <u>payroll clerk / supervisor</u>.

c. Her <u>deductions / wages</u> are $800.

d. Irina Sarkov's signature is on the <u>paycheck / pay stub</u>.

e. The time clock is near the <u>receptionist / entrance</u>.

4. Look at the pay stub. *True* or *False*?

**IRINA'S
COMPUTER SERVICE**
7000 MAIN STREET
HOUSTON TX 77031

ENRIQUE GUTIERREZ
000-23-5473

PAY PERIOD:
10/17/18 to 10/23/18

Salary		$860.00
Deductions		
Federal	$94.60	
State	$23.65	
Social Security	$53.32	
Medicare	$12.47	
SDI	$ 8.06	
Net		**$667.90**

a. Irina is Enrique's supervisor. _____*false*_____

b. Enrique is an employee at Irina's Computer Service. _____

c. This pay stub is for one month. _____

d. His wages are $667.90 after deductions. _____

e. Enrique pays five different deductions. _____

f. The pay stub shows the office phone number. _____

g. The Social Security deduction is $8.06. _____

[CHALLENGE] Go to page 261 in this book. Follow the instructions.

1. **Look in your dictionary. In which department(s) do employees . . . ?**

   a. talk on the phone a lot   _customer service, logistics_

   b. wear a uniform   _____

   c. wear a hard hat   _____

   d. work with numbers   _____

   e. solve computer problems   _____

   f. make repairs   _____

2. **Look in your dictionary. In which department can you hear . . . ?**

   a. "These are the healthcare benefits in our plan."   _human resources_

   b. "Look at that monitor. A man without ID just entered the building!"

   _____

   c. "Solar Now. How can I help you?" _____

   d. "How can we get the product from our warehouse to the customer in one week?"

   _____

   e. "We can put ads online and give free samples." _____

   f. "You need to restart your computer." _____

   g. "The lights are out at headquarters. I'm going over there right now."

   _____

   h. "I'm preparing the tax forms now." _____

   i. "As you can see, we are selling more and more products." _____

   j. "We need to make a better, new product." _____

3. **What about you? Look in your dictionary. Complete these sentences.**

   a. I'd like to work in the _____ department because

   _____.

   b. I wouldn't like to work in the _____ department because

   _____.

| CHALLENGE | What job skills do people need to work for marketing? Accounting? Information technology? |

1. Look in your dictionary. *True* or *False*?

a. The factory manufactures lamps. _____true_____

b. The factory owner and the designer are in the warehouse. _____

c. A worker is operating a yellow forklift. _____

d. The line supervisor is pushing a hand truck. _____

e. There are three boxes on the pallet. _____

2. Cross out the word that doesn't belong.

a. **People** designer shipping clerk ~~forklift~~ packer

b. **Places** factory owner warehouse factory loading dock

c. **Machines** hand truck forklift order puller conveyor belt

d. **Jobs** ship parts assemble design

3. Complete the Lamplighter, Inc. job descriptions. Use the words in the box.

~~designer~~ factory worker line supervisor order puller packer shipping clerk

LAMPLIGHTER, Inc.

a. design the lamp _____designer_____

b. watch the assembly line _____

c. assemble parts _____

d. count boxes on the loading dock _____

e. move boxes on a hand truck _____

f. put lamps in boxes on the conveyor belt _____

4. What about you? Look at the jobs in Exercise 3. Which one would you like? Which one wouldn't you like? Why?

Example: *I would like to be a line supervisor. I like to supervise people.*

CHALLENGE Rewrite the false sentences in Exercise 1. Make them true.

1. Look in your dictionary. *True* or *False*?

    a. The gardening crew leader is talking to the landscape designer.   *true*

    b. One of the gardening crew has a wheelbarrow.   _____

    c. The landscape designer is holding a leaf blower.   _____

    d. The shovel is between the lawn mower and the rake.   _____

    e. The pruning shears are to the right of the trowel.   _____

    f. The hedge clippers are to the left of the weed whacker.   _____

2. Look at the Before and After pictures. Check (✓) the *completed* jobs.

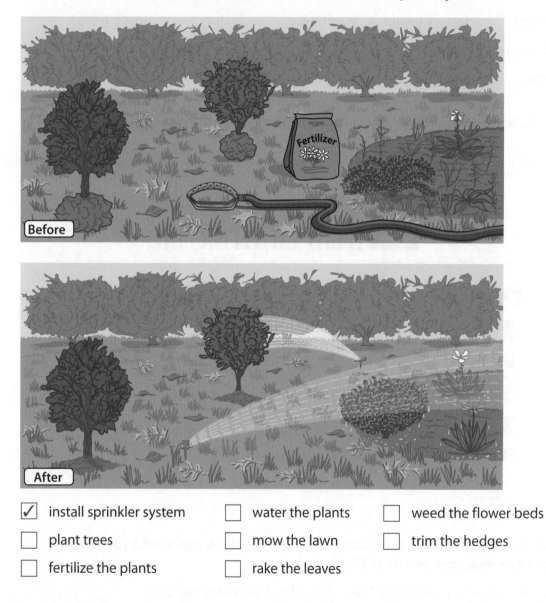

Before

After

✓ install sprinkler system	☐ water the plants	☐ weed the flower beds
☐ plant trees	☐ mow the lawn	☐ trim the hedges
☐ fertilize the plants	☐ rake the leaves	

CHALLENGE What can people use these tools for: shovel, hedge clippers, trowel, pruning shears? **Example:** *shovel—to plant a tree*

1. **Look in your dictionary. Circle the words to complete the sentences.**

   a. A farmer / <u>rancher</u> is on a horse.

   b. In Picture C, a farmworker is <u>milking / feeding</u> a cow.

   c. There is <u>hay / alfalfa</u> near the fence of the corral.

   d. There is <u>farm equipment / livestock</u> next to the vegetable garden.

   e. A farmer is in the <u>orchard / vineyard</u>.

   f. In Picture B, two hired hands are <u>harvesting / planting</u> lettuce.

2. **Look at the bar graph. Number the crops in order. (1 = the biggest crop)**

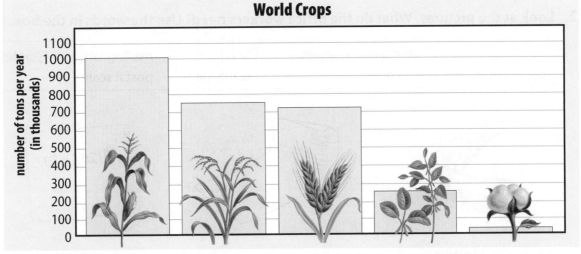

Based on information from: *Food and Agricultural Organization of the United Nations, 2013 World Production*

   ____ **a.** wheat   ____ **c.** cotton   ____ **e.** soybeans

   _1_ **b.** corn   ____ **d.** rice

3. **What about you? Have you ever been in . . . ? Check (✓) Yes or No.**

	Yes	No	If *yes*, where?
a. a field	☐	☐	_____
b. an orchard	☐	☐	_____
c. a barn	☐	☐	_____
d. a vineyard	☐	☐	_____
e. a vegetable garden	☐	☐	_____

   CHALLENGE Work with a classmate. List products that are made from wheat, soybeans, corn, cotton, and cattle. **Example:** *wheat—bread*

Office Work

1. Look in your dictionary. *True* or *False*? Correct the <u>underlined</u> words in the false sentences.

a. The receptionist is in the ~~conference room~~.   *reception area*   ____false____

b. The office manager is at his desk in a <u>cubicle</u>.   _____

c. The <u>clerk</u> is cleaning the floor.   _____

d. The computer technician is working on a <u>scanner</u>.   _____

e. The <u>executive</u> is at a presentation.   _____

f. The <u>file clerk</u> is at the file cabinet.   _____

2. Look at the pictures. What do the office workers need? Use the words in the box.

calculator	electric pencil sharpener	file folder	mailing label	~~staples~~
paper cutter	photocopier	fax machine	postal scale	

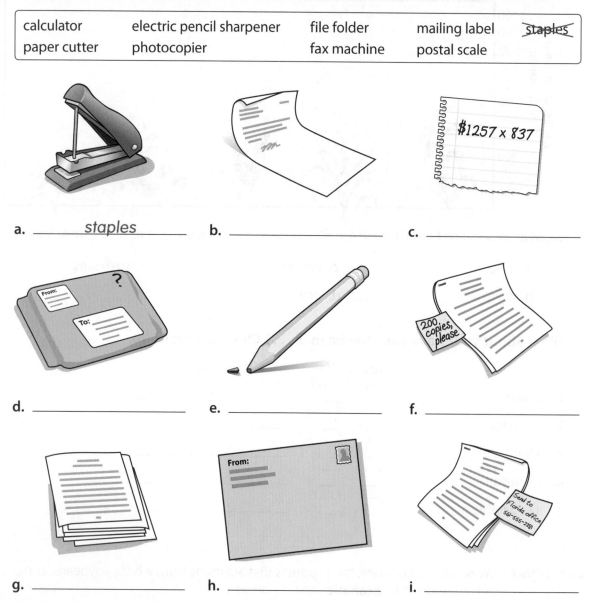

a. ____staples____   b. _____   c. _____

d. _____   e. _____   f. _____

g. _____   h. _____   i. _____

3. Look at the supply cabinet. Complete the office inventory.

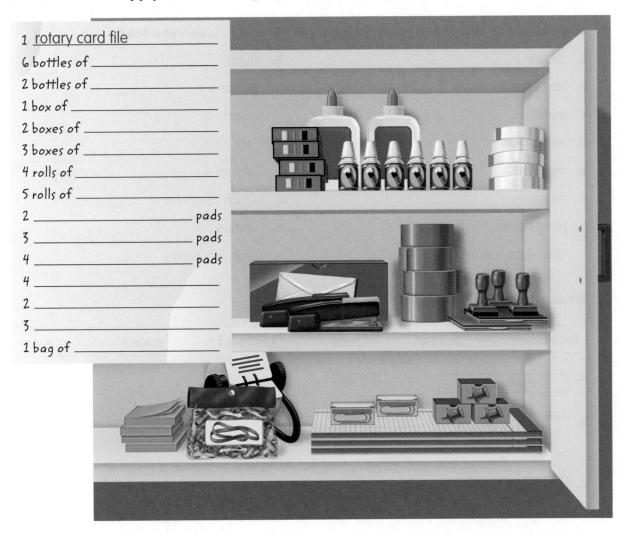

1 <u>rotary card file</u>
6 bottles of _____
2 bottles of _____
1 box of _____
2 boxes of _____
3 boxes of _____
4 rolls of _____
5 rolls of _____
2 _____ pads
3 _____ pads
4 _____ pads
4 _____
2 _____
3 _____
1 bag of _____

4. What about you? How often do you use . . . ? Check (✓) the columns.

	Often	Sometimes	Never
a fax machine			
sticky notes			
an inkjet printer			
a laser printer			
an organizer			
an appointment book			
a rotary card file			
a paper shredder			

CHALLENGE   Make a shopping list of office supplies you need for your home. What will you use them for? **Example:** *envelopes—to pay bills.* Discuss your list with a classmate.

Information Technology

1. Look at pages 190–191 in your dictionary. How many . . . can you see?

a. cables   <u>6</u>

b. keyboards   ___

c. mice*   ___

d. microphones   ___

e. modems   ___

f. monitors   ___

g. power cords   ___

    *plural for *mouse*

h. routers   ___

i. speakers   ___

j. towers   ___

k. track pads   ___

l. USB ports   ___

m. laptop computers   ___

n. printers   ___

o. surge protectors   ___

2. What are they using? Write the word.

flash drive	headset	hub	keyboard	~~mouse~~	speaker

a. | Double click! | <u>mouse</u>

b. | Save it on this and take it home. | _____

c. | Where is the backspace key? | _____

d. | This is too big for me. | _____

e. | I'll plug it in here. | _____

f. | I'll make it louder. | _____

3. Cross out the word that doesn't belong.

a. **Inside the tower**   hard drive   motherboard   ~~mainframe~~

b. **Software programs**   word processing   RAM   spreadsheet

c. **Hardware**   DVD drive   Wi-Fi connection   CPU

d. **Outside the tower**   power supply unit   external hard drive   router

4. Look in your dictionary. *True* or *False*? **Correct the underlined words in the false sentences.**

desktop computer

a. The ~~mainframe computer~~ has a virus alert. _____false_____

b. The computer operations specialist is looking at <u>data</u>. _____

c. The hub is connected to the <u>keyboard</u>. _____

d. The external hard drive is connected to the hub and the <u>desktop</u> computer. _____

e. The <u>printer</u> has paper in it. _____

f. The man with the <u>headset</u> is web conferencing. _____

g. The webcam is on top of the <u>modem</u>. _____

5. Circle the words to complete the conversations between IT support and a caller.

A: The printer <u>can't stream video / (won't print)</u>!
  a.
B: Is there paper in it?

A: My desktop computer won't start!

B: Check the <u>hard drive / power cord</u>. Is it plugged into a wall outlet or surge protector?
  b.
A: I can't <u>log on / install the update</u>!
  c.
B: Do you have the correct username and password?

A: The <u>screen / power supply unit</u> froze.
  d.
B: Shut your computer down. Wait a few seconds. Then turn it back on.

A: All of our computers have a virus!

B: *All* of them? I'll connect you to our <u>computer operations / cybersecurity</u> specialist.
  e.

CHALLENGE   What do people use these things for: presentation programs, spreadsheet programs, webcams, flash drives, headsets? Discuss your answers with a partner.

1. Look in your dictionary. Circle the words to complete the sentences.

a. The (concierge) / parking attendant is on the phone.

b. The elevator is across from the gift shop / luggage cart.

c. One of the guest rooms has two double / king-size beds.

d. The housekeeping cart is in the hallway / ballroom.

e. Maintenance / The desk clerk is repairing the ice machine.

f. There are two bell captains / guests in the suite.

g. The doorman isn't opening the door / revolving door.

2. Look at the hotel directory in the guest room. What number do you call for . . . ?

HOTEL EDISON ☎ DIRECTORY

HOTEL EDISON

a. room service _3_

b. gift shop ___

c. pool ___

d. meeting room ___

e. front desk ___

f. housekeeper ___

g. bellhop ___

h. gym ___

3. What about you? Would you like to be a guest at the hotel in your dictionary?

☐ Yes   ☐ No   Why? _____

CHALLENGE Look in your dictionary. Write five questions that you can ask the desk clerk about the hotel. **Example:** *What time does the pool open?*

1. Look in your dictionary. Who is . . . ?

a. leaving the walk-in freezer   _food preparation worker_

b. washing dishes   _____

c. sitting near the buffet   _____

d. talking to the bus person   _____

e. working in the banquet room   _____ and _____

f. carrying food to a diner   _____

g. seating a diner at a table   _____

2. Look in your dictionary. Where are they? Check (✓) all the correct columns.

	Dining Room	Banquet Room	Kitchen
a. servers	✓	✓	
b. diners			
c. short-order cook			
d. sous chef			
e. caterer			
f. bus person			
g. head chef			
h. maitre d'			
i. runner			

3. Look in your dictionary. Who said . . . ?

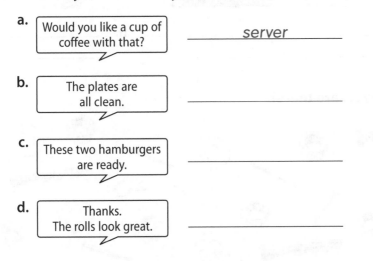

a. Would you like a cup of coffee with that?   _server_

b. The plates are all clean.   _____

c. These two hamburgers are ready.   _____

d. Thanks. The rolls look great.   _____

CHALLENGE   Imagine you own a hotel. Make a list of food to have at a breakfast buffet. Compare your list with a classmate's. Do you have any of the same items?

Tools and Building Supplies

1. Look in your dictionary. Cross out the word that doesn't belong.

a. Hardware	nail	eye hook	~~outlet cover~~	wood screw
b. Plumbing	C-clamp	plunger	pipe	fittings
c. Power tools	circular saw	hammer	router	electric drill
d. Paint	wood stain	paint roller	spray gun	chisel
e. Electrical	wire stripper	plane	wire	extension cord
f. Hand tools	hacksaw	work light	pipe wrench	mallet

2. Look at the pictures. What do you need? Choose the correct tool from the box.

drill bit	~~electrical tape~~	level	paintbrush
Phillips screwdriver	sandpaper	scraper	screwdriver

a. ___electrical tape___   b. _____   c. _____   d. _____

e. _____   f. _____   g. _____   h. _____

3. Look at the picture. How many . . . are there?

a. nuts   _6_
b. nails   ___
c. screws   ___
d. washers   ___
e. bolts   ___
f. hooks   ___

194

4. Look at the chart. *True* or *False*?

Multi-use Knife Features						
Deluxe	✓	✓	✓	✓	✓	✓
Traditional	✓	✓	✓		✓	
Micro	✓		✓			✓

a. The "Traditional" has a blade.   *false*

b. The "Micro" has a Phillips screwdriver.   _____

c. All three models have screwdrivers.   _____

d. All three models have a tape measure.   _____

e. The "Deluxe" has pliers.   _____

f. Only the "Deluxe" has a wire stripper.   _____

5. What about you? Check (✓) the tools and supplies you have.

☐ hammer   ☐ plunger

☐ handsaw   ☐ vise

☐ power sander   ☐ ax

☐ electric drill   ☐ masking tape

☐ adjustable wrench   ☐ duct tape

☐ jigsaw   ☐ plane

☐ yardstick   ☐ chisel

☐ screwdriver   ☐ Other: _____

[CHALLENGE] Look at the chart in Exercise 4. Which model would you buy? What can you use it for?

Construction

1. **Look in your dictionary. Put the words in the correct category.**

Heavy Machines	Tools	Building Material	
cherry picker	_jackhammer_	_concrete_	_____
_____	_____	_____	_____
_____	_____	_____	_____
_____	_____	_____	_____

Things To Stand On   _____   _____   _____

ladder   _____   _____

_____

_____

2. **Look at the items. Match.**

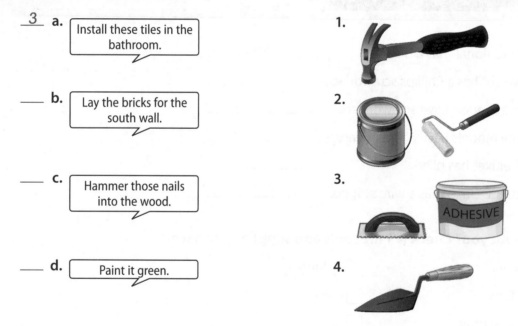

_3_ **a.** Install these tiles in the bathroom.

1.

____ **b.** Lay the bricks for the south wall.

2.

____ **c.** Hammer those nails into the wood.

3. ADHESIVE

____ **d.** Paint it green.

4.

3. **What about you? Check (✓) the materials your school building has.**

☐ concrete   ☐ stucco

☐ shingles   ☐ tile

☐ bricks   ☐ wood

CHALLENGE Look in your dictionary. What are the construction workers doing? Write sentences. **Example:** _One construction worker is using a jackhammer._

1. Look in your dictionary. Match.

1.    2.    3.   4.   5.

_3_ **a.** frayed cord

____ **b.** slippery floor

____ **c.** poisonous fumes

____ **d.** flammable liquids

____ **e.** radioactive materials

2. Look at the worker. Check (✓) his safety equipment.

Super Safe Sam

Job Safety
Better safe than sorry!

- ✓ back support belt
- ☐ earmuffs
- ☐ ear plugs
- ☐ fire extinguisher
- ☐ hard hat
- ☐ knee pads
- ☐ particle mask
- ☐ respirator
- ☐ safety boots
- ☐ safety glasses
- ☐ safety goggles
- ☐ safety visor
- ☐ two-way radio
- ☐ work gloves

3. What about you? Which safety equipment do you use at work? At home? Write a list for each. Discuss your list with a classmate.

At Work

_____

_____

_____

_____

_____

At Home

_____

_____

_____

_____

_____

CHALLENGE Imagine you work at the place in your dictionary. Which safety equipment will you wear or use?

1. Look in your dictionary. *True* or *False*?

a. The contractor is holding a floor plan.   _false_

b. Three bricklayers called in sick.   _____

c. One construction worker is going to the clinic.   _____

d. The man operating the crane is not being careful.   _____

e. The wiring is dangerous.   _____

f. The budget is three thousand dollars.   _____

g. There's an electrical hazard in the office.   _____

2. Look in your dictionary. Check (✓) the things at the construction site.

☐ ladder	☐ insulation	☐ bricks
✓ I beams	☐ hard hats	☐ pickax
☐ forklift	☐ shovel	☐ trowel
☐ scaffolding	☐ crane	☐ tiles
☐ tractor	☐ jackhammer	☐ sledgehammer
☐ cherry picker	☐ backhoe	☐ safety regulations
☐ bulldozer	☐ wheelbarrow	☐ wood

3. Look at the list in Exercise 2. Choose two items. What do people use them for?

Example: *You can use a ladder to reach high things.*

_____

_____

4. Look in your dictionary. Circle the words to complete the sentences.

a. There is an electrical hazard in the clinic / at the construction site.

b. One worker isn't wearing a hard hat / shoes.

c. One worker fell into bricks / concrete.

d. Another worker dropped a hammer / jackhammer.

e. An I beam / Drywall is going to hit two workers.

f. A piece of tile / wood is going to fall on a worker.

g. The worker with the headphones and red hard hat is very careful / careless.

5. **Look in your dictionary. Answer the questions.**

a. Who is Sam Lopez? _____ *contractor* _____

b. Who are Jack and Tom? _____

c. What is the name of the clinic? _____

d. How much will the wiring cost? _____

e. How many months does the schedule give the workers from start to finish? _____

6. **Complete the building owner's report. Use the words in the box.**

bricklayer	budget	careful	clinic	contractor
~~dangerous~~	electrical hazard	floor plan	sick	wiring

7/2

I went to the construction site today. It's a _____ *dangerous* _____ place! I saw some
                                                      a.

_____ coming out of a box. This is a real _____ .
        b.   **c.**

Some of the workers are not very _____ . One
                                              d.

_____ fell in cement and needed to go to the _____!
        e.   **f.**

Other workers didn't have hard hats on. Two workers called in _____
                                                                          g.

and weren't at work. Sam, the _____ , said it was a bad day. Then
                                        h.

I showed Sam the new _____ with more offices. He looked very upset.
                              i.

He's worried about the schedule. *He's* worried about the schedule, and *I'm* worried about the

_____ . Sam doesn't think three million dollars is enough!
        j.

7. **What about you? Would you like a job at the construction site in your dictionary? Why or why not?**

CHALLENGE Look in your dictionary. What safety equipment do the workers need? Why do they need it? Make a list. Use <u>page 197</u> in your dictionary for help.

199

Schools and Subjects

1. **Look in your dictionary. In which school can you hear . . . ?**

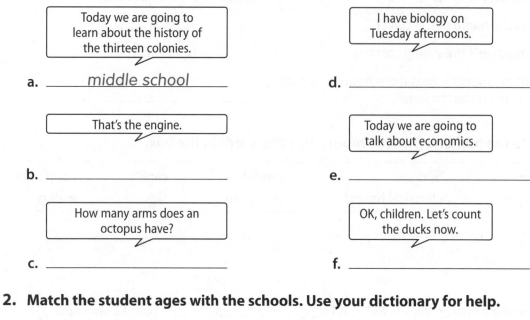

> Today we are going to learn about the history of the thirteen colonies.

a. _middle school_

> I have biology on Tuesday afternoons.

d. _____

> That's the engine.

b. _____

> Today we are going to talk about economics.

e. _____

> How many arms does an octopus have?

c. _____

> OK, children. Let's count the ducks now.

f. _____

2. **Match the student ages with the schools. Use your dictionary for help.**

_2_ **a.** 20 years old   **1.** high school

____ **b.** 3 years old   **2.** college

____ **c.** 7 years old   **3.** preschool

____ **d.** 16 years old   **4.** adult school

____ **e.** 12 years old   **5.** elementary school

____ **f.** 30 years old   **6.** middle school

3. **What about you? Complete the chart.**

Check (✓) the schools you have attended:	Name	Location	Dates
☐ elementary school			
☐ junior high school			
☐ high school			
☐ vocational school			
☐ adult school			
☐ college / university			
☐ community college			
☐ Other: _____			

4. **Look in your dictionary. In which class can students . . . ?**

   a. learn about World War II   _history_

   b. work with numbers   _____

   c. do exercises outside   _____

   d. learn French   _____

   e. sing   _____

   f. talk about books   _____

   g. paint   _____

   h. use this workbook   _____

5. **Label the class notes. Use the words in the box.**

Math	Science	World Languages
Music	English Language Instruction	~~History~~

a. _History_

1914-1918,
  World War I

1941-1945,
  World War II

1954-1972
  Civil Rights Movement

b. _____

$\sqrt{934} =$

c. _____

d. _____

学校
教師

e. _____

come came come

go went gone

write wrote written

f. _____

CO_2

CHALLENGE   Go to page 261 in this book. Follow the instructions.

English Composition

1. **Look at the essay in your dictionary. How many . . . are there? Check (✓) the columns.**

	0	1	2	3	4
a. words in the title					✓
b. paragraphs					
c. sentences in the last paragraph					
d. quotation marks					
e. commas in the first paragraph					
f. exclamation marks					
g. apostrophes					
h. parentheses					
i. colons					
j. hyphens					
k. question marks					
l. footnotes					

2. **Look at the essay. Check (✓) the things the writer did.**

Another Move

My family and I came to this country five years ago. At first I was lonely and missed my own country, but now I feel at home here.

Next september we're moving again—to san diego, california. I'm worried. Will I like it? Where will we live. My father says, "Don't worry." My mother says that soon San Diego will feel like home. "But I'm happy here?" I exclaim. I watch my father's face and listen to my mother's words, and I feel better. My new city will soon be my new home.

a. ✓ The writer gave the essay a title.

b. ☐ He wrote an introduction.

c. ☐ He indented the first sentence in a paragraph.

d. ☐ He capitalized names all the time.

e. ☐ He used correct punctuation all the time.

f. ☐ He wrote a conclusion.

3. Look in your dictionary. *True* or *False*?

a. The writing assignment is due on September 3.   *false*

b. The student has time to think about the assignment.   _____

c. He brainstorms ideas with other students.   _____

d. He organizes his ideas in his notebook.   _____

e. He writes a first draft on his computer.   _____

f. He edits his paper in red.   _____

g. He revises his paper before he turns it in.   _____

h. The student gets feedback from his teacher.   _____

i. He turns in his paper late.   _____

j. The composition is about his job.   _____

4. Put the words in the box into the correct columns.

~~edit~~   brainstorm   get feedback   organize   rewrite

Prewriting	Writing and Revising	Sharing and Responding
_____	*edit*	_____
_____	_____	

5. What about you? Check (✓) the columns.

When I write a composition, I	Always	Sometimes	Never, but I would like to try this!
think about the assignment			
brainstorm ideas			
organize my ideas			
write a first draft			
edit my draft			
revise my draft			
get feedback			
write a final draft on a computer			

CHALLENGE Write a three-paragraph essay about your life in this country. Write a first draft, edit your paper, get feedback, rewrite your essay, and turn it in to your teacher.

Mathematics

1. **Look in your dictionary. Cross out the word that doesn't belong.**

a. Shapes	~~endpoint~~	rectangle	circle	square
b. Parts of a circle	radius	right angle	diameter	circumference
c. Types of math	geometry	algebra	calculus	parallelogram
d. Geometric solids	triangle	cone	sphere	cylinder
e. Lines	straight	perpendicular	pyramid	curved
f. Math operations	add	subtract	variable	divide
g. Answers to math operations	base	difference	sum	product
h. Types of integers	even	odd	positive	quotient
i. Types of angles	acute	obtuse	rectangle	right

2. **Complete the test. Use the words in the box.**

denominator	equation	negative	numerator
~~odd~~	product	sum	variable

MATH 103   TEST

Complete the sentences.

1. 121 is an _____ *odd* _____ number.

2. –7 is a _____ number.

3. The _____ in 1/2 is 2.

4. The _____ in 1/2 is 1.

5. The _____ of 10 + 3 is 13.

6. The _____ of 10 x 3 is 30.

7. An _____ has an equal (=) sign.

8. In an equation, *x* is a _____.

3. **Look in your dictionary. Circle the words to complete the sentences.**

   a. A triangle has three <u>curved / straight</u> lines. *(straight circled)*

   b. A <u>graph / parallelogram</u> has a horizontal and vertical axis.

   c. Perpendicular lines make <u>acute / right</u> angles.

   d. For $18 \div 2 = x$, $x = 9$ is the <u>product / solution</u>.

   e. <u>A word problem / An equation</u> ends with a question.

4. **Label the pictures. Use the words in the box.**

~~circle~~	cube	curved line	cylinder	triangle
cone	pyramid	sphere	square	

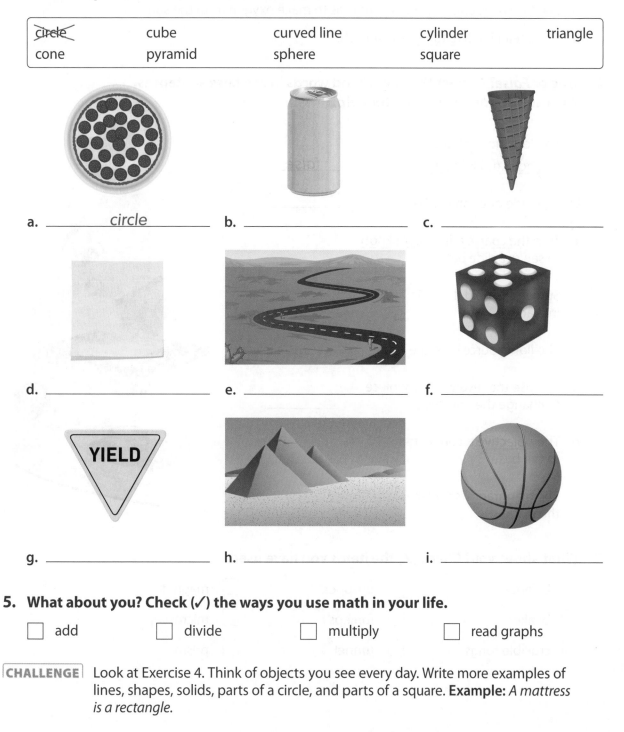

   a. _____ *circle* _____   b. _____   c. _____

   d. _____   e. _____   f. _____

   g. _____   h. _____   i. _____

5. **What about you? Check (✓) the ways you use math in your life.**

   ☐ add   ☐ divide   ☐ multiply   ☐ read graphs

   CHALLENGE Look at Exercise 4. Think of objects you see every day. Write more examples of lines, shapes, solids, parts of a circle, and parts of a square. **Example:** *A mattress is a rectangle.*

1. Look in your dictionary. Circle the words to complete the sentences.

a. The (biologist) / chemist is observing something through a microscope.

b. The chemist / physicist has a formula on the board.

c. The chemist is using the periodic table / a prism.

d. An atom has chromosomes / protons.

e. Birds are vertebrates / invertebrates.

f. Plants use organisms / photosynthesis to make oxygen from the sun.

g. The ocean is a habitat / stage for fish.

2. *True* or *False*? Correct the underlined words in the false sentences. You can use your dictionary for help.

a. You look through the ~~fine adjustment knob.~~ eyepiece   _____false_____

b. The slide goes on the base.   _____

c. Turn the coarse adjustment knob to see the slide better.   _____

d. Stage clips hold the slide in place.   _____

e. The light source is on the stage.   _____

f. You use the revolving nosepiece to change the objective.   _____

g. The objective is connected to the base.   _____

h. The diaphragm is under the stage.   _____

3. What about you? Check (✓) the items you have used.

☐ balance   ☐ dropper   ☐ magnet

☐ beaker   ☐ forceps   ☐ microscope

☐ crucible tongs   ☐ funnel   ☐ prism

4. Complete the inventory. Write the number of items in the science lab.

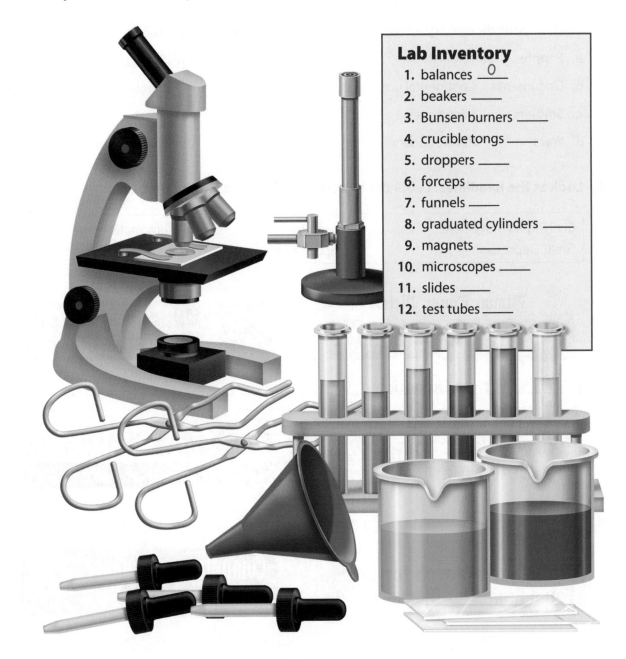

Lab Inventory
1. balances ___0___
2. beakers _____
3. Bunsen burners _____
4. crucible tongs _____
5. droppers _____
6. forceps _____
7. funnels _____
8. graduated cylinders _____
9. magnets _____
10. microscopes _____
11. slides _____
12. test tubes _____

5. Number the steps of an experiment in the correct order. (1 = the first step)

___ **a.** Observe.

_1_ **b.** State a hypothesis.

___ **c.** Draw a conclusion.

___ **d.** Do an experiment.

___ **e.** Record the results.

CHALLENGE Find out about three items in Exercise 4. What are they used for? Make a list.
Example: *crucible tongs—to hold hot items*

1. Look in your dictionary. Cross out the word that doesn't belong.

    a. People   colonists   founders   ~~Bill of Rights~~

    b. Documents   Continental Congress   Constitution   Declaration of Independence

    c. Soldiers   minutemen   thirteen colonies   redcoats

    d. Wars   Revolutionary   Civil   Industrial Revolution

2. Look at the headlines. Label the events. Use the words in the box.

Civil Rights Movement	Jazz Age	Information Age
Great Depression	Space Age	~~Western Expansion~~

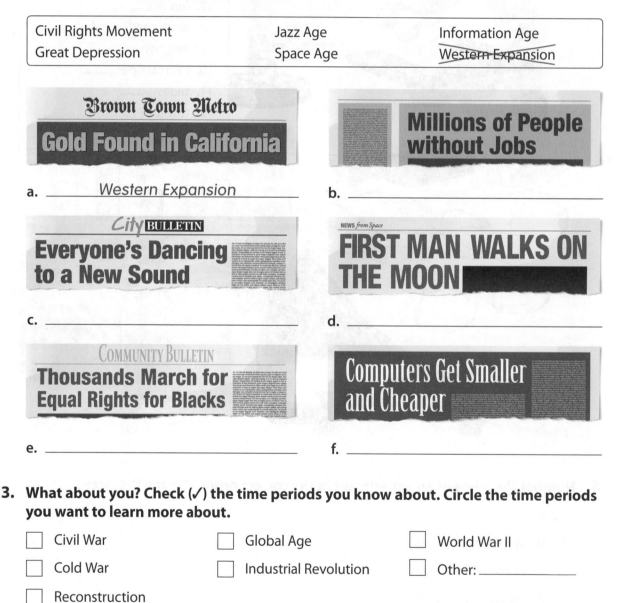

    a.   _Western Expansion_   b. _____

    c. _____   d. _____

    e. _____   f. _____

3. What about you? Check (✓) the time periods you know about. Circle the time periods you want to learn more about.

    ☐ Civil War   ☐ Global Age   ☐ World War II

    ☐ Cold War   ☐ Industrial Revolution   ☐ Other: _____

    ☐ Reconstruction

CHALLENGE   Choose a time period from Exercise 3. Look online, or in an encyclopedia or history book. Write a short paragraph about that time period. When was it? What are two interesting events from that period?

1. Look in your dictionary. Match.

_4_ **a.** president   1. Shinzo Abe

___ **b.** prime minister   2. Benito Mussolini

___ **c.** emperor   3. Qin Shi Huang

___ **d.** dictator   4. Benito Juárez

2. What are these photos of? Use the words in the box.

ancient civilization	composition	exploration	monarch	war
modern civilization	~~invention~~	political movement	immigration	

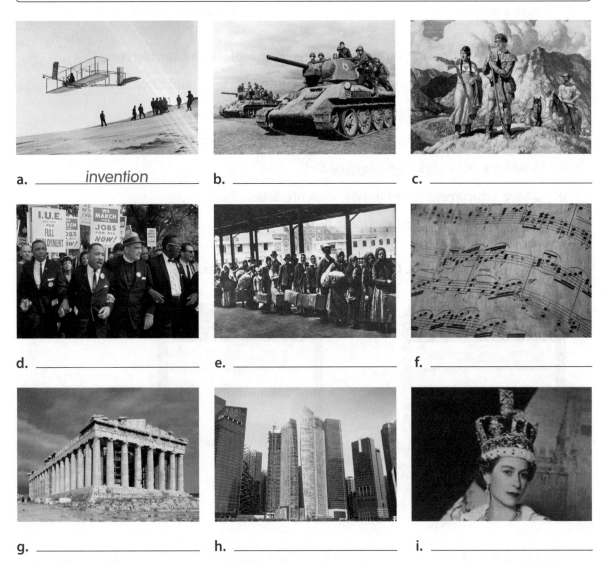

a. _____invention_____   b. _____   c. _____

d. _____   e. _____   f. _____

g. _____   h. _____   i. _____

CHALLENGE Write the name of a famous explorer, an inventor, and an immigrant. Where did they come from? What are they famous for? **Example:** *Albert Pujols is a famous baseball player from the Dominican Republic.*

1. **Look at page 210 in your dictionary. Which comes first? Number the steps in order (1 and 2).**

   a. Change text.   2   **e.** Open the program.   ___

       Select text.   1   Quit the program.   ___

   b. Save the document.   ___   **f.** Save the document.   ___

       Close the document.   ___   Type the document.   ___

   c. Delete a word.   ___   **g.** Delete text.   ___

       Double-click on a word. ___   Drag to select text.   ___

   d. Copy a word.   ___   **h.** Create a new document. ___

       Paste a word.   ___   Click on the screen.   ___

2. **Look in your dictionary. Circle the words to complete the sentences.**

   a. Remember to delete a word / **save the document** on your hard drive.

   b. Click on the X to **close** / create a document.

   c. You need a mouse or track pad to type a word / **double-click**.

   d. To select a word, click / **double-click** on it.

   e. To save a document, **click** / double-click on "Save."

   f. To move text, quit / **copy and paste** it.

3. **Look at Rosa's message. Check (✓) the things Rosa did.**

Before	After
12:34 PM	12:34 PM
New Message	New Message
To:	To:
Cc:	Cc:
Subject:	Subject:
I'll meet you tomorrow at 4:00 in the school cafeteria.	I'll meet you tomorrow at 4:00 in the cafeteria.
Rosa	Rosa

   ✓ typed her name   ☐ deleted a question   ☐ deleted a word

   ☐ selected a word   ☐ typed the date   ☐ quit the program

4. Look at page 211 in your dictionary. Complete the Q (questions) and A (answers).

Q: How do I go to the top or the bottom of the screen?

A: _____Use the arrow keys_____ or _____ up or down.
     a.   **b.**

Q: How do I confirm my password?

A: _____.
                              c.

Q: How do I send my registration information?

A: _____.
                              d.

Q: How do I show the computer that it is really me?

A: _____. Then _____.
                      e.   **f.**

5. Look at the email. *True* or *False*?

| My Mail |
| New | Forward | Send | Delete | Junk | Spell Check | Attach |

tomorow
tomorrow ×

To:

Subject: Tomorow

Here's my new bike. What do you think?

Do you want to go for a ride in the park tomorrow?

Let me know.

Todd

a. Todd logged in to his email account. _____*true*_____

b. He addressed the email. _____

c. He typed the subject. _____

d. He composed the message. _____

e. He attached a picture. _____

f. He attached a document. _____

g. He checked his spelling. _____

h. He sent the email. _____

CHALLENGE   Compose an email and send it to a classmate. Then describe the steps you took.
Example: *First, I wrote the message. Then I . . . .*

Internet Research

1. Look at pages 212–213 in your dictionary. Match.

_7_ a.    **1.** date

___ b. (magnifying glass icon)   **2.** back button

___ c. (back arrow button)   **3.** URL

___ d. www.money.wwnews.org   **4.** video player

___ e. (refresh icon)   **5.** search icon

___ f. (play button)   **6.** refresh button

___ g. January 8, 2017   **7.** bookmark

2. Look in your dictionary. Circle the words to complete the sentences.

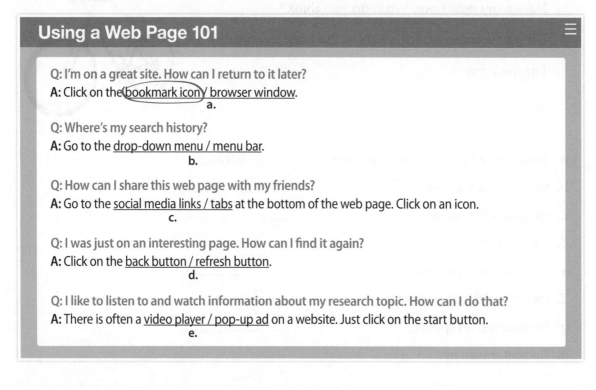

Using a Web Page 101   ☰

Q: I'm on a great site. How can I return to it later?
A: Click on the (bookmark icon) / browser window.
                        a.

Q: Where's my search history?
A: Go to the drop-down menu / menu bar.
                        b.

Q: How can I share this web page with my friends?
A: Go to the social media links / tabs at the bottom of the web page. Click on an icon.
                        c.

Q: I was just on an interesting page. How can I find it again?
A: Click on the back button / refresh button.
                        d.

Q: I like to listen to and watch information about my research topic. How can I do that?
A: There is often a video player / pop-up ad on a website. Just click on the start button.
                        e.

3. What about you? What do you do on the Internet?

4. Look at pages 212–213 in your dictionary. *True* or *False*? Correct the underlined words in the false sentences.

a. The woman's ~~menu bar~~ *research question* is about jobs.   _false_

b. She selected Google as her research question.   _____

c. She typed in the phrase "top jobs in the U.S."   _____

d. The woman clicked on a link about the best jobs.   _____

e. The woman kept a record of sites and books.   _____

f. She clicked on the star to cite sources.   _____

g. The web page has three social media links.   _____

h. The content is about the 25 best jobs.   _____

i. The source is January 8, 2017.   _____

j. The video player is below the pop-up ad.   _____

k. The woman clicked on the Career tab.   _____

5. Complete the teacher's instructions for an Internet research paper. Use the words in the box.

cite	click on	keep	look at	~~research~~	search box	search engine	type

Class: English 101   Due Date: November 11

Instructions for your Internet research paper

1. Choose a ___**research**___ question to write about.
   a.

2. Select a _____ . (Google, Firefox, Internet Explorer)
   b.

3. _____ key words or a phrase in the _____ .
   c.   d.

4. _____ the search results and _____ interesting links.
   e.   f.

5. Remember to _____ a record of your sources.
   g.

6. Don't forget to _____ your sources!
   h.

CHALLENGE   Choose a research question. Then conduct research. Which search engine did you use? What did you type in the search box? Which sources did you use? What did you learn?

Geography and Habitats

1. Look in your dictionary. Put the words in the correct columns.

Land		Water
rain forest	_____	_____	_____
_____	_____	_____	_____
_____	_____	_____	_____
_____	_____	_____	_____
_____	_____	_____	_____
			_____

2. Complete the chart. Use words from Exercise 1.

a. largest	_lake_		Caspian Sea (Asia/Europe)	143,244 sq. miles
b. highest	_____		Everest (Asia)	29,078 feet
c. largest	_____		Sahara (N. Africa)	3,500,000 sq. miles
d. largest	_____		Greenland (Denmark)	840,000 sq. miles
e. longest	_____		Nile (Africa)	4,160 miles
f. deepest	_____		Pacific	35,837 feet
g. largest	_____		Bengal (S. Asia)	839,000 sq. miles

3. What about you? Check (✓) the places you've visited.

☐ waterfall   ☐ desert   ☐ ocean

☐ canyon   ☐ bay   ☐ mountain range

CHALLENGE   Search online for a world map. Write the names of two islands and two oceans. Do not use the ones from Exercise 2.

1. Look in your dictionary. *True* or *False*?

a. There are nine planets in our solar system.   _____false_____

b. The sun looks dark during a solar eclipse.   _____

c. The astronaut is looking through a telescope at the space station.   _____

d. The astronomer is at an observatory.   _____

e. There are six stars in the constellation.   _____

2. Complete the chart with the names of the planets. Then answer the questions.

Which planet . . . ?

a. is closest to the sun   ___Mercury___   e. has many rings around it   _____

b. is farthest from
   the sun   _____   f. is between Saturn
                                                  and Neptune   _____

c. is the largest   _____   g. is our home   _____

d. is between Mercury
   and Earth   _____

3. What about you? Check (✓) the things you see in the sky tonight.

☐ planets   Which one(s)? _____

☐ the moon   Which phase?   ☐ new   ☐ full   ☐ quarter   ☐ crescent

☐ stars   ☐ constellations   ☐ comets   ☐ satellites

CHALLENGE   Find out the names of three different constellations. What do they look like? Talk
            about your answers with a classmate.

Trees and Plants

1. **Look in your dictionary. *True* or *False*?**

   a. A tree has roots, limbs, branches, and twigs. _____true_____

   b. Holly is a plant. _____

   c. The birch tree has yellow leaves. _____

   d. The magnolia and dogwood trees have flowers. _____

   e. The cactus has berries. _____

   f. Poison sumac has a trunk. _____

   g. Poison ivy has three leaves. _____

   h. The willow has pinecones. _____

   i. A vine has needles. _____

2. **Look at the bar graph. Number the trees in order of height. (1 = the tallest)**

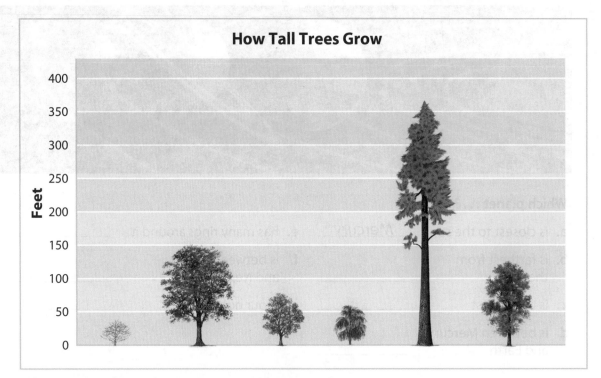

Based on information from: Petrides, G.: *Peterson Field Guides. Trees and Shrubs.*
(NY: Houghton Mifflin Co., 1986)

____ **a.** dogwood   ____ **d.** oak

____ **b.** elm   _1_ **e.** redwood

____ **c.** maple   ____ **f.** willow

CHALLENGE   Which trees grow near your home? Make a list.

216

1. **Look in your dictionary. Circle the words to complete the sentences.**

   a. The <u>bouquet</u> / (marigold) is orange.

   b. The <u>tulip / crocus</u> and the <u>gardenia / poinsettia</u> are red.

   c. The <u>chrysanthemum / daffodil</u> and the <u>houseplant / lily</u> are yellow.

   d. The <u>carnation / jasmine</u> and the <u>daisy / orchid</u> are white.

2. **What goes below the ground? What goes above the ground? Put the words in the box in the correct part of the diagram.**

   | ~~bud~~ | ~~bulb~~ | leaves | petals | roots | seed | stems | thorn | shoot |

   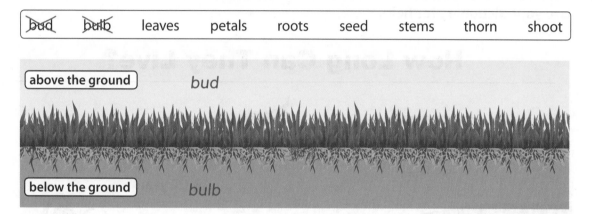

   above the ground   *bud*

   below the ground   *bulb*

3. **Complete the sentences. Use the names of the flowers in the box.**

   a. Because of their color, these flowers are called _____*violets*_____.

   b. _____ grow from bulbs. The one in the picture is red.

   c. _____ are large yellow flowers. They grow very tall. You can eat their seeds.

   d. People love the smell of _____. But be careful! Their stems have thorns.

   e. _____ are usually yellow. They have six petals around a "cup." They grow early in the spring.

   f. _____ are plants with large leaves. The red leaves look like petals, but they are really leaves!

4. **What about you? Which flowers do you like? Why?**

   Example: *I like roses. They smell good and they grow in many different colors.*

   [CHALLENGE] Make a list of three flowers that grow in your city, town, or country. Describe them. Which is your favorite? Why?

Marine Life, Amphibians, and Reptiles

1. **Look in your dictionary. Cross out the word that doesn't belong. Write the category.**

   a. _____Reptiles_____   turtle   alligator   ~~seal~~   crocodile

   b. _____   fin   gills   scales   scallop

   c. _____   seahorse   frog   toad   newt

   d. _____   sea lion   dolphin   lizard   sea otter

   e. _____   tuna   whale   bass   swordfish

2. **Look at the chart. Circle the words to complete the sentences.
   Use your dictionary for help.**

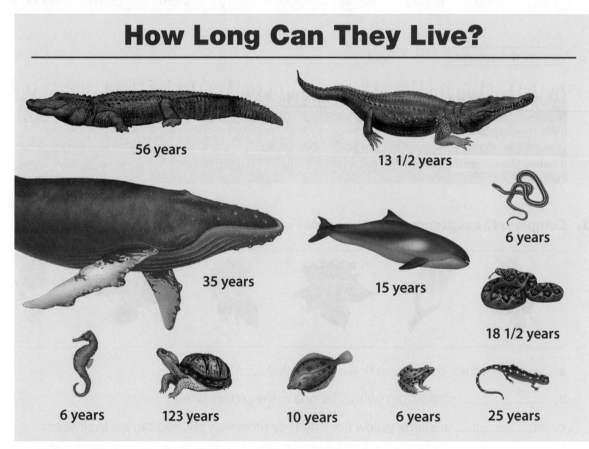

How Long Can They Live?

56 years

13 1/2 years

6 years

35 years

15 years

18 1/2 years

6 years   123 years   10 years   6 years   25 years

Based on information from: Texas Parks and Wildlife http://www.tpwd.state.tx.us/publications/
nonpwdpubs/young_naturalist/animals/animal_life_spans/

a. The (alligator) / crocodile can live fifty-six years.

b. The flounder / garter snake can live ten years.

c. The garter snake / rattlesnake can live eighteen and a half years.

d. The porpoise / seahorse can live fifteen years.

e. The frog / salamander can live twenty-five years.

f. The turtle / whale can live 123 years!

3. Find and circle 12 more sea animal words. The words go across (→) and down (↓).

```
J  E  L  L  Y  F  I  S  H  A  R
P  E  R  B  O  S  T  Q  L  W  A
E  L  S  W  O  R  M  U  P  E  D
S  Y  S  A  R  M  M  I  M  A  T
E  O  T  R  A  P  O  D  U  S  O
A  C  A  M  Y  E  T  Y  S  H  R
H  T  R  E  L  J  U  D  S  A  T
O  O  F  L  O  U  N  D  E  R  O
R  P  I  M  S  N  A  I  L  K  I
S  U  S  X  I  D  R  B  A  S  S
E  S  H  R  I  M  P  O  L  O  E
```

4. What about you? Make two lists using the words from Exercise 3.

Things I Eat	Things I Don't Eat

CHALLENGE   Add to your lists in Exercise 4. Use your dictionary for help.

1. Look in your dictionary. Complete the chart.

	Name of Bird	Habitat*	Physical Appearance
a.	robin	■ ■ ■ ■	brown with orange breast
b.		■ ■	blue with white on wings, head, and breast
c.		■ ■	large; brown with white head and tail; big yellow beak and claws
d.		■	large head, flat face with big eyes; brown and white feathers
e.		■ ■	blue-black feathers with purple throat
f.		■ ■	green with red throat; long, thin bill
g.		■	large; long black neck and head; white "chin" and breast
h.		■	black and white with small red spot on head; small bill
i.		■	green head and neck; white neck "ring"; brown chest and tail
j.		■ ■	small; brown, white, and gray feathers

*where the bird lives: ■ = forests ■ = water ■ = mountains ■ = farms ■ = suburban gardens ■ = cities

2. Look at the picture. Check (✓) the things you see.

✓ honeybee	☐ scorpion	☐ grasshopper	☐ ladybug	☐ mosquito
☐ fly	☐ moth	☐ spider	☐ wasp	☐ tick
☐ beetle	☐ butterfly	☐ caterpillar	☐ nest	

CHALLENGE Make a list of the birds and insects you can see near your home.

1. **Look in your dictionary. Cross out the word that doesn't belong.**

a. Pets   dog   goldfish   guinea pig   ~~prairie dog~~

b. Farm animals   horse   cow   gopher   pig

c. Rodents   rat   mouse   squirrel   goat

d. Birds   parakeet   donkey   rooster   hen

2. **Look at the ad. Check (✓) the animals you see.**

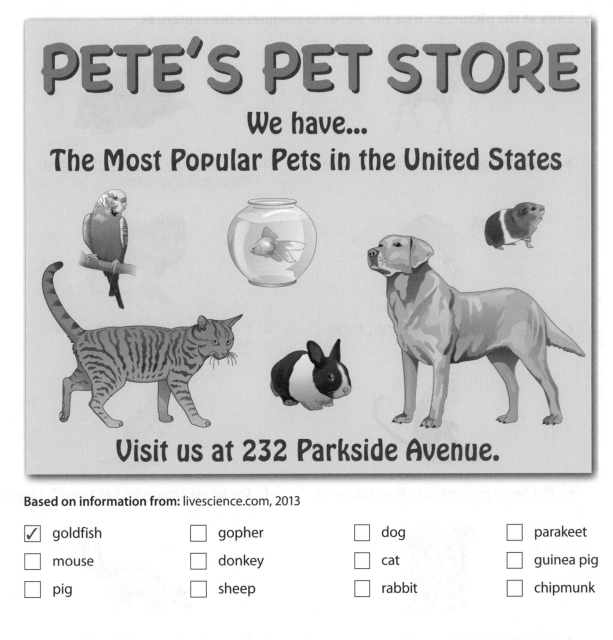

Based on information from: livescience.com, 2013

✓ goldfish   ☐ gopher   ☐ dog   ☐ parakeet

☐ mouse   ☐ donkey   ☐ cat   ☐ guinea pig

☐ pig   ☐ sheep   ☐ rabbit   ☐ chipmunk

CHALLENGE Survey your classmates. Find out if they had pets in their native countries. Which pets are popular?

1. Look in your dictionary. *True* or *False*?

  a. The beaver lives in North America.   _____*true*_____

  b. The lion lives in South America.   _____

  c. The chimpanzee lives in Africa.   _____

  d. The orangutan lives in Asia.   _____

  e. The llama lives in Australia.   _____

2. Look at the pictures. Circle the words to complete the sentences.

  a. The <u>antelope</u> / (<u>deer</u>) has <u>antlers</u> / <u>horns</u>.

  b. The <u>platypus</u> / <u>porcupine</u> has long, sharp <u>quills</u> / <u>whiskers</u>.

  c. The <u>camel</u> / <u>llama</u> has a <u>hump</u> / <u>trunk</u>.

  d. The <u>lion</u> / <u>mountain lion</u> has four <u>hooves</u> / <u>paws</u>.

  e. The <u>bear</u> / <u>monkey</u> has a long <u>tail</u> / <u>neck</u>.

  f. The <u>hyena</u> / <u>kangaroo</u> has a <u>pouch</u> / <u>trunk</u>.

  g. The <u>elephant</u> / <u>rhinoceros</u> has <u>horns</u> / <u>tusks</u>.

  h. The <u>raccoon</u> / <u>skunk</u> has a black and white <u>coat</u> / <u>mane</u>.

3. Look at the chart. Check (✓) the mammals that are endangered.*

SOME ENDANGERED* MAMMALS

endangered = very few are still living; they may not continue to live.

Based on information from: *The World Almanac and Book of Facts 2016.* (NY: World Almanac Books, 2016)

☐ anteater	✓ armadillo	☐ baboon	☐ black rhinoceros
☐ brown bear	☐ buffalo	☐ camel	☐ coyote
☐ elephant	☐ giraffe	☐ gorilla	☐ gray bat
☐ hippopotamus	☐ kangaroo	☐ koala	☐ leopard
☐ moose	☐ mountain lion	☐ opossum	☐ panda
☐ panther	☐ red wolf	☐ tiger	☐ zebra

CHALLENGE Look online or in an encyclopedia for information about one of the mammals in your dictionary. Where does it live? What does it eat? How long does it live? Is it endangered? Write a paragraph.

1. **Look in your dictionary. Which energy sources come from . . . ?**

Atoms	The Earth	Water
nuclear energy	_____	_____
_____	_____	**The Sun**
Air	_____	_____
_____	_____	

2. **Look at the newspaper headlines. Match them with the types of pollution.**

1. **AS IT HAPPENS** / **Beaches Safe for Swimming This Summer**

2. **COMMUNITY BULLETIN** / **CARS GET NEW ANTI-SMOG DEVICE**

3. **Media WATCH** / **Farmers Stop Using Dangerous Chemicals on Grapes**

4. **WORLD NEWS** / **Countries Agree to Stop Making Atomic Bombs**

5. **DAILY OBSERVER** / **Petroco Cleans up Water after Boating Accident**

6. **MOUNTAIN POST** / **Hospitals More Careful with Medical Garbage**

____ **a.** oil spill   _1_ **c.** water pollution   ____ **e.** hazardous waste

____ **b.** pesticide poisoning   ____ **d.** radiation   ____ **f.** air pollution

3. **Look at the bar graph. Number the energy sources in order. (1 = used the most)**

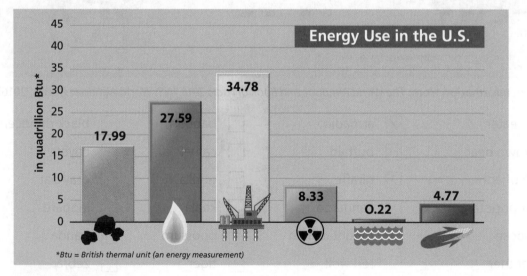

Energy Use in the U.S.

in quadrillion Btu*

17.99   27.59   34.78   8.33   0.22   4.77

*Btu = British thermal unit (an energy measurement)

Based on information from: *The World Almanac and Book of Facts 2016.* (NY: World Almanac Books, 2016)

_1_ **a.** oil   ____ **c.** coal   ____ **e.** natural gas

____ **b.** biomass   ____ **d.** hydroelectric power   ____ **f.** nuclear energy

4. Look in your dictionary. What do these people do to conserve energy and resources?

> I never leave lights on
> when I leave a room.

a. _turn off lights_

> I always keep it at 68°
> in the winter.

f. _____

> I really don't need to use hot or
> warm water to get my shirts clean.

b. _____

> I drive to work with three
> people from my office.

g. _____

> I don't use paper cups
> for my coffee.

c. _____

> This plastic bottle goes in
> one of the blue containers.

h. _____

> I turn off the faucet when
> I brush my teeth.

d. _____

> I always bring
> my own bag.

i. _____

> I *never* throw things out
> the car window!

e. _____

> I repair our faucets
> so they use less water.

j. _____

5. What about you? How often do you . . . ? Check (✓) the columns.

	Always	Sometimes	Never
buy recycled products			
save water			
turn off lights			
use energy-efficient bulbs			
adjust the thermostat			
carpool			
compost food scraps			
plant trees			
Other: _____			

CHALLENGE   List three other ways to conserve water or electricity. **Example:** *I don't water my lawn.*

Go to page 258 for Another Look (Unit 11).

225

1. **Look in your dictionary. *True* or *False*?**

    a. Adelia is wearing a red cap and gown.   *false*

    b. The photographer is upset with the students.   _____

    c. Adelia is crying in the serious photo.   _____

    d. The guest speaker is taking a picture.   _____

    e. The mayor is standing at the podium.   _____

    f. The ceremony is funny.   _____

    g. The students celebrate after the ceremony.   _____

2. **Look at the pictures and the captions. Match.**

    _5_ a. Here's my Dad taking pictures.   ____ d. Hey! Where's the guest speaker?

    ____ b. Nice cap and gown!   ____ e. A serious ceremony.

    ____ c. My Mom cries when she's happy!   ____ f. It's time to celebrate!

3. Look at the photos in Exercise 2. Circle the words to complete the email.

My Mail
To: Paljo@eol.us
Subject: Graduation

I'm attaching some photos from my graduation day.

Do you remember my father? There he is with his camera. He's the family

guest speaker / (photographer.)
        a.

That's a picture of the cap / podium before the mayor spoke. She was the
        b.

guest speaker this year.

The woman is my mother. She always celebrates / cries at ceremonies.
        c.

The funny / serious photo of me is at the ceremony. I'm getting
        d.

my diploma / gown.
    e.

Finally, it was time to celebrate / take a picture! That's me with Adelia and
        f.

another classmate. Don't we look happy?

I wish you had been there, too!

M

4. What about you? Answer the questions.

a. Were you ever at a graduation? ☐ Yes ☐ No

b. Who was there? ☐ a photographer ☐ a guest speaker
   ☐ Other: _____

c. Did you cry? ☐ Yes ☐ No   If *yes*, why? _____

d. Did you celebrate after the graduation? ☐ Yes ☐ No   If *yes*, how? _____

CHALLENGE Look in your dictionary. Read the comments on page 227. Write five more comments about the photos on Adelia's web page.

1. **Look at page 228 in your dictionary. Put the words in the correct columns.**

Inside Events	Outside Events
_____	_____zoo_____
_____	_____
_____	_____
_____	

2. **Look at the events in Exercise 1. Where can you go to . . . ?**

   a. listen to music   _____rock concert_____

   b. see animals   _____

   c. see fish   _____

   d. buy clothes   _____

   e. watch a movie   _____

   f. see flowers and plants   _____

   g. play a game   _____

3. **Circle the words to complete the sentences.**

   a. It's nice to walk through the (botanical gardens) / movies.

   b. Elissa bought a used T-shirt at the bowling alley / swap meet.

   c. There's a new baby elephant at the aquarium / zoo.

   d. The music was very loud at the botanical gardens / rock concert.

4. **What about you? How often do you go to . . . ? Complete the chart.**

	Often	Sometimes	Never	Never, but I'd like to go
a zoo				
the movies				
a botanical garden				
a bowling alley				
a swap meet				
a rock concert				
an aquarium				

5. **Look at page 229 in your dictionary. Complete the event listings below.**

WHAT'S HAPPENING

ART

NEWPORT ___Art Museum___

                 a.
Special exhibit of sculpture and paintings by local artists. Through August 25. **$5.00.**

MUSIC

CITY CENTER

Adriana Domingo sings the leading role in Antonio Rivera's new _____,

                b.
Starry Night. 8:00 P.M., August 14 and 15.

Tickets $10–$30.

PLUM HALL

Oakland Chamber Orchestra, with Lily Marksen at the piano, performs a _____

                c.
featuring works by Beethoven, Bach, and Brahms. 8:00 P.M., August 15.

Tickets $20–$30.

THEATER

CURTAINS UP

The Downtown Players perform _The Argument_, a new _____ by J.L. Mason, starring

            d.
Vanessa Thompson and Tyrone Williams as a married couple. Through August 20. **Tickets $20.**

CHILDREN

CROWN _____

                        e.
Roller coaster, merry-go-round, and other rides provide fun for kids and adults. Great popcorn, too! Open daily.

10:00 A.M. to 5:00 P.M. **Free admission.**

GENERAL INTEREST

Newport _____

                        f.
Food, exhibitions, and prizes for best cow, quilt, and more.

August 14–15, 10:00 A.M. to sunset. **Free.**

Sal's _____

                        g.
Dance to the music of the rock band, Jumpin' Lizzards. 8:00 P.M. to midnight. Must be 18 or older (ID required). **$10.00** (includes 1 beverage).

---

6. **Look at the events in Exercise 5.** _True_ or _False_?

a. The play is free.   ___false___

b. You can see an opera at City Center.   _____

c. The county fair is open nights.   _____

d. A seventeen-year-old can go to Sal's.   _____

e. There's an afternoon concert at Plum Hall on August 15.   _____

f. Tickets to the amusement park are expensive.   _____

g. You can see the special art exhibit for $5.00.   _____

CHALLENGE Look at the listings in Exercise 5. Talk to two classmates and agree on a place to go. Write your decision and give a reason.

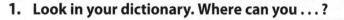

The Park and Playground

1. Look in your dictionary. Where can you . . . ?

    a. have a picnic   *picnic table*

    b. play baseball   _____

    c. see a cyclist   _____

    d. get a drink   _____

    e. push a swing   _____

    f. sit and read   _____

2. Look at the map. Complete the legend. Use the words in the box.

ball field   bike path   fountain   picnic table   playground   ~~tennis court~~   water fountain

a. *tennis court*
b. _____
c. _____
d. _____
e. _____
f. _____
g. _____

3. Look at the map in Exercise 2. *True* or *False*?

    a. There's a water fountain in the playground.   *true*

    b. The tennis court is to the left of the ball field.   _____

    c. There's an outdoor grill near the fountain.   _____

    d. There are benches near the swings.   _____

    e. The bike path goes around the fountain.   _____

4. What about you? Check (✓) the activities you did as a child.

    ☐ ride a tricycle   ☐ go down a slide   ☐ use a jump rope

    ☐ climb the bars   ☐ pull a wagon   ☐ picnic in the park

    ☐ play in the sandbox   ☐ ride a skateboard   ☐ Other: _____

CHALLENGE Look at the park in your dictionary. What are people doing? Write eight sentences.
                Example: *A little boy is riding a tricycle.*

1. Look in your dictionary. What are people using to . . . ?

a. play in the sand   _____pail_____

b. sit on the sand   _____ and _____

c. keep drinks and food cold   _____

d. protect their skin from the sun   _____ and _____

e. stay warm in the ocean   _____

f. breathe underwater   _____

g. see underwater   _____

2. Look at the chart. *True* or *False*?

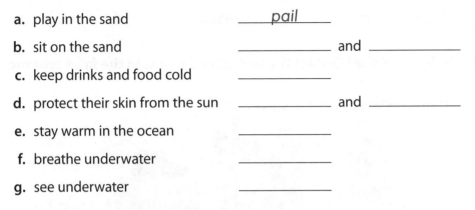

Charles Beach	●		●		●	●	●
Moonstone Beach				●	●		●
Town Beach	●	●	●			●	

a. You can swim at Charles Beach.   _____true_____

b. Surfers can use their surfboards only at Moonstone Beach.   _____

c. You can go out in your sailboat at Town Beach.   _____

d. You can use a scuba tank at Charles Beach.   _____

e. You can rent a beach umbrella at Moonstone Beach.   _____

f. There's a lifeguard at all three beaches.   _____

g. There's a pier at Town Beach.   _____

3. What about you? How important are these things to you? Circle the number.

	Very Important				Not Important
clean sand	4	3	2	1	0
big waves	4	3	2	1	0
seashells	4	3	2	1	0
lifeguard station	4	3	2	1	0

[CHALLENGE] Look at the chart in Exercise 2. Which beach would you like to go to? Why?

1. **Look in your dictionary. How many people are . . . ?**

   a. backpacking _1_ **b.** rafting ___   **c.** camping ___   **d.** canoeing ___

2. **Look at the graph.** *True* or *False*? **Correct the <u>underlined</u> words in the false sentences.**

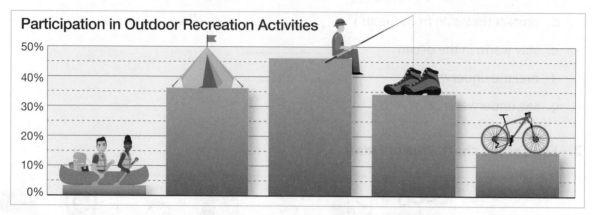

Participation in Outdoor Recreation Activities

   Based on information from: www.outdoorfoundation.org/pdf/ResearchParticipation2013.pdf

   a. Only 3.4% of people go <u>rafting</u>.   *canoeing*   _false_

   b. More than 40% go <u>fishing</u>.   _____

   c. Almost 15% go <u>horseback riding</u>.   _____

   d. A little more than 35% go <u>camping</u>.   _____

   e. Almost 35% go <u>hiking</u>.   _____

3. **Read the sentences. What do the people need? Match.**

   _5_ **a.** It's too dark in this tent. I can't read.   **1.** camping stove

   ___ **b.** It's cold. Let's build a campfire.   **2.** canteen

   ___ **c.** Where's my backpack? I'm thirsty.   **3.** fishing pole

   ___ **d.** Ouch! These mosquitoes keep biting me!   **4.** insect repellent

   ___ **e.** Brian's afraid of the water. He can't swim.   **5.** lantern

   ___ **f.** Everyone's hungry. I'll start the hamburgers.   **6.** life vest

   ___ **g.** I'm tired. Good night.   **7.** matches

   ___ **h.** I'd like to catch some of those trout in the lake.   **8.** sleeping bag

4. **What about you? Check (✓) the activities you like.**

   ☐ camping   ☐ mountain biking   ☐ fishing   ☐ canoeing

   [CHALLENGE] Choose your favorite outdoor activity. What do you need to do it? Make a list.

1. **Look in your dictionary. Circle the words to complete the sentences.**

   a. The man in the red vest is cross-country skiing / downhill skiing.

   b. Two people are snowboarding / sledding.

   c. The skater with the white skates is figure skating / ice skating.

   d. A woman and man are scuba diving / snorkeling.

2. **Look at the hotel information. Where should people stay? Write the number(s).**

   a. Ana likes water sports. _____1, 2_____

   b. Mei-yuan likes winter sports. _____

   c. Jason loves downhill skiing. _____

   d. Crystal wants to go snorkeling. _____

   e. Paulo wants to take his children sledding. _____

   f. Kyle wants to go waterskiing and sailing. _____

   g. Olga wants to go surfing. _____

   h. Taro loves sailing and windsurfing. _____

3. **What about you? Look at Exercise 2. Where would you like to stay? Why?**

   Example: *I want to stay at the Wicker Inn or Hillside Lodge. I like ice skating.*

   CHALLENGE Interview two people. Which winter or water sports do they like? Recommend a
   hotel from Exercise 2.

1. **Look in your dictionary. Put the words in the correct columns.**

Outdoor Sports	Indoor Sports	
archery		

2. **Look at the chart. List the sports in order of popularity. (1 = the most popular)**

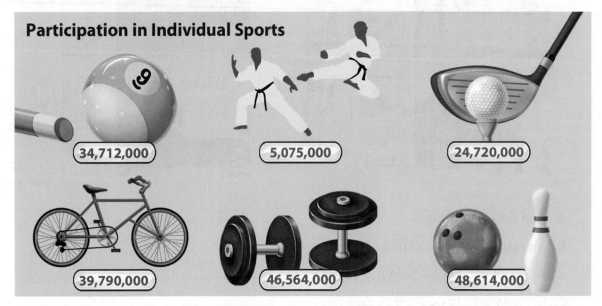

Participation in Individual Sports

34,712,000 5,075,000 24,720,000

39,790,000 46,564,000 48,614,000

Based on information from: *Sports and Fitness Industry Association Activities Topline Participation Report,* 2013 and Statista, 2013

1. _____*bowling*_____   3. _____   5. _____

2. _____   4. _____   6. _____

3. **What about you? Check (✓) the sports you like.**

☐ boxing   ☐ wrestling   ☐ horse racing   ☐ Other: _____

CHALLENGE Interview four people in your class. Which individual sports do they like? Make a list. **Example:** *Two students like weightlifting.*

1. **Look at the basketball court at the top of your dictionary page. Write the numbers.**

   a. How many teams are there? _2_

   b. How many fans are holding a sign? ___

   c. How many players can you see? ___

   d. How many coaches can you see? ___

   e. How many referees can you see? ___

   f. What's the score for the home team? ___

2. **Look at the bar graph. *True* or *False*? Correct the <u>underlined</u> words in the false sentences.**

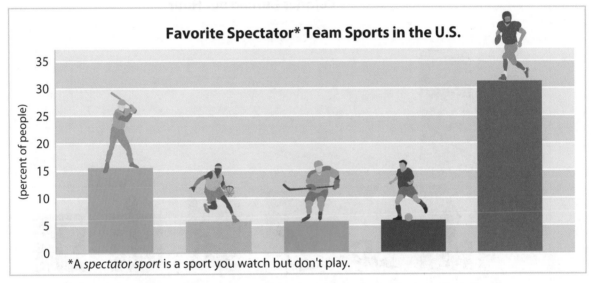

Favorite Spectator* Team Sports in the U.S.

*A spectator sport is a sport you watch but don't play.

Based on information from: Harris Poll, 2014. http://www.harrisinteractive.com/NewsRoom

   a. Almost 16% said ~~ice hockey~~ *baseball* is their favorite sport. _____

   b. <u>Basketball</u> is the number 1 favorite sport. _____

   c. About 6% said <u>ice hockey</u> is their favorite sport. _____

   d. The same percent of people said basketball, ice hockey, and <u>football</u> is their favorite sport. _____

3. **What about you? Circle the sports you play. <u>Underline</u> the sports you watch.**

   softball   football   basketball   baseball

   volleyball   ice hockey   water polo   soccer

CHALLENGE   Go to page 261 in this book. Follow the instructions.

Sports Verbs

1. Look in your dictionary. Circle the words to complete the sentences.

   a. One man is (kicking) / passing / throwing a football.

   b. A woman is <u>bending / swimming / racing</u> at the gym.

   c. The woman at the gym is <u>jumping / tackling / exercising</u>.

   d. The man on the tennis court is <u>pitching / serving / swinging</u>.

   e. A man in orange shorts at the track is <u>finishing / dribbling / stretching</u>.

   f. A man on the baseball field is <u>catching / hitting / swinging</u> with his glove.

2. Look at the bar graph. Complete the sentences.

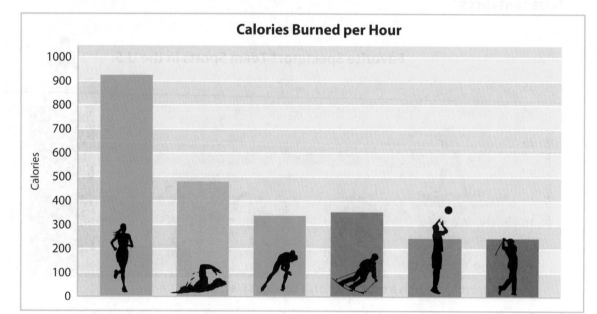

Calories Burned per Hour

Based on information from: *Fitday.com*.

   a. When you ___swim___ , you burn 490 calories per hour.

   b. When you _____ a golf club, you burn 245 calories per hour.

   c. When you _____ baskets, you also burn 245 calories per hour.

   d. When you _____ in track and field, you burn 911 calories per hour.

   e. When you _____ , you burn 350 calories per hour.

   f. When you _____ , you burn 346 calories per hour.

3. What about you? Check (✓) the activities you do.

   ☐ work out   ☐ swim   ☐ race   ☐ skate   ☐ dive   ☐ ski

CHALLENGE Look in your dictionary. Which activities need more than one person?
         Example: *pass*

1. Look in your dictionary. What do you see? Put the words in the correct categories.

arrow	bat	boots	bow	catcher's mask
club	glove	helmet	poles	racket
inline skates	~~uniform~~	shoulder pads	target	shin guards

Baseball   **Skiing**   **Golf**   **Skating**

__*uniform*__   _____   _____   _____

_____   _____   **Tennis**   **Archery**

_____   **Football**   _____   _____

_____   _____   **Soccer**   _____

_____   _____   _____

2. Look at the chart. Number the items in order of size. (1 = the biggest)

How Big* Are They?

26"

28.5"

9"

28"

27"

* regulation circumference size

a. ___ baseball   c. ___ soccer ball   e. ___ volleyball

b. _1_ basketball   d. ___ bowling ball

3. What about you? Check (✓) the sports equipment you have used.

☐ bowling ball   ☐ ice skates   ☐ flying disc   ☐ snowboard

☐ weights   ☐ football   ☐ skis   ☐ Other: _____

☐ volleyball   ☐ hockey stick

CHALLENGE Look at <u>pages 234 and 235</u> in your dictionary. What kinds of sports equipment do you see? Make a list. You have only three minutes!

1. Look in your dictionary. Cross out the word that doesn't belong.

a. Types of paint   acrylic   ~~glue stick~~   oil   watercolor

b. Things to collect   action figures   baseball cards   clubs   figurines

c. Games   cards   checkers   chess   crochet

d. Cards   hearts   diamonds   checkers   spades

e. Painting   canvas   easel   paintbrush   dice

2. Look at the chart. Circle the words to complete the sentences.

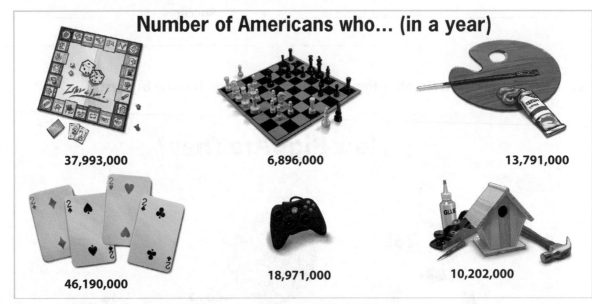

Number of Americans who... (in a year)

37,993,000   6,896,000   13,791,000

46,190,000   18,971,000   10,202,000

Based on information from: *Statistical Abstract of the United States,* 2012.

a. 37,993,000 people play (board games)/ chess.

b. 18,971,000 people play cards / video games.

c. 13,791,000 people draw or paint / quilt.

d. 10,202,000 people use video game controllers / woodworking kits.

e. 6,896,000 play checkers / chess.

f. 46,190,000 people play chess / cards.

3. What about you? Look at the hobbies in Exercise 2. Write them in the correct column.

Hobbies I Do	Hobbies I Don't Do	Hobbies I Would Like to Do
_____	_____	_____
_____	_____	_____
_____	_____	_____

4. Unscramble these hobby and game words. You can use your dictionary for help.

a. DEMLO STIRAN   M O D (E) L   T R A I N S

b. DIVOE MAGE   __ __ Ⓞ __ __ __ __ Ⓞ __

c. RANY   Ⓞ __ __ __

d. TUILQ CLOBK   __ __ Ⓞ __ __ Ⓞ __ __ __

e. TROARY TRUTEC   __ Ⓞ __ __ __ __ __ __ __ __ __ Ⓞ

f. TREASH   __ Ⓞ __ Ⓞ __ __

Put the letters into the circles.

Ⓞ Ⓞ Ⓞ Ⓞ Ⓞ Ⓞ Ⓞ Ⓞ Ⓞ Ⓞ

Unscramble the letters in the circles.

A hobby: __ __ __ __ __ __ __ __ __ __

5. What is it? Use unscrambled words from Exercise 4 to write what people are talking about.

I'm going to play *it* for hours.

a. _____video game_____

I love to put *them* on the track.

c. _____

It's one of the red cards.

b. _____

I'm using *it* to knit a sweater.

d. _____

6. What about you? How much do you like to . . . ? Check (✓) the columns.

	I love it.	I like it.	It's OK.	I don't like it.	I don't know.
paint					
do crafts					
play cards					
collect things					
play games					
pretend					

CHALLENGE What can you do with construction paper? **Example:** *You can make posters.*

1. Look at pages 240–241 in your dictionary. Cross out the word that doesn't belong.

a.	Things you carry	boom box	~~Blu-ray player~~	video MP3 player
b.	Things you watch	flat screen TV	camcorder	microphone
c.	Things that are small	video MP3 player	memory card	tuner
d.	Things for music	screen	speakers	turntable
e.	Things for a camera	dock	tripod	zoom lens
f.	Things you wear	earbuds	headphones	portable charger
g.	Things you put in the wall	battery pack	plug	battery charger

2. Look at the ad. How much money can you save?

Super Sam's Super Sale!

$47.99 ○Sale! $37.99

$199.99 ○Sale! $189.99

$399.99 ○Sale! $299.99

$319.99 ○Sale! $259.99

$199.99 ○Sale! $147.99

$84.99 ○Sale! $59.99

$84.99
-59.99
You save $25.00!!!

a.	speakers	$25.00	**d.** boom box	_____
b.	noise-canceling headphones	_____	**e.** video MP3 player	_____
c.	camcorder	_____	**f.** digital camera	

3. Look at the universal remote buttons. Write the function. Use the words in the box.

fast forward	pause	play	~~rewind~~

a. _rewind_ b. _____ c. _____ d. _____

4. Look at the pictures. Which one is . . . ? Write the number.

1.

2.

3.

4.

a. overexposed   _2_   c. out of focus   ___

b. good for a photo album ___   d. underexposed   ___

5. What about you? Check (✓) the items you have. Circle the items you want.

☐ boom box   ☐ DVD player   ☐ tripod

☐ Blu-ray player   ☐ digital camera   ☐ universal remote

☐ personal CD player   ☐ dock   ☐ zoom lens

☐ flat-screen TV   ☐ camcorder   ☐ photo album

[CHALLENGE] Look in the newspaper or online. Find out today's prices for three of the items in Exercise 2. Compare the prices with the prices in the ad.

1. **Look in your dictionary. Circle all the dictionary words in the TV schedule.**

Saturday Evening

	8:00	8:30	9:00	9:30	10:00	10:30	11:00
2	**It's Family!!** Eddie goes to the office in the last show of this popular (sitcom)	**Lisa!** Talk show host interviews a soap opera star.	**Movie: There He Goes!** (2011 comedy) Karl Chaps looks for a job in the big city, but finds many problems along the way–including a banana peel! Lots of laughs. **				**News**
4	**Italy v. France** Final game of the World Cup				**Movie: Jersey Jim** (2016 action-adventure) Snakes, rocks, waterfalls, and much more. With Johnny Diamond. ***		
5	**Wild World** Nature program looks at the endangered panda.	**Mystery!** Holmes investigates a murder in a small town. Filled with suspense.			**The Truth is Out There** Visitors from Mars.		**News**
6	**Movie: Marta** (2018) Two lonely people find romance in this sweet movie by director Emanuel Soto. ****				**Home** The camera follows 16 real people as they do their daily activities, such as brushing their teeth. But do they floss, too?		
7	**Time's Up!** New game show	**Max and Minnie** Cartoon	**Movie: The Shadow** (2018) A mysterious stranger terrorizes a town. Directed by Hideaki Tanaka. **				

2. **Look at Exercise 1. Write the time and channel to watch these types of shows. You can use your dictionary for help.**

   a. watch a funny program _____ _8:00, Channel 2_

   b. watch a sports program _____

   c. see a program about animals _____

   d. watch a funny movie _____

   e. see a reality show _____

   f. watch a science fiction story _____

   g. see a love story _____

   h. learn what's happening in the world _____ or _____

   i. be scared by a movie _____

3. **What about you? Work with a partner. Look at the TV schedule in Exercise 1. Try to find a program you both want to watch.**

4. What kind of entertainment is it? Match.

_4_ **a.** "Romeo and Juliet are dead!"   **1.** children's program

____ **b.** "And the score is: Alicia 25, Todd 12."   **2.** shopping program

____ **c.** "You can buy this for just $29.99 plus shipping." **3.** game show

____ **d.** "Goodbye, boys and girls. See you tomorrow."   **4.** tragedy

____ **e.** "Get off your horses, cowboys!"   **5.** western

5. Look at the chart. Circle the words to complete the sentences. Use your dictionary for help.

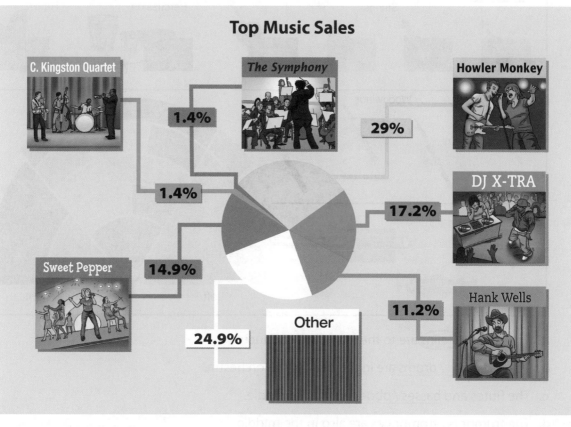

Top Music Sales

C. Kingston Quartet — 1.4%

The Symphony

Howler Monkey — 29%

1.4%

DJ X-TRA — 17.2%

Sweet Pepper — 14.9%

Hank Wells — 11.2%

Other — 24.9%

Based on information from: Nielsen Music U.S. Report (2014)

a. (Rock) / Hip-hop was 29% of the total sales.

b. Classical / Country was 11.2%.

c. Pop / Jazz was only 1.4%.

d. The most popular music was rock / pop.

e. Classical was as popular as jazz / country.

f. Hip-hop and R&B were more popular than country / rock.

6. What about you? What kind of music do you listen to? When do you listen to it?

CHALLENGE   Take a survey. Find out your classmates' favorite kind of music.
Example: *Five students prefer reggae.*

1. Look in your dictionary. Which instruments have . . . ?

   a. strings   _violin_   _____ _____ _____ _____

   b. a keyboard   _piano_   _____ _____ _____

2. Look at the orchestra seating plan. Circle the words to complete the sentences. Use your dictionary for help.

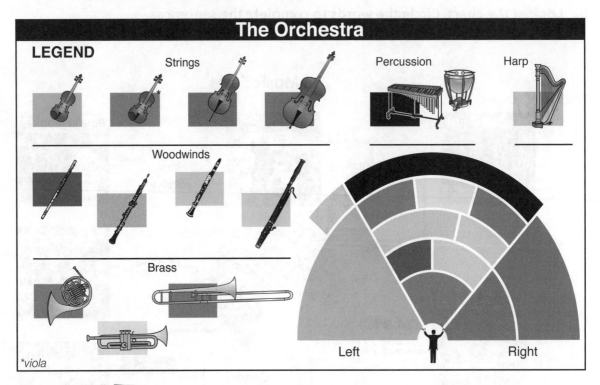

   a. The cellos / (violins) are to the left of the conductor.

   b. The bassoons / drums are in the back of the orchestra.

   c. The flutes and basses / oboes are in the middle.

   d. The trumpets / trombones are also in the middle.

   e. The trumpets are between the French horns and the tambourines / trombones.

   f. The cellos / clarinets are to the right of the conductor.

   g. There are no harmonicas / xylophones in this orchestra.

3. What about you? What would you like to do? Check (✓) the items.

   ☐ sing a song   ☐ conduct an orchestra

   ☐ be in a rock band   ☐ play an instrument (Which one?) _____

  CHALLENGE Find out about these instruments: viola, harmonica, harp, and bugle. What kinds of instruments are they? Look at the categories in your dictionary for help.

1. Look in your dictionary. *True* or *False*?

   a. There's a parade on New Year's Day.   _____true_____

   b. Children get candy canes on Halloween.   _____

   c. Couples use string lights on Valentine's Day. _____

2. Write the names of the holidays on the cards. Then circle the words to complete the sentences.

Happy _____New Year's Day_____ *!*   **SEND**

a. The card shows (confetti) / fireworks.

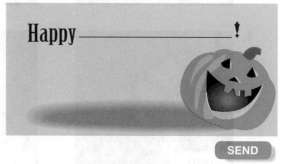

Happy _____ *!*   **SEND**

b. There's a <u>float / jack-o'-lantern</u> on the card.

Happy _____ *!*   **SEND**

c. There's <u>candy / turkey</u> on the plate. It's part of a holiday <u>costume / feast.</u>

Happy _____ *!*   **SEND**

d. There's a red <u>heart / mask</u> on the card.

Merry _____ *!*   **SEND**

e. There's a <u>flag / tree</u> with <u>confetti / ornaments</u> on the card.

Happy _____ *!*   **SEND**

f. The card shows <u>fireworks / string lights</u>.

CHALLENGE   Make a holiday card.

Go to page 259 for Another Look (Unit 12).   **245**

A Birthday Party

1. Look in your dictionary. Who is . . . ? Match.

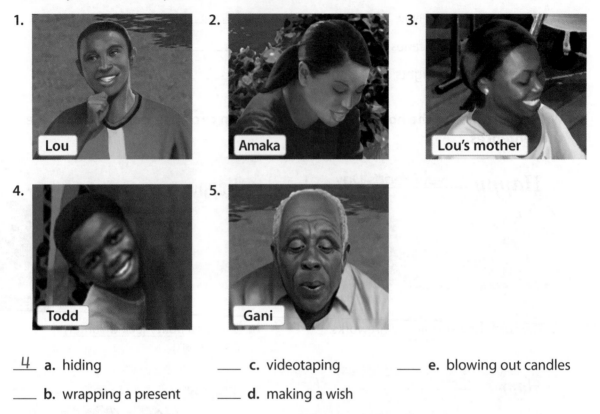

1. Lou
2. Amaka
3. Lou's mother
4. Todd
5. Gani

__4__ **a.** hiding   ___ **c.** videotaping   ___ **e.** blowing out candles

___ **b.** wrapping a present   ___ **d.** making a wish

2. Melissa is planning a party. Look at her list and the picture. Check (✓) the things Melissa did.

For The Party

- ✓ buy decorations
- ☐ hang decorations
- ☐ buy a present
- ☐ wrap the present
- ☐ buy candles
- ☐ sweep the deck
- ☐ bake a cake

3. **Look in your dictionary. Where are they? Check (✓) the columns.**

	Backyard	Deck
a. decorations	✓	✓
b. presents		
c. cakes		
d. lemonade		
e. tables		
f. candles		
g. the woman videotaping		
h. the boy hiding		
i. the girl wrapping		

4. **Complete Lou's sister's diary entry. Use the words in the box.**

blow out	brought	~~deck~~	hid
make	presents	videotaped	wrapped

March 3

Today was Lou and Grandpa Gani's birthday party! It was great. Mom made hamburgers

on the ___deck___ , and we all ate at a big table in the backyard. Lou got a lot of cool
　　　　　a.

_____. One man _____ two boxes—one for Lou and one for
　　b.　　　　　　　　　**c.**

Grandpa. He _____ them with pretty blue paper. Best of all, there were two
　　　　　d.

cakes! I wanted Lou and Grandpa to hurry up and _____ a wish and
　　　　　　　　　　　　　　　　　　　　　　　　e.

_____ the candles so we could eat them! Mom _____ the whole
　f.　　　　　　　　　　　　　　　　　　**g.**

party. Poor Todd. He _____ because he doesn't like to sing. This year Lou is
　　　　　　　　　h.

18 and Grandpa is 80. Next year, I'll be 14! I hope I get two cakes, too.

5. **What about you? Think about a party you went to. Check (✓) the things that happened. Did people . . . ?**

☐ bring presents ☐ videotape the party ☐ blow out candles ☐ make a wish

CHALLENGE Look in your dictionary. Imagine you were at Lou and Gani's birthday party. Write a paragraph about it. Who was there? What did they do?

"C" Search

Look at the picture. There are more than 20 items that begin with the letter **c.** Find and circle them. Make a list of the items that you circled.

Example: *coins*

Picture Crossword Puzzle

Complete the puzzle.

			¹B	A	L	²D					
³							⁴				
	⁵				⁶						
⁷									⁸		
				⁹							
							¹⁰				
			¹¹								
¹²											
			¹³								

Across →

Down ↓

Another Look (Unit 3)

Picture Word Search

There are 15 housing words in the word search. They go across (→) and down (↓). Find and circle 13 more.

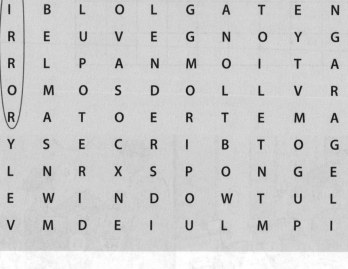

M	A	I	L	B	O	X	A	K	Y
I	B	L	O	L	G	A	T	E	N
R	E	U	V	E	G	N	O	Y	G
R	L	P	A	N	M	O	I	T	A
O	M	O	S	D	O	L	L	V	R
R	A	T	O	E	R	T	E	M	A
Y	S	E	C	R	I	B	T	O	G
L	N	R	X	S	P	O	N	G	E
E	W	I	N	D	O	W	T	U	L
V	M	D	E	I	U	L	M	P	I

250

"C" Search

Look at the picture. There are more than 25 items that begin with the letter **c**. Find and circle them. Make a list of the items that you circled.

Example: *coconut*

Another Look (Unit 5)

Picture Word Search

There are 17 clothing words in the word search. They go across (→) and down (↓). Find and circle 15 more.

S	W	E	A	T	S	H	I	R	T
O	A	T	S	I	O	A	B	I	U
C	L	A	V	E	S	T	E	N	R
K	L	O	A	F	E	R	S	G	T
S	E	T	E	N	N	O	R	O	L
S	T	H	R	E	A	D	O	B	E
B	R	A	O	E	N	I	R	O	N
E	L	M	E	D	I	U	M	O	E
L	O	R	A	L	R	P	A	T	C
T	E	N	J	E	A	N	S	S	K

252

Picture Crossword Puzzle

Complete the puzzle.

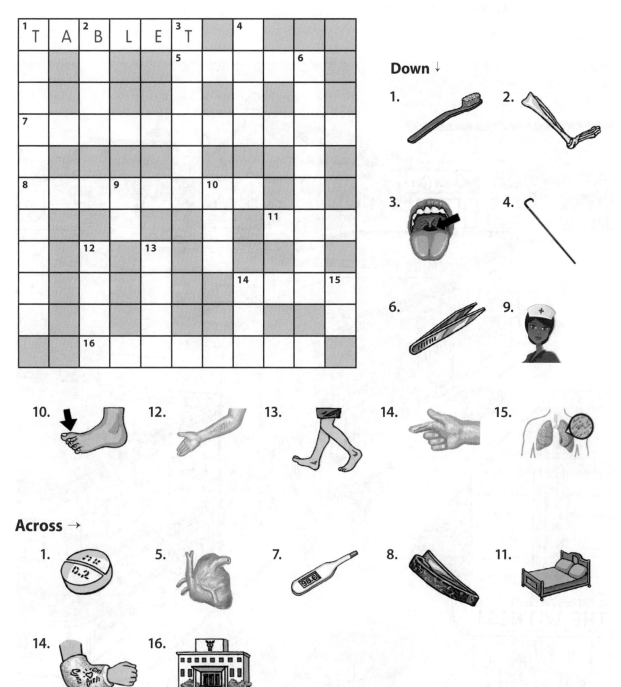

Down ↓

1. 2.

3. 4.

6. 9.

10. 12. 13. 14. 15.

Across →

1. 5. 7. 8. 11.

14. 16.

"C" Search

Look at the picture. There are more than 10 items that begin with the letter **c**. Find and circle them.
Make a list of the items that you circled.

Example: *coffee shop*

Where Have All the Flowers Gone?

Look at the picture. Circle all the flowers. Write the locations of the flowers.

Example: *on the bus*

Another Look (Unit 9)

Job Search

There are 14 jobs in the box. They go across (→) and down (↓). Find and circle 12 more.

```
A  S  S  E  M  B  L  E  R  Y
R  O  O  N  I  A  O  M  E  L
T  L  N  G  N  K  S  O  P  A
I  D  C  I  T  E  I  V  O  W
S  I  A  N  U  R  S  E  R  Y
T  E  S  E  R  V  E  R  T  E
A  R  H  E  W  E  L  D  E  R
N  O  I  R  E  N  O  O  R  A
A  M  E  S  S  E  N  G  E  R
G  A  R  D  E  N  E  R  Y  E
```

256

Where are the Sticky Notes?

Look at the picture. There are 15 sticky notes. Find and circle them. Write the location.

Example: *on the computer monitor*

Picture Crossword Puzzle

Complete the puzzle.

			¹S									
²			T						³			
			A		⁴			⁵				
	⁶		R									
			F			⁷	⁸					
⁹			I		¹⁰							
			S									
			H		¹¹			¹²				
		¹³										
							¹⁴					
	¹⁵											

Across →

2.

4.

5.

7.

9.

11.

14.

15.

Down ↓

1.

4.

8.

12.

3.

6.

10.

13.

"C" Search

Look at the picture. There are more than 25 items and activities that begin with the letter *c.* Find and circle them. Make a list of the items and activities that you circled.

Example: *cooler*

Challenge Exercises

CHALLENGE for page 27

Complete the receipt.

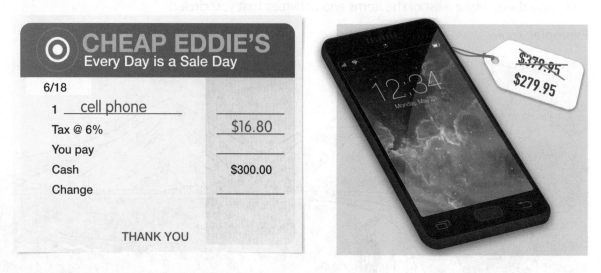

CHEAP EDDIE'S
Every Day is a Sale Day

6/18

1	cell phone	
Tax @ 6%		$16.80
You pay		
Cash		$300.00
Change		

THANK YOU

~~$379.95~~
$279.95

CHALLENGE for page 75

Look at Exercise 2 on page 75 in this book. Convert the U.S. measures to metric measures. Use the charts in your dictionary for help.

a. _____1 1/2 pounds_____ = _____about 680.4 grams_____

b. _____ = _____

c. _____ = _____

e. _____ = _____

CHALLENGE for page 171

Ask four people about their jobs. What do they do? How many hours a week do they work? Fill in the chart below. Then write sentences about them. Follow the example below.

What is your name?	What do you do?	How many hours a week do you work?
Meng	cashier	25
1.		
2.		
3.		
4.		

Example: *Meng is a cashier. She works twenty-five hours a week.*

CHALLENGE for page 183

Complete Enrique Gutierrez's paycheck from page 183. Use the information in Exercise 4 and your dictionary for help.

IRINA'S COMPUTER SERVICE

Check number:
123456789 999999999 124

7000 Main Street
Houston, TX 77031

Pay to the order of _____ Enrique Gutierrez _____ $ _____

Six hundred _____ and _____/100 dollars

Town Bank

Irina Jarkov

CHALLENGE for page 201

Think of different types of schools in another country. List in order the schools and students' ages. Follow the example below.

Country	School	Ages
Peru	preschool	2 to 5 years old
	primary school	6 to 11 years old
	secondary school	12 to 17 years old

Country	School	Ages

CHALLENGE for page 235

How many players are there on a . . . team? If you don't know, try to find out.

basketball _____ 5 _____   ice hockey _____

soccer _____   football _____

baseball _____   volleyball _____

Verb Guide

Verbs in English are either regular or irregular in the past tense and past participle forms.

Regular Verbs
The regular verbs below are marked 1, 2, 3, or 4 according to four different spelling patterns.
(See page 264 for the irregular verbs, which do not follow any of these patterns.)

Spelling Patterns for the Past and the Past Participle	Example	
1. Add -ed to the end of the verb.	ASK	ASKED
2. Add -d to the end of the verb.	LIVE	LIVED
3. Double the final consonant and add -ed to the end of the verb.	DROP	DROPPED
4. Drop the final y and add -ied to the end of the verb.	CRY	CRIED

The Oxford Picture Dictionary List of Regular Verbs

accept (1)
add (1)
address (1)
adjust (1)
agree (2)
answer (1)
apologize (2)
appear (1)
applaud (1)
apply (4)
arrange (2)
arrest (1)
arrive (2)
ask (1)
assemble (2)
assist (1)
attach (1)
attend (1)
bake (2)
bargain (1)
bathe (2)
block (1)
board (1)
boil (1)
bookmark (1)
borrow (1)
bow (1)
brainstorm (1)
breathe (2)
browse (2)
brush (1)
bubble (2)
buckle (2)
burn (1)
bus (1)
calculate (2)
call (1)

capitalize (2)
carpool (1)
carry (4)
cash (1)
celebrate (2)
change (2)
check (1)
chill (1)
choke (2)
chop (3)
circle (2)
cite (2)
claim (1)
clarify (4)
clean (1)
clear (1)
click (1)
climb (1)
close (2)
collate (2)
collect (1)
color (1)
comb (1)
comfort (1)
commit (3)
compare (2)
complain (1)
complete (2)
compliment (1)
compose (2)
compost (1)
conceal (1)
conduct (1)
consult (1)
contact (1)
convert (1)
convict (1)

cook (1)
cooperate (2)
copy (4)
correct (1)
cough (1)
count (1)
create (2)
cross (1)
cry (4)
dance (2)
debate (2)
decline (2)
delete (2)
deliver (1)
design (1)
dial (1)
dice (2)
dictate (2)
die (2)
direct (1)
disagree (2)
discipline (2)
discuss (1)
disinfect (1)
distribute (2)
dive (2)
divide (2)
double-click (1)
drag (3)
dress (1)
dribble (2)
drill (1)
drop (3)
drown (1)
dry (4)
dust (1)
dye (2)

earn (1)
edit (1)
empty (4)
end (1)
enter (1)
erase (2)
evacuate (2)
examine (2)
exchange (2)
exercise (2)
expire (2)
explain (1)
explore (2)
exterminate (2)
fast forward (1)
fasten (1)
fax (1)
fertilize (2)
fill (1)
finish (1)
fix (1)
floss (1)
fold (1)
follow (1)
garden (1)
gargle (2)
graduate (2)
grate (2)
grease (2)
greet (1)
hail (1)
hammer (1)
hand (1)
harvest (1)
help (1)
hire (2)
hug (3)

identify (4)
immigrate (2)
indent (1)
inquire (2)
insert (1)
inspect (1)
install (1)
introduce (2)
investigate (2)
invite (2)
iron (1)
jaywalk (1)
join (1)
jump (1)
kick (1)
kiss (1)
knit (3)
label (1)
land (1)
laugh (1)
learn (1)
lengthen (1)
lift (1)
list (1)
listen (1)
litter (1)
live (2)
load (1)
lock (1)
log (3)
look (1)
mail (1)
manufacture (2)
match (1)
measure (2)
microwave (2)
milk (1)
misbehave (2)
miss (1)
mix (1)
monitor (1)
mop (3)
move (2)
mow (1)
multiply (4)
negotiate (2)
network (1)
numb (1)
nurse (2)

obey (1)
observe (2)
offer (1)
open (1)
operate (2)
order (1)
organize (2)
overdose (2)
pack (1)
paint (1)
park (1)
participate (2)
pass (1)
paste (2)
pause (2)
peel (1)
perm (1)
pick (1)
pitch (1)
plan (3)
plant (1)
play (1)
polish (1)
pour (1)
praise (2)
preheat (1)
prepare (2)
prescribe (2)
press (1)
pretend (1)
print (1)
program (3)
protect (1)
pull (1)
purchase (2)
push (1)
quilt (1)
race (2)
raise (2)
rake (2)
receive (2)
record (1)
recycle (2)
redecorate (2)
reduce (2)
reenter (1)
refuse (2)
register (1)
relax (1)

remain (1)
remove (2)
renew (1)
repair (1)
replace (2)
report (1)
request (1)
research (1)
respond (1)
retire (2)
return (1)
reuse (2)
revise (2)
rinse (2)
rock (1)
sauté (1)
save (2)
scan (3)
schedule (2)
scroll (1)
scrub (3)
search (1)
seat (1)
select (1)
sentence (2)
separate (2)
serve (2)
share (2)
shave (2)
ship (3)
shop (3)
shorten (1)
shower (1)
sign (1)
simmer (1)
skate (2)
ski (1)
slice (2)
smell (1)
smile (2)
smoke (2)
solve (2)
sort (1)
spell (1)
spoon (1)
staple (2)
start (1)
state (2)
stay (1)

steam (1)
stir (3)
stop (3)
stow (1)
stretch (1)
study (4)
submit (3)
subtract (1)
supervise (2)
swallow (1)
tackle (2)
talk (1)
taste (2)
thank (1)
tie (2)
touch (1)
transcribe (2)
transfer (3)
translate (2)
travel (1)
trim (3)
try (4)
turn (1)
type (2)
underline (2)
undress (1)
unload (1)
unpack (1)
unscramble (2)
update (2)
use (2)
vacuum (1)
videotape (2)
visit (1)
volunteer (1)
vomit (1)
vote (2)
wait (1)
walk (1)
wash (1)
watch (1)
water (1)
wave (2)
weed (1)
weigh (1)
wipe (2)
work (1)
wrap (3)
yell (1)

Verb Guide

Irregular Verbs

These verbs have irregular endings in the past and/or the past participle.

The Oxford Picture Dictionary List of Irregular Verbs

simple	past	past participle	simple	past	past participle
be	was	been	make	made	made
beat	beat	beaten	meet	met	met
become	became	become	pay	paid	paid
bend	bent	bent	picnic	picnicked	picnicked
bleed	bled	bled	proofread	proofread	proofread
blow	blew	blown	put	put	put
break	broke	broken	quit	quit	quit
bring	brought	brought	read	read	read
buy	bought	bought	rewind	rewound	rewound
catch	caught	caught	rewrite	rewrote	rewritten
choose	chose	chosen	ride	rode	ridden
come	came	come	run	ran	run
cut	cut	cut	say	said	said
do	did	done	see	saw	seen
draw	drew	drawn	seek	sought	sought
drink	drank	drunk	sell	sold	sold
drive	drove	driven	send	sent	sent
eat	ate	eaten	set	set	set
fall	fell	fallen	sew	sewed	sewn
feed	fed	fed	shake	shook	shaken
feel	felt	felt	shoot	shot	shot
find	found	found	show	showed	shown
fly	flew	flown	sing	sang	sung
freeze	froze	frozen	sit	sat	sat
get	got	gotten	speak	spoke	spoken
give	gave	given	stand	stood	stood
go	went	gone	steal	stole	stolen
hang	hung	hung	sweep	swept	swept
have	had	had	swim	swam	swum
hear	heard	heard	swing	swung	swung
hide	hid	hidden	take	took	taken
hit	hit	hit	teach	taught	taught
hold	held	held	think	thought	thought
keep	kept	kept	throw	threw	thrown
lay	laid	laid	wake	woke	woken
leave	left	left	win	won	won
lend	lent	lent	withdraw	withdrew	withdrawn
let	let	let	write	wrote	written
lose	lost	lost			